America Adrift

Restoring the Promise of Our Democracy

LAWRENCE ROSENCRANTZ

ISBN: 1466263091
ISBN-13: 9781466263093

Preface

Picture a great ship on stormy seas, drifting relentlessly toward a rocky shore. Its engine is badly malfunctioning, and its crew and captain are so engrossed in rancorous argument about every aspect of the voyage that no one is at the helm to steer the ship, and there is no agreement about how to repair the engine. The ship's badly misinformed owners, each with their own perspective and unaware of the full extent of the ship's plight, send conflicting messages to the ship that only perpetuate the turmoil.

Like that ship, America is drifting inexorably onto the shoals of lessened national security, a declining standard of living, diminishing world influence, and even the longer-term potential for civil unrest. Like that crew, our elected representatives seem utterly incapable of coming together to meet the challenges we face. And like that ship's owners, we are badly misinformed and sending conflicting messages.

Not only is there bitter disagreement in the United States over solutions to our national and local problems, there is shockingly little agreement as to what the most important problems are to begin with. Indeed, we are being driven further into separate camps by a withering array of pundits, academicians, and politicians, each with their own perspective and platform. Some see government as the solution provider, while for others government *is* the problem.

While it is tempting to blame one political party or another, one president or another, the fact is that our disunity and disarray have deeper, more complex roots. If we are to alter the current situation in our country, then it is crucial that we understand these roots. That understanding is also critical to the process of bringing us together upon common ground so that we can begin solving the host of difficult problems we are now confronting, before they become our undoing. Understanding the genesis of our current plight and how we can come together to constructively address the issues that divide us form this book's subject matter.

The events of 9/11 and their political aftermath have had a profound effect upon our national psyche, suffusing our once "can do" attitude with corrosive apprehension, anger, and negativity. Criticism, rather than any attempt to seek consensus, has become the primary focus of the day for commentators, politicians, and citizens alike. Attempts to provide thoughtful, long-term solutions are being swept aside by the bellicose clamor and vapid commentary that appear in all media, including the internet. As a consequence of all this distraction, we have permitted our political system to become structurally flawed to such an extent that it functions more as a plutocracy than a democracy in meeting the needs of our people. Merely electing new politicians, or creating new political parties, whether they promise more government action, or less government interference, will not move us forward if they are products of the same broken system. And our democracy is badly broken. To use an analogy, merely substituting game pieces in a defective game does not alter the dynamic of the game or prevent the faulty outcomes.

While the political and social aftermath of 9/11 has contributed to all this discord, there are other major factors at work here. Our disarray has been the byproduct of carefully executed, manipulative, and fear-based efforts designed to turn hearts and minds into believing that the public interest is best served by supporting various private and corporate interests—and, obliquely, the politicians and legislation that serve these interests. The misdirection and misinformation are furthered by profit-conflicted media conglomerates that benefit far more from selectivity and sensationalism than from completeness and candor. This pandering to emotion casts aside facts and full knowledge while elevating unfounded belief to the level of assumed legitimacy.

Greed is a critical underpinning of capitalism, but an imperfect servant of the common good. It must be counterbalanced, or its excesses can cause much harm. As citizens we have wittingly or unwittingly allowed the balance point to shift to our nation's long-term disadvantage. Money's powerful influence is insidiously corrupting our access to information, our politics, and our priorities to a level never before seen. How and why this has occurred and what can be done to restore the promise of America are some of the vital issues that this book will address.

The path forward offered here is not the product of a particular political persuasion, nor is it defined by the simplistic labels of liberal or conservative, capitalist or socialist. On the contrary, our democracy's salvation will be found in the search for bridges between our differences—in the ability to open our minds and choose what best moves us forward regardless of economic doctrine, political party, or associated label. Answers will come not from party or polemic, but from a whole cloth woven with new thinking. That is the end we will pursue here, although the path is neither straight nor simple. Quick palliatives or reinforcement of so-called conventional wisdom will not be found here. For that reason a degree of patience and open-mindedness is called for in this book's early chapters, which cover critical background and perspective.

Let there be no mistake, though. The disturbing trends of structural unemployment, stagnating incomes, growing wealth disparity, declining international competitiveness, and declining education levels relative to other countries are accelerating. This situation will only intensify if we fail to change our current state of discord and disarray. Let there be no illusions, either. The promise of our democracy is relentlessly, perhaps all too soon irretrievably, slipping from our grasp. We have neither time to waste, nor the luxury of inflexibility in a world that waits for no man, woman, or country.

Chapter One

Freedom

The only freedom which deserves the name is that of pursuing our own good, in our own way, so long as we do not attempt to deprive others of theirs, or impede their efforts to obtain it.
—*John Stuart Mill*

People demand freedom only when they [believe they] have no power.
—*Henry Wadsworth Longfellow*

This book's principal purpose is to bring us together as Americans, so that we can restore the promise of our democracy and ensure a brighter future for our country. Achieving that objective will require that we overcome the discord and division that has paralyzed our nation. Instead of working together toward solutions to the challenges confronting us, we seem to be at odds with one another at every turn. Social issues, such as abortion and gay marriage, inspire strong passions that often divert us from more pressing problems. There is even deep disagreement about the fundamental role of government in our lives; is it an instrument of social and economic change, or should it be much more limited in scope? Ironically, one of the things that most unites us, freedom, is also one of the things that most divides us. As a concept, freedom suffuses our politics and our actions. It is the underpinning of our constitutional system and the repeated justification for blood being shed and treasure expended throughout our history. It is the oft-used rallying cry for causes emanating from every point on the political spectrum. As an ideal, freedom has been defined as political independence and the license to do as one chooses. Few would disagree with that ideal, and thus its broad appeal.

It is when we move from the ideal of freedom to practical reality that the difficulty begins. Freedom is never unlimited. In the words of Thomas Jefferson, "Rightful liberty is unobstructed action according to our will within limits drawn around us by the equal rights of others." And there's the chafe. In the real world, one person's freedom comes into conflict with the freedom of others; one's freedom to swing one's fist ends at someone else's nose. The issue then becomes resolving the conflicts—determining the level of restrictions to put upon freedom so it doesn't impinge upon the "equal rights of others." And that is where we find our most fervent disagreements as Americans. What restrictions should there be on our freedom to own lethal weapons, our freedom to control medical decisions about our body, our freedom to marry whomever we choose, or our freedom to speak and act however we wish? The disagreements are not about freedom as a general right in America, but about what restrictions are justified to limit individual and collective freedom. The source of much of this conflict comes from a failure to agree on the standards as to what constitutes an *appropriate* restriction and how to apply it. So instead of discussing objective standards we often become embroiled in irreconcilable emotional arguments about the freedom itself. These emotional arguments are the product of strongly held beliefs that cannot be reconciled. The end result is that the appropriateness of the underlying restriction being sought, whether grounded in legality, morality, religion, or some combination thereof, becomes lost in the passion of the moment.

Those who most ardently espouse a particular freedom often do not see an apparent contradiction in opposing "the equal rights of others," in Jefferson's words. So we find some arguing against government intrusion into our lives from surveillance or reporting requirements while supporting government expansion through bloated government programs designed to alleviate some social ill. Those who feel their religious beliefs, for example, decry abortion may feel vindicated restricting the freedom of others whose religious or personal beliefs do not support such restriction. These ostensibly contradictory points of view are the product of differing standards as to what should compel restriction and what should be left unrestricted. In the absence of discussion and ultimate agreement about the standard to be applied, individuals are hard-pressed to agree about the restriction, or the lack thereof, or even about the conduct of any debate on the subject. The fallback is raw emotion and anger. This emotional state of affairs is symptomatic of much of the division within our society today. We get caught up in broad concepts like freedom and liberty that offer us no discernible path to solution when they are used to justify or negate actions.

Despite being a legalistic society, we find our judicial system offers little comfort when we seek to use the concept of freedom to determine what actions or prohibitions are appropriate. American courts have applied differing standards to differing freedoms, making the whole issue of freedom even murkier. We thus have one set of legal standards for freedom of speech and another for a subset of that, freedom of the press. There are legal standards for privacy, our freedom to do what we want in isolation and to be free from prying eyes, and another set of standards for freedom of expression, such as art versus pornography. It's no wonder Americans argue about who gets to do what. It's all quite confusing. When emotion is finally cast aside, some people resort to supposed logic, some to religious tenets, and others to presumed mores of our society in an effort to support their own view of appropriate restriction. What is left lacking is any effort to reconcile the competing justifications, and more importantly, the *needs* underlying the opposing positions. Even once we venture beyond our noses, and into the realm of the harm to others, all of it is quicksand. We get bogged down because, as is the case with abortion, we do not always have agreement about applicability. In the case of abortion, when is there harm to a living being? There is a legal standard for life, viability outside the womb, but not complete societal acceptance of that standard as an appropriate one. The debate about overturning *Roe v. Wade* is really about substituting a standard borne of religious criteria in favor of the present legally accepted medical standard. In other words, even established legal standards do not always inhibit people's belief in the correctness of their efforts to restrict freedoms sought by others.

So where does this leave us with freedom in America? First, we need to be careful about abstract appeals to freedom as a rallying cry for anything. Waving placards emblazoned with the word, naming political parties, and attaching causes to some notion of freedom may incite passion, but such practices do little to explain and justify support for the underlying need. They are too simplistic and unfocused. They polarize viewpoints and prevent discussion of the real issue: the appropriateness of the restriction, or the removal thereof, in question. To further the point, hardly anyone would disagree that increased profits would flow from complete freedom for businesses from all forms of regulation. Allowing a manufacturing business the freedom to dump its production by-products into the air and water and to hire people with no restrictions on working conditions would greatly enhance earnings *and* international competitiveness. So if our standard is that we need to have profitable businesses without regard to anything else, then all is good. Profitable businesses provide jobs, so people spend and create more jobs, etc. You know the story. But maximum profit without regard to anything else is not our standard in the United States. We want young children in school, not working in factories. We want to have clean water for drinking and fish habitat. Most of us want profits earned fairly without fraud. And we want our air free of things that could make us sick or worse.

This simple example is at the heart of a great deal of the economic discord and disagreement in our country; namely, what level of restriction upon economic freedom results in the most public benefit? And closely related is the question, what level of economic *support* ought to be provided by government, again ostensibly for the ultimate benefit of the public? Standing in the shadow of one of the greatest financial crises in our history, as the wealthy grow wealthier while the middle class declines economically, questions of business regulation, economic growth, taxation, and wealth distribution deeply divide us. There are those who argue for laissez faire, asserting that capitalism is self-regulating; that business should be free from all but the most basic of restrictions. On the other end of the spectrum are those who contend that every aspect of business must be regulated, lest greed run amok, trampling the rights and well-being of individuals. It is interesting to note that both of these polar positions use public benefit as their justification. The inability to reconcile them lies in our inability to agree on what actions and limitations create "public benefit." That is at the core of arguments, for example, about tax cuts for wealthy Americans versus "priming the pump" with government spending in order to best achieve economic growth. All agree that economic growth is a worthy goal, but there is deep division among us as to how to achieve it.

In succeeding chapters we will discuss why these issues of business freedom and government involvement are so important and yet so difficult for us to resolve. We will explore how we can reach a degree of consensus that will preserve business prosperity and competitiveness without unduly impinging upon other American values. Similarly, we will address some of the emotionally charged issues of individual freedom that confound agreement among us, like abortion, gun control, and gay marriage. Our objective will be to chart a path to common ground and resolution. All of these issues, whether economic or political, collective or individual, ultimately impact our national priorities.

When we are bitterly divided about government's role, national priorities become impossible to establish. As a result of our division we have become politically schizophrenic about education, infrastructure, the environment, taxation, national security, and other societal needs. We will address that schizophrenia by finding a path to agreement about what our national priorities ought to be. Without such agreement we are a ship of state without a course to follow, adrift in a violent, unforgiving world.

Before we can proceed to the foregoing issues, there are a few important precursors we need to cover. These will not only help us get at our current situation's "complex roots" that the Preface alluded to, they will also aid us in finding a path forward. First, we first need to adopt some basic assumptions that will allow us to loosen our grip a bit upon even our most fervently held beliefs. A more open perspective is crucial to our ability to move beyond labels and political dogma toward a degree of consensus. That will in turn enable us to adopt approaches and viewpoints we might have otherwise failed or been unwilling to consider previously. We will address this in the next chapter. Second, we need to consider the powerful effect that fear has had, consciously and unconsciously, on our national psyche. Fear, in the form of distrust and apprehension, real or conjured, has become the single most powerful determinant of political decision making in the United States today. In its various forms, it is at the heart of much of the negativism and intransigence that pollutes our politics. Such a powerful influence deserves our attention and comprehension if we are to alter its impact. We will address that in Chapters Three and Four.

In our effort to simplify the complex in America, we routinely resort to labels like "liberal," "conservative," bleeding heart," "right winger," "Bible thumper" and literally hundreds of other pejorative characterizations that do violence to both understanding and our ability to talk *with* one another as opposed to *at* each other. This propensity to label is such an important element of national discord that it is the subject of Chapter Five. Chapter Six explores the primary source of our inability to find common ground: our focus upon beliefs rather than needs. Collecting all of this together, we will address the thorny issues of education, economic and business freedom, social programs, leadership, and other contentious issues in America. We will also discuss our political system in the context of corporate America today, and how we can restore the balance between achieving a robust economy, and serving *pragmatic* social objectives in a fiscally responsible manner. Together, these and related topics will lead us to the basis for greater understanding of one another, dialogue, and ultimately a way to achieve agreement between us where little or none may have existed before.

If the public interest is to be truly served, we need to restore our democracy in terms of a better informed electorate capable of making wise and hard choices. That will require changes to what we expect of our media and our approach to education. Sound decisions can be made only when learning is applied to factual and complete information. We will also need to make structural changes to our political and legislative processes so that citizen votes, rather than special-interest dollars, drive public perception and legislative decision making. Lessening the influence of the entrenched oligarchy of powerful special interests currently disproportionately shaping our national agenda will be the hardest task of all. An important tool will be our understanding of freedom, both economic and personal, as well as an understanding of the forces that immobilize and divert us.

A puppet has no freedom. It moves only at the will of the puppeteer. Whether we want to acknowledge it or not, too many of us have become like puppets, moved by the subtle tugs of public relations campaigns, political rhetoric, and an increasingly concentrated and controlled mainstream media driven more by dollars than by full disclosure. If we are to truly restore the freedom to control our destiny, then we must cut the strings of apprehension and discord. We must also summon the will to alter the dynamics that misguide and divide us so that we may stand together in support of what is best for us all as a nation. Only in that way can we prevent plutocracy from supplanting our democracy. Only in that way can we resist that which diminishes us and pursue that which inspires and achieves greatness for us individually and for our country.

Chapter Two

Some Very Basic Assumptions

It ain't what you don't know that gets you into trouble.
It's what you know for sure that just ain't so.
—Mark Twain

All …breakthroughs begin with a change in beliefs.
—Anthony Robbins

If you lived in Columbus's day, and the great explorer announced to you that the world was round, you would have looked out at the ocean and thought him quite daft. For as you could plainly see with your own eyes, the world appeared essentially flat. And it was equally clear that if you sailed far enough out, you would fall off the edge at the horizon line. We laugh at that notion today because we know better. Over time we acquired knowledge that refuted the former belief. But back then your belief in the world's edge and flatness would have been quite strong, because it defined the world around you as you "actually" saw it. Because beliefs provide order to our universe and the ability to be safe within it, as we perceive it, they can be quite firmly held. A challenge to our beliefs is a challenge to our security, to our sense of what we can trust as correct so that we will be protected. Beliefs form the basis for what we desire and what we fear, what we find meaningful and what we do not.

But the rest of the world often has very different perceptions, values, and beliefs than many Americans. As a consequence far more people see things differently than we do. Billions of people, in fact, hold largely different religious, ethical, and governmental beliefs than do the majority of Americans. Yet we maintain our beliefs with a degree of assuredness. And we have essentially had the luxury of doing so. Most of America's history has followed a certain insularity—a belief that we had it right and the rest of the world was playing catch-up, or at least ought to follow our example. Until recently our capitalistic economy accomplished growth and a rising standard of living like no other has before. Many of the resources we have required in the past were conveniently found largely within our borders. We have had vast amounts of arable land to grow food and animal feed. We have had coal, oil, iron ore, and other raw materials in abundance. And as immigrants flowed into the country, we have had a continuing supply of both skilled and unskilled workers to devise and build the products we desired. We have also been insulated because our military might has essentially kept foreign invaders from our shores in modern times. All the while our constitutionally based systems and relative homogeneity fostered a rare stability of government. This insularity has not required us to understand the people and cultures of other countries, or to depend significantly upon resources outside the United States, at least until recent times. Nor has it caused much questioning of the beliefs and understandings we hold as a people. With the winding down of the Cold War, our limited attention to the beliefs of those outside our country lessened even further, until the rude awakening of September 11, 2001. While that event heightened our consciousness of the ethnic presences behind the attacks occurring on that day, it did little to expand our understanding of them. Ironically, it encouraged a turning inward for many.

We derive our beliefs from the things we see and hear, and from our other sensory perceptions. If I do not believe what I see, such as a large hole in the sidewalk in front of me, I may fail to take the action needed to avoid the harm from falling into it. In those instances where beliefs are tied directly to our personal safety or well-being, the beliefs can be quite intractable. Some beliefs are so strong that people are willing to die for those beliefs, or commit grievous harm to others, and feel entirely justified because of their beliefs. Yet such beliefs can very often be quite wrong, even where our well-being is concerned, and even when based on what we perceive to be the obvious.

For over thirteen hundred years after Aristarchus of Samos determined that the sun, and not the earth, was at the center of our universe, people continued to hold the opposite view. For centuries, when people looked up at the sun moving across the sky, it appeared obvious that the sun revolved about our earth. That "common sense" view and the weight of the Aristotle's and Ptolemy's influence held sway until Copernicus demonstrated otherwise in the mid fifteen hundreds. In fact, it has been argued that Copernicus waited until near death to publish his findings to avoid the ridicule that was sure to follow such scientific blasphemy as that the earth revolved around the sun. The point here is that what we often believe quite strongly as "common sense" or as abundantly obvious may not even be reality.

Given the importance and vehemence of beliefs, it will be useful to our discourse here to begin with certain fundamental assumptions that suspend our preconceptions and beliefs for a while. That will enable a better examination of not only the basis of our beliefs, but also allow a better understanding of the beliefs, needs, and motivations of others in the world. With a degree of such open-mindedness it will be possible to begin listening to one another in the search for agreement as to the nature of, and solutions to, our problems. From listening comes understanding, and from understanding can come agreement. If we are to make progress against the myriad of problems facing our country, it will begin with a greater level of agreement, facilitated by greater understanding of one another's beliefs and, most importantly, the needs they support.

In the context of our values and beliefs, we also need to deal with the complexity of our world. There is much around us that appears incomprehensible. That incomprehensibility engenders anxiety and sometimes outright fear. Fear is an emotion that has been manipulated throughout time with devastating consequences, and is being used with increasing frequency today in American society and elsewhere to compel allegiance and sway views. Our world has become a more frenetic, isolating, and threatening place. The very technology that opens new relationships, at the same time reaffirms and adds to the physical and emotional distance that separates us as we communicate from miles apart through pseudonyms and e-mails. The visual media that assault us at every turn—the internet, television, newspapers, magazines, and reader boards—remind us continually of the brutality and injustice visited upon the innocent and the defenseless. The overwhelming difficulties presented daily in our world compel a degree of indifference or avoidance in order for us just to function. We have to become inured to a degree, or we would drown in the horror that occurs daily in the world. While we can turn down the volume and focus inwardly upon ourselves through noble efforts to achieve personal redemption or less noble self-aggrandizement, the dissonance around us does not lessen. The distracting complexity of our lives is why it will be useful to get very basic in our assumptions. Sometimes out of simplicity comes the profound. When the complexity and our fear-based beliefs are finally put aside in favor of some very basic assumptions about our existence, a degree of clarity can be forged. Bedrock simplicity can then enable small steps to make great strides toward a clearer path to national consensus about the changes we must make.

So what are these basic assumptions? First, that there are no provable absolutes in life. The history of mankind has been a search for absolutes: an attempt to find an unswerving set of truths to guide our way. Absolutes are reassuring. We can "trust" them to keep us safe. Yet when all is considered, even so-called proven scientific absolutes depend upon what our senses appear to tell us, or upon theories that stand because testing has not yet disproven them. In fact, new scientific discoveries continually alter our previous scientific beliefs about such monumental issues as the origin of our universe and the basis of life.

It is difficult, if not impossible, for many of us to comprehend the concepts of infinity, time having no beginning or end, and parallel universes, because we have no reference points in our experience. If one believes in an "organizing intelligence," as Dr. Wayne Dyer calls it, or a Creator, the logical question becomes who or what created the Creator and when? If we are truly honest with ourselves, we do not even know with absolute certainty that we individually exist in the way we experience life. We only "know" what we perceive through our various senses such as sight, taste, sound, touch, and smell. One might then ask, "Isn't perception reality?" And that brings us to our second assumption, that perception is only a relative reality. Seeing may be believing, but that belief is not necessarily founded upon something absolute either; only upon what we *think* we see. Once again, consider the analogy to the belief that the world was flat or that the sun revolved about the earth. Those beliefs were based on what people actually thought they saw. They thought they saw the world as flat and the sun revolving around the earth.

When a photographer takes a picture, he or she brings to that instant when the shutter is opened and closed, all of their beliefs, biases, and training to determine what is photographed, how it will be composed, the mediums used (digital or film, color or black and white), and the intended purpose. What is created is not reality but an image that represents what the photographer saw as his or her reality. In some cases the image is so overtly manipulated that it does not even represent that. The photographer consciously or unconsciously wants us to believe something, to see what they saw or believed, and so the image expressly reinforces the perception or belief of the photographer. A photographer can even selectively choose the image, such as when capturing a demonstration. He or she can photograph an assemblage of those in the minority on an issue and represent it as the majority, for example, perhaps even believing it to be the majority. A reporter can report those aspects of a story that he or she feels represent the truth, but it is simply their truth.

When I was in law school a famous trial attorney gave us a telling demonstration. He randomly selected several of my fellow students to enact a shooting incident. After the enactment he selected several other students and asked them to leave the classroom. One at a time, they were summoned back to the class to tell what they saw. Each one saw the same incident differently, until even the rest of us were unsure what had actually been portrayed in the enactment, even though we had previously seen it with our own eyes. We all saw the exact same thing but our individual "realities" were different and subject to manipulation, even though occurring without any overt attempt to change our minds. What we individually so definitely thought we saw had become riddled with doubt.

The attorney then handed to one of my fellow students a police officer's written description of a crime. It had been prepared by the attending officer from witness accounts. The student was then given ample time to read and assimilate what it said. Next he was asked to return the written account and relay its contents orally to a second student, privately, outside of the classroom. That student then relayed it privately to a third until it had been relayed orally to a fifth student. The fifth student, with the written statement displayed on a screen behind him that he could not see, was then asked to tell us the details of the incident about which he had been informed. His recitation bore no resemblance whatsoever to the written piece on the screen behind him. He was quite confounded by our looks of amazement and disbelief as he recounted what he "knew" of the incident. But the telling from one person to the next had interposed each person's values and beliefs (they each seized upon and interpreted different aspects of the story), so that the final version was much changed from the first.

Our expectations also affect what we perceive as reality. Anyone who has ever used purple-lens ski goggles knows how the snow at first looks purple. But our mind "knows" that snow is white, and soon the snow appears quite white through the purple lenses. Our brain has "corrected" our eyes to account for the reality we expect. This effect is hard at work in the "Puzzle of the Six Extra Words." In that puzzle we are presented with a written paragraph and asked to count the number of times the word *and* was doubled. Even after knowing that there were six times the word *and* was doubled in the paragraph, and after enlarging the text on my computer screen to meticulously track every word, I could not find all six times *and* was doubled in the text. My mind kept altering my perception to eliminate unexpected usage of the word *and*, but all six were in fact there when subsequently highlighted in bold type.

We can also all see the same things, yet perceive them differently. And our perceptions of the same object or thing can change, even though there is no change at all in the object. Look at the two drawings below. Some will see the left lowermost corner of the wire frame cube to be in the front. Others will perceive it as one of the back corners of the cube. For some the dark object is a vase. For others it is the dark space between two opposing faces.

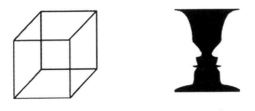

In the end perception is not "true" or absolute reality, and what we believe as reality can often be easily altered, even through the innocent actions of others. There does not have to be evil intention to color our beliefs for us to perceive the same thing differently from one another. All it takes is enough preconditioning or peer pressure for us to conform our reality to the beliefs or expectations of others. Once we know the alternative view of the objects above, we are then able to see the objects differently. Regrettably, alternative views are not often made available by those who seek to preserve a view that benefits them. Corporate conglomerate news media, for example, often have a strong financial disincentive to present alternative views that might anger a news source or be detrimental to an advertiser or affiliate.

All of this has profound implications on a global scale as well as microcosmically. When we view things with other people of common beliefs and values we are less likely to have significantly divergent "realities." But when people of different cultural predispositions and backgrounds are involved, the "ski goggle adjustment" and peer pressure effects are magnified. Contrast the reality of an AIDS-orphaned and starving child in Africa with the reality of a child living with both parents on a farm in the Midwestern United States. Contrast the reality of an out-of-work Palestinian youth who has witnessed the death of his father and brother at the hands of Israeli soldiers with the reality of an Israeli mother whose child was blown to pieces by one so certain of his reality that he willingly gave up his life in order to take the lives of innocent human beings he did not even know. These people will see and interpret the world in ways vastly differently from one another.

Our discourse here asks that you suspend your beliefs and preconceptions for a while so we might achieve greater clarity and understanding. You are asked to suspend for a time your most fervently held beliefs, even those at your very core. For the moment, be a little less certain of your own correctness and virtue. Seek first to understand the realities of others and question your own assumptions, values, and beliefs. It is ultimately in all of our own self-interests to do so.

It is in our self interest because, despite our greatness as a people and a nation, we face unparalleled challenges. The economic and social stresses of American daily life are having a profound effect upon all of us and our children. We have become a deeply divided society, trying to cope with the complex internal and external forces that impact the quality of our lives and even our very existence.

Violence at home and threats abroad terrorize American lives. Our educational systems are struggling to compete with those of third world countries, which now account for more than half of the world's output of goods and services. Corruption and greed in our institutions, such as Congress and major American corporations, rob us of confidence in the efficacy of these institutions. All the while our political systems have become largely unresponsive and hugely ineffective in terms of meeting the needs and desires of the majority of our people. Confidence in our leadership is at historic lows. These threats to our very way of life compel us to examine further what we have become and what we can be. That is the element of self-interest that needs to be pursued. Such an examination does not mean an abandonment of our ideals. Rather, it compels a return to those of our ideals that we can reaffirm through a better understanding of them, their value, and their applicability. And it may compel new approaches that grow out of a less ideological, less dogmatic sense of ourselves and our objectives. Such an examination can also lead us to more meaningful lives and a more peaceful world. This is not idealistic prattle. What we will discuss here involves the pragmatic and the achievable. What we will explore is not merely criticism, but constructive approaches well within our grasp if we have the will to make the needed changes personally and nationally.

A word or two about religion is appropriate here. Religion will be discussed at various points in this book, but hopefully construed by the reader in a manner that neither advocates nor denigrates a particular religion or non-belief. Denigration or advocacy is not the intention or objective. Whether that will be perceived as such will be a function of the beliefs and willingness of the reader to consider different perspectives. Religions serve useful purposes until their belief systems are perverted by those with personal agendas, or until they become exclusionary by highlighting differences rather than similarities. In the latter instance, the desire for conformity and fear of nonbelievers can foster great harm. When religions focus on limiting the lives of others by trying to control the conduct of believers and nonbelievers alike, they can foster conflict and division. When religions focus on expanding the lives of others by charitably helping to feed, educate, and house, they create much good in this world. But so much evil and horror have been perpetrated throughout history in the name of religion. How can it then be that belief in the directions of a divine Creator has resulted in so much suffering? How can it be that nearly all religions believe they alone know absolute truth? These questions also compel a degree of openness to divergent thought—at least, hopefully, to a recognition that your beliefs do not have to be mine, or mine yours.

I do not pretend that loosening our grip on deeply held beliefs will be an easy task. But clinging to them is not working for us as a country. There is a much larger national need here that is being poorly served by unbending adherence to dogma, ideology, and perception. For now let us adopt the two assumptions we have outlined: that there are no absolutes, and that perception is only relative reality. That degree of open-mindedness will allow us to consider much that we might have otherwise closed our minds to or simply overlooked. As we shall see, the beneficial implications will be substantial.

Chapter Three

The Problem of Fear

"In my experience," Teabing said, "men go to far greater lengths to avoid what they fear than to obtain what they desire."
—Dan Brown, The Da Vinci Code

There is perhaps no greater motivator of human behavior than fear. It is rooted in our very basic instincts for survival, serving as the warning of potential harm. It is so central to our being that it can even invoke psychological and physical reactions such as perspiration, elevated blood pressure, rapid heartbeat, and outright panic. All of these things aided more primitive beings in coping with threats and assessing whether to fight or to flee. In our more modern world, some of these reactions are less than helpful, and can be even dangerous at times. Fear can often foster desperate acts generated by the reflex to do something as opposed to letting the dangerous situation persist. A panicked person with a gun, for example, can commit some terrible acts when those acts are dispassionately viewed in calmer moments. Central to fear is the unknown: unknown actions to take and unknown consequences about to occur. When a ball comes flying at our head at a sporting event we simply react instinctively by ducking before we even sense any fear. Then relief is the sensation if we are successful avoiding the ball, or pain if we are not. It is when we are confronted by the lack of a clear path to safety that fear takes hold and the body prepares all systems for action yet to be determined. Senses and other bodily operations are heightened as the mind searches for actions that will yield relief from the threat. Where the danger is perceived as ongoing, the search for relief is ongoing and can even become quite frenzied when no obvious answer is found, and the danger becomes more imminent.

Fear is also not always apparent to us and takes its most insidious form when it is subconsciously acting upon us. Thus we can become edgy or even quite neurotic without understanding why. This occurs where our mind has perceived a threat but has not elevated it to the level of consciousness. Without delving too deeply into human psychology, the kind of fear that comes from distrust is the most relevant here. Simply put, we fear that which is different from ourselves and our sense of what is right or true. Someone who acts, believes, or looks differently than we do can be perceived as a threat to our sanguinity about our own beliefs, appearance, and actions. Return to your childhood and the merciless treatment accorded children who were considered different, who wore out-of-fashion clothes, who stuttered or were intellectually "slow." Perhaps you were even one of those perpetrating or receiving the acts of hostility and unkindness. But no one acknowledged or sensed that there was any fear of these different children. What they perceived instead was a sense of superiority or smugness about their own correctness or appropriateness. Look beyond that overt smugness and you will find conscious relief from shared ridicule of the outlier, tinged with doubt and ultimately unconscious apprehension and self-doubt.

Some societies have even taken this form of fear to the point of killing innocent individuals perceived as a threat to their own well-being because of nonconformity. Two such societies were ancient Sparta and the more modern era of Hitler's Germany. Those who had anointed themselves as the definers of the human standard in Spartan society caused newborn children, deemed to not conform to the desired standard, to be left to die of the elements in the mountains or hurled to their deaths at the bottom of a ravine. The rationale was that the remaining Spartan society would not be tainted by those determined to be weak and inferior beings, thereby flushing the gene pool of inferior progeny. What is the most remarkable thing about this is that other Spartans, including mothers and fathers, approved of this slaughter of innocents as perfectly acceptable and even appropriate. A similar process occurred in Nazi Germany with the "benevolent" killing of gays, the deformed, and the mentally ill. With our beliefs and values today we look back on Sparta and the atrocities of World War II Germany in horror. Parenthetically, our revulsion in turn is part of our fear of this happening again or even to us individually. Simply calling these people "evil" does not aid us. Those were people whose horrendous acts were motivated by their beliefs at the time about what they perceived to be truth, and their fear of the consequences of inaction.

When we castigate people as "evil," it simplistically creates only a label. It does not lead to a true understanding of why people throughout time can, in their minds, logically and appropriately commit acts of what is later deemed to be unspeakable cruelty upon their fellow beings. This all of course assumes a degree of rational thought by the perpetrators as opposed to the actions of the truly psychotic. Yet we often resort to the "psychotic" label to explain cruelty. So we argue that the Spartans had to be insane to do what they did, or that Hitler was a madman. Yet there is no evidence that the very advanced Spartan civilization suffered from mass psychosis. On the contrary, they saw their asceticism and rigidity as crucial to their survival. The murder of "weak" children was a clearly thought-out part of an overall societal structure. It also does not serve us well to define people such as Hitler or Stalin as madmen. The more useful reference is why these people attracted a following. Underlying their actions, and that of their followers, was fear. And their leaders were masters at manipulation of that human emotion to achieve conformity with their wishes arising from their own fears and insecurities.

The pervasiveness of fear as a motivator of human behavior throughout time simply cannot be overstated. Yet fear is seldom if ever publicly acknowledged as the rationale for action. No one wants to admit or concede that they are fearful. Instead the ostensible reason for acts later deemed monstrous is often couched in noble terms such as the commandment of a higher being, justice, putting people out of their misery, self-preservation, or honor. Even where fear is acknowledged, such as fear of starvation, creating the "need" to seize more arable land (and thus a perceived need to subjugate or kill all or many of the inhabitants of that land), the true fear is not expressed. The true fear is the sense of one's own helplessness in the face of a perceived threat. That fear allows us to succumb to the fears and needs of others even to the point of sanctioning substantial harm. The end justifies the means.

When we are tempted to surrender our well-being to the dictates of others, individually or collectively, a warning flare should be fired across the bow of our consciousness. While it may seem comforting in the short run to relinquish responsibility to others who display bravado, the reality is that we ultimately bear the consequences. Fear should never drive us, individually or as societies, to abrogate our responsibility to make rational and humane decisions and to insist upon the same from our representatives and leaders. Problems are often complex and require time to resolve. Too often we are willing to accept the quick, simplistic, aggressive response of another in order to quiet the discomfort of our own fear and sense of helplessness.

It is always of great value to question whether actions are affirmative or fear-based. To the extent they are fear-based, our lives are diminished or worse. Protecting ourselves from harm as part of an overall strategy for advancement is entirely appropriate. But fear as the sole determinant of action is shortsighted and often leads to impulsive rather than thoughtful outcomes. Leaders who play upon our fears and exhort us to support them or their goals solely because they will protect us from some purported evil or harm do not thereby advance the cause of humanity or protect our longer-term interests. We do not create by tearing down or disparaging. We do not increase or protect our freedoms by diminishing them in the name of security. Business leaders whose only answer to competitive challenge is to pare expenses and cut staff do not thereby address the long-term best interests of stakeholders (stockholders and employees), or address fundamental issues of better management. Rather they acknowledge in such a fear-driven course of action their own failure as managers and their own lack of creativity and resourcefulness. Those who focus on disciplining their children's shortcomings, rather than supporting their unique strengths, create fearful adults rather than individuals with strong self esteem and the confidence to deal with life's challenges.

Fear cannot be avoided. It is, however, our reaction to fear that will determine our individual and collective quality of life. The customary reaction to fear is defensive. Thus, to the extent we make fear-based decisions, we often take defensive actions rather than actions that build up and enhance our lives. Solely defensive reactions avoid solutions and can prolong the difficulty. Much of the opposition to action in the public interest today is defensively based. Whether decrying a perceived loss of freedom or a supposed government takeover, such responses are purely defensive and do not move us toward solutions to the underlying problems. That is not to suggest that all efforts to reduce government are bad. Rather, government is typically introduced to solve a problem, whether that is to provide a service or to afford a protection. Naked appeals urging us to remove or reduce government involvement in an area, without also offering a viable alternative, leave us worse off than before.

Where positive action *is* taken, the discomfort of fear can create a desire for immediate action that may prevent the ability to take a longer-term, more inclusive view. When we fear that a levee will break, for example, the rush to patch the levee may leave the larger issue of flood control for later, or abandon it altogether. Once the immediate threat has passed, we often turn our attention to the next pressing need without completing the prior task. When national security is threatened, the first response is typically tactical and specifically military rather than strategic. Time is a precious commodity in America; we don't believe we have time to look over the fence until someone has tunneled under it. And then the response is usually to plug the tunnel rather than to try and comprehend those doing the tunneling and what will address and stop the motivation of those tunneling. It has been part of our American character to be reactive, to seek quick fixes. More contemplative approaches are often brushed aside in the rush to action. It is a trait we ought to consider. That does not mean "analysis paralysis." It simply means we have much to gain from listening more to alternative voices of caution and reason before we take action. And it means stepping back and considering whether we are being fear-driven or solution-driven.

As a nation we have a remarkable lack of knowledge about other cultures. We are regrettably not alone among the peoples of the world in this deficiency. While many Americans like to see themselves as worldly, the reality is otherwise. We know very little about the geography, history, and cultural makeup of most of the world's nations. Study after study confirms the ignorance of our populace, not merely about world geography and culture, but even of the location and capitals of states within the United States itself. This kind of nativism and cultural ignorance are endemic in this world. In countries large and small, millions of people, often focused on basic survival rather than geopolitics, live in relative ignorance of the people and cultures beyond their borders,. Only now, for example, is China guardedly beginning to open its vast country to other viewpoints and information outside itself. It is shocking to think of such a huge country filled with so many people who have little or no direct experience beyond their communities. The implications of this are disquieting for a country whose economic and military strength is growing dramatically. North Korea is an example of the potential for harm that exists when a people are isolated, impoverished, and ruled by fear. Similar examples of enforced or situational isolation abound elsewhere around the globe. We know so little about ourselves and even less about our fellow inhabitants of this planet Earth. The problem of cultural ignorance is even greater in countries where many of the inhabitants lack access to non-ethnocentric education and mass media. This cultural captivity is often manipulated by religious and secular leaders to maintain their power. What is critically important about all of this is that cultural ignorance is the petri dish of fear. And fear breeds distrust and ultimately conflict.

The Cold War grew out of immense distrust between Russia and the United States, two countries who had previously been reluctant allies in World War II. The wartime alliance was one of necessity, but the distrust grew out of ignorance. Only when cultural and business interaction expanded the connections between the United States and Russia did the Cold War begin to subside. That too grew out of necessity, as Russia's economic system foundered badly in the 1960s, and there was then a willingness to "peer over the fence." One fear conquered another. The fear of economic and social collapse conquered Russia's distrust of the West. As Russians came here and Americans traveled in Soviet countries, and we talked more to each other rather than at each other, we discovered our commonalities and began to overcome our fear of each other. We discovered mutual benefit in bridging our differences. This is by no means a completed process, but significant progress has been made. Another driving factor in the warming of relations between the United States and Russia has been that corporate opportunity has become greater by doing business *with* Russia than by opposing it militarily.

The pattern of cultural ignorance and consequent fear have widespread applicability. The roots of the Israeli-Palestinian conflict are complex, but one element has been mutual fear. Previously living side by side, Muslim and Jew largely coexisted, albeit uncomfortably at various times over the ages. Their religions even sprang from a common forefather, Abraham, and they share many other commonalities. Jews, Christians, and Muslims coexisted in Spain until Queen Isabella expelled non-Catholics in 1492 AD. But when immigrants began to settle in the Holy Land, the cultural differences were striking, and so were the resentments and distrust.

After 1948, displaced and impoverished former residents of Israel became resentful and angry flash points for existing, deep dissatisfaction and cultural hatred. *Zionist* became an attractive label toward which to direct the discontent festering there and among the subjects of sheiks and kings awash in their respective countries' oil wealth. Resentment that might have been directed at the few who possessed such massive oil wealth, or against the corrupt governments that did little to provide for their people, was turned instead toward Jews in general and Israel specifically. The external peril, creating and playing upon the fear of one's neighbor, has been the tool of demagogues throughout history. It has been used successfully in the Middle East to maintain a host of self-aggrandizing leaders at the expense of their people. Once the cycle of hatred has started, the search for righteousness is hopelessly lost to vengeance.

Fear is a central theme in religion. It has sometimes been used to attract and hold converts and to enforce compliance with the will of spiritual leaders. Fear of the deity's wrath in life and fear of eternal suffering in an afterlife, or no afterlife, are powerful motivators to assure spiritual compliance. Religion itself also serves to calm the disquiet felt about our world and our place in it. Religion fills a void by answering the otherwise unanswerable through faith. It is not a purpose of this book to denigrate religion or any peaceful, mainstream form of religion. But we cannot ignore the atrocities and terrors perpetrated in the name of religion throughout history.

How can it be that something which seeks goodness in us all can be an instrument of harassment, torture, and depravity? From the Crusades to the Spanish Inquisition to the Salem witch trials, to Sunni and Shiite conflict, religion-justified suffering has permeated nearly every people and country. Most religions do not condone external violence within their teachings. Thus, while the Catholic Papacy has had an army for over five hundred years, it has been largely ceremonial and protective (the Papacy was not above engaging others to war in its interests, however). Religion has not been so much an instigator of war, but of persecution by those who pervert the religion's teachings to their own ends. And persecution, whether in the schoolyard or the Serengeti, finds its motivation from fear.

Those who are already insecure and thus fearful can see competing religious beliefs as a threat to their own sense of security. Because religion can be such a powerful answer to our most fundamental doubts and fears about our very existence and our place in the universe, any threat to our absolute beliefs reawakens those doubts and fears. This is especially so for those with a limited worldview or limited access to competing ideas with which to broaden their views and assuage their fears. Those who live in relative isolation from science and world events are all the more easily influenced. In contrast, the more we comprehend that various things are rectifiable, rather than the work of evil, the less fearful we are and the less susceptible we become to efforts to manipulate those fears. The more we understand the peaceful beliefs of others who believe differently than ourselves, the more likely we are to coexist in peace.

Religions have meaningful purposes in this world. It is when religions are perverted and used to justify violence wrought upon nonbelievers that religion becomes an instrument of harm to others. We must learn to talk *with* one another, not *at* each other, and learn to appreciate our commonalities. Religion-inspired violence is borne of fear and intolerance, fertilized by ignorance and the resources of those who stand to benefit from the conflict.

As people become more aware of their differences, they can acquire comfort, rather than fear, in the sheer diversity of religious belief or non-belief, as well as in their shared values and views of the universe. The antipathy between Muslim and Jew is all the more remarkable given the vast range of shared history and cultural origins. Religious leaders truly imbued with holy ideals must have the courage to step forward and stress acceptance and knowledge rather than hatred and myopia. If those leaders have real faith in their beliefs, then they should not fear exposure to the beliefs of others. The carnage wrought upon believer and nonbeliever alike should be cause enough to oppose violence in the name of God. We must come to understand that my belief does not have to be your belief; and that we can find safety in our common beliefs rather than fear in our differences. Faith is just that. No religion has yet demonstrated with absolute certainty that it alone is the one true religion. Even within each religion there are sects and interpretations that may vary widely. Lacking such certainty, no religious leader or individual should ever feel anointed to condemn the beliefs of others, pious, agnostic, or atheist. And as believers and nonbelievers we must demand this of ourselves and our religious leaders. We must also be vigilant to any attempts to pervert our own religion, whatever that might be, to justify the abridgement of the freedom of others or to do outright harm in God's name. This is the element of personal responsibility that takes us from the idealistic to the pragmatic. Demagogues do not function in a vacuum. It is only when the rest of us retreat in fear that the distortion and harm can occur. No matter what our religion, we have an obligation to ensure that it respects the universal tenants of peace and tolerance. The famous words of Pastor Martin Niemoller are as relevant today as they were in the time of Hitler's Germany when he wrote them:

> When the Nazis came for the communists,
> I remained silent;
> I was not a communist.
>
> When they locked up the social democrats,
> I remained silent;
> I was not a social democrat.
>
> When they came for the trade unionists,
> I did not speak out;
> I was not a trade unionist.
>
> When they came for me,
> there was no one left to speak out for me.

That element of personal responsibility is a good place to end this chapter. When we understand the insidious and pervasive role fear plays in our lives, we can begin to create positive change. The benefits are enormous. Just consider the losses to science, the arts, and humanity from all the beings, and their never-to-be-born progeny, who perished in the Holocaust, or died in suicide bombings and at the hands of other religious and political zealots throughout history. What enormous advances could we have made had those people not died? How many potential Einsteins, Beethovens, Al-Batanis, and Da Vincis have we lost? And what great accomplishments could we have achieved in our personal lives if our energies were focused more on the positive rather than defensively based out of reaction to fears?

Chapter Four

The Politics of Fear and Diversion

The people can always be brought to the bidding of the leaders . . . All you have to do is to tell them they are being attacked and denounce [those opposed to war] for lack of patriotism and exposing the country to danger.
—Nazi propagandist Herman Goering from his jail cell
during the Nurnberg War Crimes trials, April 18, 1946

We are all of us connected. What we do affects others and what they do affects us. What happens in our house is impacted by what happens in the State House. Regardless of our interest in civic affairs or politics, the decisions made by our school board, our mayor, governor, and our President, and all of the people in between, deeply affect the quality of our lives, even to the point of affecting our individual security and freedom of choice. A modern-day Thoreau seeking the solitude of Walden Pond would today find his attempt limited by zoning and other land use laws, property tax issues, building codes, and a host of other external "interference." The world intrudes upon us whether we seek it or not. Functional isolation in a telecommunicated, interconnected, industrialized world is all but impossible. In this context the desire by some for less government is quite understandable.

When our involvemnt, however, takes the form of expressions of anger and actions that merely oppose, we are not helpful to the effort to achieve national consensus and direction. What we should seek is a way forward, not backward. That suggests that solutions, rather than angry denunciation and opposition, is what is needed from us. Our behavior—whether to opt out, oppose, or advocate—is a product of our beliefs and our perceptions. We have previously discussed the need for openness in our beliefs. It is also fundamentally important to understand the forces that affect our perceptions of the world around us and the forces that impact our lives. These forces and perceptions not only impact us personally; they shape us collectively as a country. We have talked about how fear and anxiety play upon us, but understanding the politics of fear and diversion is so central to our ability to bring about meaningful change that it deserves its own discussion.

Fear has been used by demagogues throughout history to garner support and bend people to their will. Its appeal is so strong that in order to diminish their fear, people can be swept up in causes that have violent and horrific consequences. As we know, one of the most dramatic examples was Nazi Germany. Playing masterfully to their insecurities, Hitler and his sickeningly brilliant propagandist, Joseph Goebbels, manipulated the German people into stifling dissent, going to war, and even committing genocide. Some of the lessons of Nazi Germany are often overlooked by the focus on the horror of the Holocaust. But the subtleties of manipulation employed then hold equally great lessons for other countries and other generations. That manipulation did not exist in a vacuum. The beliefs and values of many Germans provided receptivity to it.

In the United States, which has traditionally prided itself in taking the moral high ground in its foreign policy, the fear of terrorist attack following 9/11 became the publicly articulated linchpin of justification for the doctrine of preemption: that we would preemptively attack another country if we *believed* that it posed a singular threat. For the first time the American people and their legislators sanctioned an attack on another country, Iraq, based on the *fear* of aggression, as opposed to actual overt attack or threatened action by the country attacked. It is not our purpose here to debate the wisdom of such a dramatic departure in American foreign policy, beyond noting that it was fear-based. Indeed, the political discussion and debate of the 2004 presidential elections turned heavily upon internal and external security anxieties and contributed mightily to how people voted. The presidential election of 2008 had a similar component, but it was overshadowed by economic concerns. The element of fear then became concern about perpetuating existing economic policies that were leading the country into deep recession or worse.

When fear becomes the determinant of democratic choice, boundaries and good judgment become harder to discern. As we have noted, fear injects an element of desperation into decision making that interferes with more thoughtful action. Panicked people running to the exits of a burning building have little time for debate about which route to safety is best. The person trying to divert the stampede away from a blocked door will likely be trampled for his or her efforts, no matter the correctness of the position.

Fear has been exerting an increasing stranglehold on political decision making in the United States at all levels from national to local. Contrast the exhortation by President John F. Kennedy in 1960 to ask what Americans could do for their country with the current focus upon limitation of government regulation, restricting immigration, limitation of medical choice (including access to care, abortion rights, and the right to die at a chosen time) and the expansion of state-sponsored or endorsed religious activity. The entire healthcare debate was peppered with fearful warnings about loss of personal freedom, government takeovers, and loss of benefits for seniors. That opened the door for a bloated piece of legislation that pleased no one, if anything moving us backward rather than forward in the healthcare debate. The immigration issue is similarly driven, rightly or wrongly, by the fear of job loss and increased crime. This resort to fear-based politics recently reached an absolute nadir in my home state, when one candidate's sole political appeal to voters was to frighten them about his opponent. He expressed no agenda or qualifications of his own in his campaign; only that his allegedly evil opponent shouldn't be elected for various reasons, therefore he, and not his opponent, should be elected.

The resort to overt or less conspicuous fear as a political tool in America finds expression in not merely the issues, or lack thereof, but endemically throughout the political system. The complaints about gridlock, partisanship, and do-nothing politicians resound throughout our country. The core reason for this inertia is fear. The citizens are anxious, politicians are afraid to take innovative positions (or special interests induce them not to), and political strategists and their public relations counterparts know how to use fear to influence elections and thereby keep incumbents in power.

Americans are fearful on several levels. Nationally, terrorism has unnerved our prior complacency about personal safety within our borders. Locally, trepidation about perceived moral decay, crime, and deep economic insecurities have all combined to put most voters in a decidedly defensive frame of mind. The near collapse of our financial system has shaken American confidence in our institutions, both government and corporate. Any illusion that we are safe, even in our homes, is impinged by the daily parade of depravity, criminality. and corruption featured in our news sources. There we see the shootings, sexual crimes, and malfeasance that has occurred only hours before or even live for us to follow. That is what attracts viewers, sells advertising, and unsettles our confidence in the future.

The media also has a role, wittingly or otherwise, in inhibiting the expression of new ideas which would otherwise lessen anxiety. Competition for airtime means most discussion is reduced to polemics and superficial reportage. News programs that ought to provide insight have become commentary from often ill-informed, opinionated talking heads of one persuasion or another. The end result is an intimidating environment that confronts anyone seeking to explain even slightly complex concepts. Politicians with even minimal political savvy know that advancing new ideas is suicidal. So they resort to simplistic platitudes or negative discourse. Even political novices are taught that new ideas are very risky. New ideas and creative thinking are thrown to the pundit and opposition wolves where selective quotes and misinformation will chew these fresh concepts to pieces and make their proponents a fool for their efforts. The current political process has little time or inclination for complete analysis. The need to attract readers, listeners, and viewers, and thus advertising profits, means focusing on the sensational. Even the best ideas get reduced to simplistic one-liners and then are ridiculed as if to demonstrate the superiority of the commentator and the foolishness of the advocate. Where "consultant" commentators of each party are presented, they are often so biased for their position, and the interchange so short, that little light is shed. Then there is the media's attempt to represent people who are little more than teleprompter readers, or "journalists," as somehow competent to debate complex and emotionally charged issues or to critique those who have real credentials in the area being discussed. The ultimate loser is the electorate who, even if they desire to be informed, are left ill-informed. The resultant uncertainty breeds distrust and apprehension.

As will be discussed in greater detail later, Americans are also fearful about economic issues. Competitive pressures from domestic and foreign businesses, technological change, high unemployment, and evolving job expectations have combined to create considerable job-related stress for American workers at all levels. Sanguinity about our technological superiority has given way to fears that innovation is finding fertile ground in other countries where education has a higher national priority and production costs are lower. Many of our cherished industries, such as automobile and consumer electronic production, have moved to other countries. Where headquarters remain, manufacturing is being outsourced. Even professional work, such as architecture and accounting, is being outsourced abroad. There is genuine concern about the impact that globalization will have on our standard of living and our ability to compete with lower-wage workers abroad.

Bombarded by all this negativity, it is no wonder the electorate is anxious and susceptible to emotional appeals to cut government spending, impose tariffs, stop alleged moral decay, and build walls around our country. Attempts to jump-start the economy and to prop up a shaky financial system are viewed through eyes that understandably fear such massive expenditures and the federal debt they incur.

With scrutiny, creativity, and positive thinking filtered out, what succeeds today is pandering to our insecurities. Smart political strategists counsel their candidates to be bland, noncommittal, and inoffensive. That's the defensive strategy. The offensive strategy attacks the opponent and also plays to our fears of the moment. Is it any wonder then that we are confronted with strident partisanship rather than leadership, regurgitated tired remedies rather than creative new ideas, and ultimately gridlock? Is it surprising then that frustrated parishioners want to take moral imperatives, as they perceive them, from their church hall to City Hall, or that many others have simply chosen to not participate in the political process at all?

The shock of the Supreme Court's decision in *Roe v. Wade* was one of the galvanizing events for religious individuals and institutions that had not previously been involved in the political process on behalf of their faith. Seeing themselves as the "moral majority," beginning in the late1960s a committed and growing cadre of devout and sincere believers began to involve themselves in the political process to address what they saw as increasing societal decay. The litmus test for their candidates was conformity to a set of religion-based beliefs about abortion, prayer in public institutions, and morality in general. Their objectives became changing the composition of the Supreme Court in order to reverse *Roe v. Wade* and altering societal conduct through legislation embodying their religious (read *moral*) beliefs. Getting people of like beliefs elected meant taking part in the political process at all levels. That involved becoming delegates at conventions, running for office, and providing financial and physical campaign support (such as making lawn signs, going from door to door, and manning phone banks). An entire industry sprang up to support this movement, often with substantial financial reward for its leaders. Centered primarily upon a receptive Republican Party, these mores-focused individuals became a force for significant philosophical change in the party.

With individual anxieties sharpened by the political system, the effort to inject religious influence in government has had great appeal for many today. After all, who can argue with morality? As is the issue with religion generally, the problem is not so much the ultimate objective but the means. While we can agree in the abstract with the need for a just and moral society, the harder part is finding agreement about what is moral and what is just when we get to specifics. The differences of view can and have become quite divisive. The rancorous debate over abortion is but one example. Even within the ranks of those opposed to abortion, there is a spectrum of opinion about when, if at all, to make exceptions, such as when the mother's life is endangered. The brilliant eighteenth-century minds who crafted the U.S. Constitution recognized the difficulties inherent in religious standards and endeavored to draw a clear line between government and religion. They posited that government ought not to interfere with the private practice of religion and that no religion should be sanctioned by government. Any debate about where that line is to be drawn ought to err on the side of separation. We are a pluralistic society with multiple religious practitioners, agnostics, and atheists within our population. They all vote. So there is no single universal American religion. We are not a theocracy, although there are those who would seek to change that.

There is a too widely held belief in our country that laws are intended to be moral or borne out of a religious directive. There is nothing moral or God-given about a stop sign. While it is true that legislators often apply lofty moral considerations to their deliberations, the real purpose of laws is practical governance and order, not morality or even justice. The application of justice is reserved for our legal system of judges and juries, charged with applying and interpreting the law. Morality is the province of religious leaders and philosophers, not the law. This statement may offend and even disturb some, but most lawyers and legal scholars would agree with the proposition. Even laws about such things as sexual predation are ultimately based upon protection of potential victims rather than imposition of some moral value. It is enough that sexual predation is extremely harmful to the defenseless victim. That said, nearly all of us would find common ground that predation is immoral, and most would find it psychologically deviant. The point, however, is that laws and regulations have practical results as their purpose, not morality. The Volstead Act (The National Prohibition Act of 1919) that attempted to limit the manufacture and consumption of alcoholic beverages in the 1920s has often been referred to as an example of the inability to legislate morality, because it did not stop alcohol consumption or alcoholism. Morality had very little to do with either its enactment or its failure. It was simply another imperfect attempt to regulate what was viewed as a potentially harmful substance, and to keep society safe from the consequences, including crime. These were practical rather than moral or religious ends.

It is entirely appropriate for people of faith to attempt to influence legislation as voters and citizens within the political process. Indeed it is their civic duty to speak their minds and vote their conscience along with other citizens. But when religion begins to co-opt the political process as a central theme, or it becomes the narrow self-interest driving decision making, we have stepped to a dangerous precipice. Candidates whose platform and raison d'être are solely faith-based can find themselves ill-equipped to address more secular issues of governance. All of this is not to say that individuals with strong religious beliefs cannot be worldly, but when the primary rationale for election is faith-based, the secular concerns may not be dealt with knowledgeably or sufficiently, if at all. The attempt to blackmail politicians into voting for a particular issue, religion-based or otherwise, by threatening to mount a campaign against them is both counterproductive and selfish. Single issues ought not to be the basis upon which we evaluate our elected officials; their total record should be. Attempting to use a religious litmus test for decision making stands things on its head, since government is a secular endeavor in the United States. Indeed, the United States was founded in part out of the desire to escape government-sanctioned religion. Without much debate that point was reaffirmed by Congress when it ratified the Treaty of Tripoli in 1797, which stated, "The government of The United States is not in any sense founded on the Christian Religion." It was not founded on any other religion, either.

Issues as mundane as land use planning and as daunting as nuclear proliferation call for special skill, knowledge, and experience. That is where the emphasis should be when evaluating candidates for office. Divisive issues such as abortion, gay marriage, school vouchers, and public prayer contribute to the legislative gridlock we are experiencing. Debate becomes polarized and diverted from other issues that need urgent attention. Because religion is founded on belief, religious debate becomes a matter of conflicting beliefs and emotion rather than about the facts or needs at hand. Finally, as we have noted, the fear-based compulsion often employed to achieve conformity within religion does not serve us well outside of religion in the secular world of politics. Our personal insecurities about our own religious beliefs (usually not consciously acknowledged) should not drive us to impose those beliefs on others.

The authors of the Constitution got it right. To the extent we allow religion to play a determinative role in politics, we will weaken our system of government and diminish the results. We will also have interjected an extraneous consideration that can cloud issues and obscure solutions. One of the exceptional things that has made this country so valued in the world in the past has been our pluralism: our openness to the different ideas and divergent beliefs of others. We cannot allow demands for conformity to the religion-based views of some to debase what is fundamentally important to us all. Yet we have seen legislators hold up important secular legislation, completely unrelated to religion, by demanding insertion of some religious precept into the bill under consideration or in exchange for support for such a precept elsewhere.

Religious freedom is only one part of personal freedom. When our religious freedom seeks to determine the boundaries of our other freedoms, it weakens all freedom, ultimately threatening religious expression itself. That was the reality understood by our forefathers, and the reality even the most religious ignore at their peril. The fear of religious backlash from one quarter or another should not be a factor in our political process. The truth, however, is that fear of religious repercussion has become an inhibiting factor that diminishes and diverts debate from other issues and reduces the quality of our choices. That is ultimately not in anyone's interest, religious or secular.

The Watergate era was a political watershed in many ways. Most noticeably it marked a further lessening of the inherent respect held for government. The power of government was less to be admired than feared. The tarnish to the office of the president has intensified over time and had a spillover effect to other offices. Poll after poll equating politicians with used-car salesmen (with apologies to used-car salesmen) tells us that we do not respect politicians very much. And, thanks to the actions of too many politicians, that view has been too often appropriate. We are also far more inclined to delve into the personal lives of public figures than in the past. Babe Ruth's sleazier side was held out of the limelight by the press in his day. That would be far less likely in this era of "gotcha" journalism and paparazzi photography.

In the political sphere, the process of delving into every aspect of one's life, relevant or not, is aided by candidates for office who are eager to expose and denigrate the personal lives of their opponent rather than have to discuss meaningful issues. Discussion of issues in depth is viewed as political suicide by every consultant in the business of advising candidates these days. In a charade of so-called issue ads, sponsored by special interest groups who support one candidate, the "issue" is some negative aspect of the opponent rather than any positive position being put forth. The most notorious of these were the "Swiftboat" ads employed effectively to denigrate the presidential candidate John Kerry in 2004 by impugning his military record. Similar ads were employed to impugn George W. Bush's National Guard service. In both instances the ads were dishonest.

Yet there is virtually no accountability for these ads. The Supreme Court recently struck down an attempt to limit such "issue ads" by declaring that element of the McCain-Feingold Campaign Finance Reform Act to be an unconstitutional abridgement of free speech.

This ugly aspect of the politics of fear creates a chilling effect on anyone contemplating running for political office today. There is hardly anyone who does not have some issue lurking in their personal or business life that cannot be exploited, truthfully or otherwise, to an embarrassing degree. It has been jokingly argued that we would not want someone in office who led such a cloistered existence as to have no foibles. But the end result is to deter otherwise qualified individuals from the rigors of campaigning and public life, even those whose transgressions have no relationship whatsoever to their functioning with distinction in public service. In fact, the "smarter" and more successful you are, arguably the less likely you would want to run the gauntlet that exists in politics today.

And then there are the opinion polls. If candidates were not reticent to speak their minds before, polling today lets them know what is safe to advocate and what is not viewed favorably by the electorate. An entire industry exists to give advice to candidates and political parties on what issues resonate with voters; how strongly these views are held, positively or negatively; trending; and about the demographics of voters and nonvoters. Constitutional issues of free speech aside, a good case could be made to eliminate polling altogether during campaign periods, so candidates for office would have to actually take positions they believed in, popular or not, rather than safe, finger-to-the-wind issues. Polling also affects the electorate's opinion by the natural inclination of people to want to be accepted and in the majority. As noted earlier in the discussion about belief, when people's views are in the minority, it can cause them to question their views and shift to the majority position. Poll results can also discourage people from advocating less popular positions or from even voting at all. This latter situation occurred in recent years when exit polling on the East Coast predicted the outcome of a presidential election was broadcast before the polls had closed in the West. That caused some people on the West Coast to not vote when the exit polls projected their candidate would lose. While it is useful and at least interesting to know public opinion, the benefits of polling during elections would seem far outweighed by the detriments to democratic choice and the free expression of ideas. Finally, public relations firms often create polls to support a desired result for their special interest group or candidate. By framing the question(s) in a specific way, the pollster can skew the result. And by the way they spin the answers, they can also shape the results to suit their purposes. We need to be far more circumspect about how we use and view polls about candidates and issues. They are nothing more than opinions, and often deeply flawed ones at that.

All of these things combine to pollute the democratic process and force conformity, lack of choice, disinterest, and gridlock. It is not just partisanship that is at the root of our inertia, but the kinds of inhibiting fears and diversions previously mentioned. The fear of taking an unpopular position, the fear of alienating major supporters, and the fear of standing alone from one's party are all significant enablers of the gridlock and conformity we are witnessing both at the state and national levels.

Finally, there is the reverse use of fear by politicians and special interests. During the 1950s, when the dangers of cigarette smoking were first being learned, the tobacco industry began one of the first disinformation campaigns. Allan Brandt, writing in *The Cigarette Century*, presented the strategy:

> Its goal was to produce and sustain scientific skepticism and controversy in order to disrupt the emerging consensus on the harm of cigarette smoking. This strategy required intrusions into scientific process and procedure....The industry worked to assure that vigorous debate would be prominently trumpeted in the media. So long as there appeared to be doubt, so long as the industry could assert 'not proven,' smokers would have a rationale to continue, and new smokers would have a rationale to begin.

Several things are worth noting here. First, the industry used the removal of fear (the reverse use of fear) to advance their interests. People inherently want to be relieved of apprehension, so when someone casts doubt upon a fear it is readily received. Secondly, the industry employed the media as an ally in their efforts. The parallels between the tobacco industry disinformation campaign of the fifties and the current efforts to create doubt about global climate change ought not to be dismissed.

As citizens we must become more involved in the political process, so it is not monopolized by powerful specific interest groups and their scare agendas. We must encourage good people to run for office, people who seek new and creative solutions rather than personal aggrandizement or personal agendas. And we must support their efforts with our time and resources. We also must be willing to subject their views to scrutiny beyond sound bites. Part of that scrutiny should be an assessment of whether their appeal is to our fears or to our aspirations and hopes— not just in terms of motivational speeches, but in terms of actual positive solutions and actions to be taken. A candidate's character is very important, but only insofar as it relates directly to their performance in the office sought. If we expect the best and brightest to be available, then their personal lives must stay personal, and we should judge their abilities, not their peccadilloes. If we are individually motivated to bring about positive change, we should consider the courageous act of running for office ourselves. The process is arduous. but the rewards. in terms of meaningful accomplishment, can be great. If we fail to do these things, then we are surrendering our country to fearmongers, the insecure, and the lowest common denominator. The prospects for our democracy if this continues are disheartening: continued erosion of personal freedoms, conformity, and fear-based withdrawal rather than positive accomplishment and leadership in the world.

All in all, it is time for America to demand excellence again from our politicians, journalists, and religious and other community leaders, and to vote with our dollars, memberships, ballots, and media choices. The quality of our lives depends upon it. If we expect to be informed, then we must support those media outlets that inform and not those which merely provide entertainment labeled as news or blindly purvey the political, economic, or religious agenda of their owners. We must support in-depth reportage, such as that offered on independent public broadcasting, and write our local stations to hold them accountable for their programming. The advertisers will get the message, and then so will the ownership of the media. Above all, we need to be aware of the politics of fear and be courageous in demanding affirmative approaches from those who seek to hold elective office. We cannot be content with palliatives, slick presentations, and both sides of the argument as equal, or the acceptance of star power as qualification while discounting the weight of scientific and historical evidence. We also need to reform the electoral process in light of the recent Supreme Court decision that granted virtually unlimited political influence to corporations, unions, and unnamed entities who can now outspend individual American citizens. We need to study the issues and candidates, taking the time to cast informed votes rather than emotional or single-issue ones. We should also not fear complexity, and instead embrace it. Most problems are not solved with slogans or simple answers.

We are at an important crossroads in our history, where the politics of fear has been elevated to new heights. The ability of private, non-citizen money to sway voters and determine outcomes has never been greater. The threats to our personal liberties, our quality of life, and our national security from fear-based decision making cannot be over-stated. We cannot afford to become so preoccupied with our daily existence and basic survival that we sacrifice our individual futures and those of our children. None of us has the luxury of living in isolation. For our lives to have real meaning we must look outside of ourselves. For the inhab-itants of a democracy, political awareness and informed participation is a crucial starting place.

Chapter Five

The Problem with Labels

Once you label me, you negate me.
—Soren Kierkegaard

The pace and complexity of life in America today is overwhelming. Just getting through each day can be a frustrating exercise in coping. Nothing is simple. We are assaulted at every turn by rules, expectations and demands, confusing and often frightening "news," and challenges from seemingly irrational people around us. Then there are the local and national political issues that clamor for our attention. In this information age, the information is overwhelming. Is it any wonder then that people try to deal with the torrent of information that confronts us by adopting summarizing mechanisms such as labels? Labeling has become convenient shorthand by which we can categorize and assimilate all of this information about people and things without having to spend valuable time delving into detail. Labels on containers are quite helpful because they inform us about the contents. But labels placed on other things can have quite the opposite effect.

When we attach a label to someone or something, we have conveniently summarized them or it in a word or two. We can index most everything around us as liberal or conservative, sexist, politically incorrect, stupid, fattening. and so forth. But much is lost in the convenient trade-off. What is lost is any degree of real understanding. No person, position, or organization is ever truly or simply a label. They are a composite of traits. Even the particular label itself can have different meaning to different people. This is nowhere more evident than in the political sphere. One person's liberal is another's moderate. But here too labels leave us wanting. What do we really mean by *liberal* or *conservative*? Even within labels such as these that we think have a universal meaning, there are great divisions and differences. Goldwater-era conservatives and Lincoln-era Republicans would be dumbfounded by today's Republican brand of conservatism. Republican conservatism once stood for strong support of constitutional liberties and fiscal responsibility. Republicans of that era would not comprehend massive federal budget deficits incurred by subsequent Republican administrations or the expedient expansion of presidential power and the diminishing of personal freedoms under the rubric of national security.

We have willingly allowed our politicians and media to carve up the political landscape in America into left and right, or their supposed respective near equivalents, liberal, and conservative. These then become fundamental litmus tests to categorize, most often pejoratively, otherwise complex people and concepts into one side or the other. As if to provide clarity, we have added "far right" and "ultra leftist" to the mix. Could anything be more simplistic, or more divisive? We have been misled into believing we basically have only two choices, liberal or conservative (with "moderates," whatever that means, typically leaning to one or the other). Democrats are customarily viewed as liberal and Republicans as conservative. But in recent years, Southern Democrats have often had more in common with Northern Republicans than with their fellow Democrats from other parts of the country.

Not only do these labels do violence to reasoned discussion and evaluation, the historical labels of *conservative* and *liberal* are in reality totally meaningless today. Classic eighteenth century liberalism supported laissez-faire: minimal government interference and the protection of property rights. These views now embody the basic tenets of present-day American conservatism. By contrast, liberalism is perceived today to argue for strong governmental involvement in order to preserve rights, provide necessary social programs, and curb the excesses of capitalism. Yet all of this governmental involvement creates more burdens upon freedom and individual rights, hardly the stuff of classic liberalism. The generalities embodied in the labels *liberal* and *conservative*, when applied to specific individuals or concepts, do more to misinform than inform. They simply predispose thought and action. In today's American political climate, where candor is anathema, labels serve to mask the details and guard against deeper examination that might disclose errors or hidden agendas. In that regard, labeling often says as much about the labeler as it does about the one being labeled. What is the motivation for reducing discussion to a cliché? Why is the labeler not willing to consider the totality of the person or thing being labeled rather than the single aspect represented by the label? Are they afraid that what they might find would give lie to their own beliefs or fears? Or perhaps what they seek is the emotional response to the label and to assign that response to the person or thing being labeled. Labelling someone as "unpatriotic" or a "Bible thumper" are examples of this kind of labeling where the label affixes a host of undesirable connotations to the person labeled.

Labeling in the political sphere has become an art form that substitutes for reasoned debate and examination. Republicans recently applied a form of labeling with great effect in their campaign against President Obama's health-care legislation. The legislation was labeled by Republicans as "Obamacare;" a "government takeover" that would create "death panels." They also portrayed the requirement to get insurance, which would spread underwriting risk and thereby theoretically bring down costs, as a loss of freedom. And here we are again, back to the issue of restrictions upon freedom and their appropriateness. Lost in the debate over compulsory health care was the host of compulsions we find in our society. You cannot drive a car without a compulsory license and, in many states, without insurance. Your children cannot attend school without compulsory vaccinations. The fear-based appeal to loss of freedom obscured the real debate that should have occurred: the appropriateness of compulsory insurance. Moreover, the fearmongering also spelled the quick demise of any discussion of the health-care system employed in nearly all other western democracies: single payer. A single-payer approach would have eliminated the costly intermediaries that insurance companies layer in. That threat to the health insurance companies spawned a major fear-based campaign to derail any consideration of such an approach, replete with fear-inducing labels like *death panels.*

As with nearly all labeling, there was a remote hint of truth to some of the labels applied to the health-care proposals. The legislation, now adopted and quite imperfect, does entail government involvement. But it is no "takeover" of health-care such as exists in the other western democracies. We will still buy insurance from private insurers, and the doctor-patient relationship of our choice is still maintained. The government will make recommendations about care, but these advisories hardly constitute "death panels." The ironic reality is that insurance companies have been making real life-and-death decisions about people's care for decades. On occasion these decisions to deny coverage for a transplant or specific treatment have resulted in the death of the patient. Yet no one has accused Aetna or United Health Group, for example, of having death panels. As far as the "loss of personal freedom" that has inspired people to form a "Tea Party" (despite the fact we are no longer taxed without representation), the fact that most states require seat belts, helmets for cyclists, and a host of other mandatory purchases has not seemed to invoke such ire.

This is not an argument for or against the healthcare legislation finally enacted. What is instructive here is that these labels were used to play upon the fears and stir the passions of well-meaning people who were not privy to the several thousand pages of this legislation. Despite repeated efforts by President Obama and his administration to inform people about the overall benefits they felt were in the legislation, what stuck most strongly, both before and after adoption, were the fear-inducing labels. The end result was to move even the president away from a simpler and more cost-effective single-payer solution toward the hodgepodge we were finally handed. We still stand as the only Western democracy with a hugely expensive private insurance middleman earning massive profits while our national health level, by many metrics, ranks lower than that of many other advanced countries.

The intimidation factor of labels cannot be overstated. Constant references to "the liberal media" or "conservative bias" have had an effect on reportage. Most members of the American press have moved far from the days of candor and challenge evoked by the likes of Edward R. Murrow. In their efforts to avoid seeming biased, some media have either leaned to the sanitized middle or bent over backwards to give equal credence to both sides, whether or not such equality of position was warranted. While there may be two sides to most issues, one is usually more persuasive than the other. The press today is reluctant to say so for fear of appearing to favor one political group or another. It says a great deal that groups like Factcheck.org have sprung up to set the record straight, one way or the other, when the mainstream media has failed to do so.

Any assertion of supposed media bias becomes immediately flawed because of its resort to a two-option (liberal or conservative) approach. As we have noted, these terms are subject to wide interpretation and application, making reference to them highly misleading. Irrespective of whether such bias (purportedly left or right, liberal or conservative) exists, the end result has been to pressure reportage to the middle and to obscure the issue of media quality. The American mainstream media is remarkably docile in its political reporting, as contrasted with more muckraking styles pursued in other democratic countries. The time constraints of deadlines and the complexity of issues all add to this tendency to keep things simplistic. It is far simpler to refer to "liberal Senator X" or "conservative Representative Y" and show us a sound bite than to take the time to present their views and voting records. We learn nothing meaningful in the process. At the same time, print, visual, and audio media can also spend an inordinate amount of time on the prurient escapades of public figures to the detriment of real news. Critical coverage is often crowded out by stories of extramarital affairs or sexually deviant behavior, all replete with shorthand labeling.

Before we leave the political arena, we should note the effective use of labeling by Republicans in recent years. Republicans seem to wear their conservative label proudly, while Democrats generally recoil from the liberal moniker. Some Democrats have even preferred to call themselves "progressives" rather than liberals, as if that label is somehow better. Republicans have used labeling to great effect in turning former Democrats into Republicans. They have associated, quite effectively, the term *liberal* with Democrats. Then they have linked a host of negative connotations with that term, implying that liberals are latte-drinking, intellectual, effete snobs who look down on the very working-class folks who were formerly Democratic supporters. Republicans then associated themselves with the labels *freedom, liberty, smaller government,* and *tax reduction.* These qualities are labels because there is no substance behind them. The Club for

Growth, which supports the most doctrinaire Republicans, ran an opposition ad against a Democrat in 2004 that read "New York Times reading, latte drinking, National Public Radio listening, Volvo driving, body piercing freak show." Should they have added, "neener-neener"? This is the stuff of kindergarten taunts, not serious political discourse.

The harm engendered by labeling is not limited to the political sphere. Labels, with their attendant connotations, do violence to relationships, psyches, careers, and attitudes. In our quest for expediency, the pejorative labels of *fat, ugly, mean, stupid, lazy* and the like inflict wounds. They are like dismissive bullets fired from places of presumed arrogance. If we truly care that someone has an unhealthy weight, then there should be caring dialogue, not attack; compassion, not ridicule. If we view someone as mentally challenged, we should try to understand why and relate to them in a positive way that will benefit us all. Nearly everyone has something positive to offer. We accomplish nothing by diminishing others. If we wish to build bridges between ourselves, we make the task harder by widening the chasm with invective labels. Shock jock programs and misogynistic, racist music that spew labels diminish us all. Labels also further the sense of isolation so many feel in contemporary America by not only pushing away the labeled, but also by disconnecting the labeler from meaningful social intercourse. When we label there is an associated assessment of "for me or against me." If I am "pro-choice" and you are "pro-life," we are automatically inapposite to each other. If I am a woman and you are sexist, we assume there is no point to our discussing either women or sexism—or much else, for that matter. We must be from different worlds. The label says it all.

Individuals and organizations, books and arguments, are complex. We do ourselves a grave disservice when we gloss over that complexity with a simplistic label. Because someone has a belief that government should be limited to the provision of basic services (conservative?), does that mean they cannot be concerned about the welfare of people? Because someone believes that government has a role to assist the less fortunate (liberal?), does that mean they cannot be fiscally attuned to wise expenditure? Because someone has the belief that women should first care for their home and children, does that mean they cannot be a deeply caring and attentive partner or wise and accomplished in other arenas?

This all gets compounded when we label organizations, because the connotations of the label then get applied to the groups' members. Can I be a member of the NRA *and* the ACLU? Can either organization have believers in a so-called strict construction of the Constitution, or the opposite? There are Sunni and Shiite Muslims; Orthodox, Conservative, and Reform Jews; Christians of many denominations, and vast differences of belief and interpretation in between. Labels serve no purpose except to stereotype or simplistically pigeonhole people into a positive or negative assessment.

Labels also dehumanize people. When we say someone is fat or poor, we have glossed over the life experiences of that human being and relegated them to lesser status. In its extreme, labeling has been used to excuse or ameliorate the horror of violence against others by dehuman-izing them. Thus in World War II Germans were "krauts" or "Jerrys." In Vietnam the enemy was called "gooks," even as we fought alongside other Vietnamese. The label obscured that these were human beings—with wives and children, sisters and brothers, and mothers and fathers—who may have been just as unclear about the war they were partici-pating in, and just as terrified of the horrors they encoun-tered. Labels take us past rational thought in the interest of expediency. They are one of the tools of demagogues, used to mindlessly foster hate of "enemies." These enemies are a collection of negative attributes bound up in a label that may bear no resemblance to the actual people. The term *fighting words* comes to mind here. Some labels are so emotionally charged that they engender an immediate reaction of anger or hatred, irrespective of the true nature of the person or thing so labeled. The term *death panels* is such an emotionally charged label.

Perhaps the most damning aspect of labeling is the fact that it cuts off important discussion that can lead to understanding and even compromise. In Portland, Oregon, a group of individuals recently proposed re-naming an important street, Interstate Avenue, to Cesar Chavez Avenue, in honor of the Mexican-American champion of California farm workers and founder of what is now The United Farm Workers of America. People who opposed the street naming were simply labeled and dismissed as racist at every public hearing on the matter. Passions ran quite high. For many business owners, however, race had nothing to do with it; it was a matter of the cost of changing signage, stationery, and other materials. Others pointed to the history of the street and its role in connecting Oregon and Washington (thus the name *Interstate*) and the future possibility of an interstate light rail line on the avenue. But all of these points, and others, were ignored by the proponents, who simply dismissed any opponent as racist. What got lost in the process was any discussion of how to best honor Chavez, the appropriateness of doing so, if it could be best done by naming a street after him, and what was the most logical street? These and other practical issues simply got pushed aside in a rancorous discussion about alleged racism. The end result was a no-win situation for all concerned at the time. The matter was tabled. The opponents did not know whether they would ultimately have to bear the expense of a street name change, and the proponents did not know if any street or other public edifice would honor Chavez. Name-calling, labeling, had postponed any hope of dialogue and any resultant progress on the issue.

In far too many instances dialogue about important issues is reduced to name-calling. Instead of trying to understand one another and find common ground, proponents of legal abortion call their opposition "Bible-thumpers," "rednecks," and "Christian extremists." Opponents of abortion, in one form or another, call their opposition "baby-killers," "the Antichrist" and "godless." If they were all forced to abandon the emotion-charged labels, they would have to express their beliefs in objective detail and to consider the needs underlying those beliefs. They would have to articulate their position instead of merely throwing out an epithet. And that would facilitate dialogue. People's views about abortion are not monolithic, simply in favor or against. Some opponents of abortion still see it as a necessary tool of medicine to protect the health of the mother or to deal with a pregnancy gone horribly wrong. Some proponents draw a line at a certain time period, beyond which they find abortion repugnant. But all attempts at resolution and compromise are lost when labels draw black-and-white lines in the sand where we shout at one another from "our side." If we return to our premise from the second chapter about the absence of absolutes in life, then we must abandon the absolute, dogmatic, and unthinking associations that labels carry.

Reasoned dialogue cannot exist in the obscuring presence of labels. Meaningful understanding of one another, and the building of bridges between us based upon recognition of our commonalities, is prevented by labeling. Labeling also inhibits developing strategies to deal with the object of the labeling. If we do not take the time to understand a perceived enemy, our ability to defend ourselves will thereby be diminished and our security compromised. Calling someone an evildoer does nothing to advance us or to help us understand our adversary so we can deal more effectively with that enemy.

There really is no alternative to knowledge. We can attempt to stay focused inwardly and pretend that our world is small and safe, but the external realities will not leave us alone. The frictions that occur at our boundaries will persist as long as we fail to extend our understanding of what is around us. Labels provide no real protection and no avenue to resolution. They are merely dismissive. We need to move beyond the use of labels and toward delving deeper. We just might make a new friend or learn something valuable.

Life begins to have meaning in connection with the relationships and associations we have with those around us in our home, in our city, our country, and the world. The more we deepen those relationships and associations with understanding, the more meaningful our lives become. The more we intelligently and fully comprehend one another, the more likely we will be friends—or at least coexist, rather than be enemies, and our world will be larger and fuller for it.

It is said that familiarity breeds contempt. That is usually not the case when we delve beyond cliché. Moreover, we do not have to share someone's views to understand and relate to them. We do not even have to like someone to coexist with them without resort to violence, or mean-spirited or resentful behavior that begets violence. But we do have to appreciate their circumstances, and they ours. That is where we can begin to find common ground, mutual benefit, and tolerance. This is not wishful thinking or idealism. Reaching out to others and engaging in dialogue reduces differences or, at the very least, provides strategies to deal with the recalcitrant. So much violence and harm flow from our ignorance of one another. Labels simply perpetuate that ignorance and impede progress. Once we look beyond a label, we can begin to see the totality of the person, or the thought, and the possibilities that we might have otherwise foreclosed. We can begin to understand one another's needs and how we can accommodate them, and they ours.

We are alone together on this planet with shared challenges such as hunger, disease, terrorism, environmental threats, poverty, and inadequate education. These common challenges can become a conduit for cooperation and solutions; but only if we move beyond labels and toward attempts at understanding.

Chapter Six

On Uncommon Ground

If you look over the course of a hundred years, I think the gradual erosion of the consensus that's held our country together is probably more serious than a few bearded terrorists who fly into buildings.

—Pat Robertson

A consensus means that everyone agrees to say collectively what no one believes individually.

—Abba Eban

By now it should be clear that no matter how fervently we hold them, our beliefs are nevertheless founded upon our assumptions. Whether we think they are handed down from God, or the product of observation and reason, our beliefs are not based upon some absolute truth, but upon underlying assumptions that we accept as absolutely true. If we accept, for example, that the Bible expresses the teaching of one whom we accept as God, then we will believe those teachings to be true. If we believe in the exactness of mathematics, then we will believe in the answers derived from mathematical formulae. Our acceptance of certain things as absolutely true is based on our need to define and explain the world around us.

In other words, beliefs are a pragmatic way of looking at life, of answering the fundamental questions of our existence and creation that enable us to function in life. Beliefs give us a degree of security. It is ultimately pragmatism that supports our beliefs, not some indisputable truth. All of the inhabitants of this world have found differing answers to the various questions that life presents to us. And as we have noted, our beliefs are also the product of peer pressure and other extraneous influences. This is not to suggest that we should abandon or doubt all beliefs. But if we understand that beliefs are pragmatic, then we should be more pragmatic in their application. Your beliefs are just as important to you as are mine to me. Thus, we should find ways to reconcile our individual beliefs in a pragmatic way, rather than an emotional one, that best serves the pragmatic bases of both our individual beliefs. This is a most important distinction. Emotion provides no basis whatsoever for reconciliation and rarely the prospect of gaining what one wishes. Anger begets anger, hatred begets hatred.

We also need to recognize that the beliefs of some Americans, despite our discussion about the fragility of belief in the second chapter of this book, simply will not change, regardless of sound argument or clear evidence of the incorrectness of those beliefs. A focus on altering beliefs can be especially unproductive and even counterproductive when the belief in question is unconditional. Such beliefs are too strongly held to consider any amount of compromise or adjustment. So much of the antagonism, disharmony, and inability to reach consensus in the United States today stems from ideological lines drawn in the sand: an unwillingness seek common ground by some because they see that effort as a threat to their beliefs. But here is a moment for reconsideration. Those who see their beliefs as threatened by efforts to accommodate the beliefs of others should understand that the effort to find common ground does not mean acquiescence to the beliefs of others or acquiescence of theirs to ours. What is required is an effort to find common ground whereby the legitimate *needs*, as opposed to the *beliefs*, of others can be accommodated. ("Legitimate needs" is used here to denote needs that are appropriate for civilized society.) The effort to find common ground should involve an attempt to meet one another's needs while respecting the beliefs.

This is such a fundamentally important point that it deserves emphasis. We have been focused far too much in this country upon arguing whose beliefs are superior, rather than attempting to address the needs that underlie those beliefs. In the process labels are lobbed about as weapons designed to demonize and discredit the opponent or object of our disagreement. "She's just a bleeding-heart liberal." "He's a right-wing nut job." Facts are marshaled, speeches are given, and emotional touch-stones like *freedom* are intoned, all in an effort to support the belief in question. And none of it will reconcile con-flicting beliefs to any significant degree. That is why we see so little willingness to compromise in our legislative bodies and so much antagonism and lines in the sand in our society today.

A focus on belief derails consensus in another way. Those who focus on belief may see any attempt at achiev-ing consensus as being a traitor to the cause or requiring an abandonment of one's principles. So ideology gets thrust to the fore and either stalemate, where power is equal, or railroading, where oppositional power is disproportionate, follows. If we are to move forward as a nation, then we must stop these ideological battles and focus instead upon meeting and accommodating needs. In order to do that, we each have to understand the pragmatic needs our own beliefs achieve. Then we can engage in productive efforts that reconcile our needs with those of others.

Understanding the needs that our beliefs address will still be a dark journey for some. For those few, whose beliefs are mean-spirited or worse, vengeful and hate-filled, any willingness to understand the source of their beliefs will be difficult or impossible. Beliefs that compel us to hate or resent others are rooted in intolerance. Intolerance is generally defined as the state of being unwilling or unable to endure the beliefs, perspectives, or practices of others. It also involves a lack of recognition of the fundamental rights and choices of others. Anyone who has scanned some of the vitriolic comments in news and other online reader comment sections on the internet can readily see that unwillingness to endure the beliefs, perspectives, or practices of others displayed in varying degrees. Hatred or enmity of this kind becomes a self-protective measure that works to maintain one's sense of identity. The greater the perceived threat is to one's identity, the greater the enmity. Intolerance can also be viewed as a defense against change, acting as a form of self-protection from the uncertainty that change portends. Attempts to make major legislative and policy changes on a national scale have as a by-product the fanning of the flames of resentment and angst within people who fear change. Those who feel their identity is threatened, or for whom change produces significant anxiety, are highly receptive to the kinds of fear-based appeals designed to oppose change that we have discussed earlier.

It is useful to consider a study by Johns Hopkins University that noted various characteristics of people *excessively* intolerant:

(a) holds a rigid set of beliefs that assert the intrinsic superiority due to race, religion, culture, or gender of the person's own group ;

(b) lacks empathy for one or more particular populations, such as Latinos, African Americans, gays, lesbians, or women;

(c) exhibits interpersonal behavior that ranges from covert or overt antagonism and hostility to exploitation toward one or more specific or targeted populations;

(d) seeks to overtly or covertly block, deny, impede, or cancel the social, organizational, psychological, or financial advancement of someone of a group believed to be inferior;

(e) uses power or other means to inhibit or prevent free expression of contrary or intolerable ideas;

(f) has a sense of entitlement based on membership in a privileged group and believes that others should recognize his or her superiority without commensurate achievements or valid credentials;

(g) manifests a pervasive pattern of disregard for the human rights of members of particular populations; and

(h) shows lack of remorse as indicated by being callous or indifferent to having hurt, restricted, mistreated, or maligned members of selective populations.

These characteristics are of value in recognizing the symptoms of lesser levels of intolerance and unwillingness to respect the rights and needs of others. An attempt to divine common ground with someone who exhibits any of the above characteristics to any significant degree will likely prove difficult at best. That is why being open-minded is so important, and why so much time was spent discussing belief earlier in this book. For without a degree of flexibility on the part of all of us to respect the rights of others, there will be no progress for any of us. We will be like that squabbling crew described in the preface that is so absorbed in rancorous debate that our ship of state runs aground. If we are to move forward, then what is called for is not a focus on the negative, upon attacking and tearing down, but an earnest and positive search for points of agreement, places where we share common interests and needs. It is from that approach, and not from bullying, labeling, or disregarding the needs of others, that positive progress toward the betterment of us all can occur.

Let's apply the approach to a practical and emotionally charged issue, abortion. This issue has two polar beliefs. Opponents of abortion believe that the act of abortion is murder, with some extending the belief all the way back to conception. They argue that this is taking the life of an unborn child who has no say in the process. This is not a legal issue, since the law currently defines a life as one that can exist on its own outside of the womb (generally felt to be twenty-four weeks or more of gestation). So the basic support for the position is based in theology, and related views of morality, rather than secular law; the commandment that "Thou shalt not kill." It is worth noting, however, that the Bible itself is silent on the issue of abortion. Those who support the right to have an abortion believe that this is a matter of individual medical choice about their own bodies and privacy, in that neither the state nor others have the right to control that freedom. These two beliefs are based upon differing needs and therefore are irreconcilable. The labels *pro-life* and *pro-choice* dress up the beliefs in false clothing, since there is hardly anyone who is anti-life or against having choices. Rather, it is again those pesky restrictions upon freedom that get in the way. We nearly all become anti-life in extreme matters of self defense or in war where our lives are at risk, for example. We nearly all become anti-choice when someone's choice is injurious to others, for example. So beliefs and labeling do not help us here.

The underlying need for those who oppose abortion is to support their religious beliefs regarding life and morality. The need for those seeking to maintain the right to abortion is to preserve individual control over medical decisions that affect people's own bodies and lives. The beliefs of abortion proponents regarding personal, as opposed to state, control over this medical decision are perceived by them as neither immoral nor inapposite to their own religious beliefs. Those who seek to deny a right to abortion can do so only by imposing their religious or moral beliefs on others. Those who favor a right to control medical decisions about their bodies are not seeking to impose such a religion-based requirement on others. Without getting into questions of rape, incest, or the health of the mother, abortion ultimately comes down to religious difference (including atheism) as to the taking of life, since the abortion or killing of a fetus that would have been viable outside the womb *is* civil murder (in the absence of other extenuating circumstances). Underlying the efforts to criminalize abortion and to deny it funding are religious beliefs that, if enacted, would impose those religious views on others who do not share such views. The point here is not to put a value on the relative beliefs of either side or to deny anyone's right to hold such beliefs. At this point we are merely trying to examine the underlying needs.

If we stand for the need to preserve freedom of religious belief, then it is inconsistent to argue for the imposition of our religious beliefs upon others. It has been argued that such reasoning would justify incest, if the belief by the one committing incest was that incest was permitted by his religion. That argument does not hold up. First, incest is unlawful in any form, so a religious belief that it is okay does not thereby legally excuse it. More importantly, incest involves harm to another legal person, not an unborn fetus. There is no religious argument here at all. And we are not dealing with the unknowable here, the beginning of life. The justification for prohibiting incest is a practical one: the protection of an *unquestioned* living being. That said, I do not expect that this will settle the argument for many. Given the deeply-seated and emotional quality of the beliefs involved here it will simply be too difficult to accept that what is at stake here is freedom of belief rather than the murder of unborn children. The term *unborn children* presupposes the issue by defining fetuses as separate living beings regardless of condition. But if we recognize that the central need here is freedom of belief, then we should accept that some will chose not to seek an abortion out of their beliefs, and others should be accorded and exercise the right, out of their need to control their own bodies free from the disconnected and unfeeling hand of the state. Those who so ardently oppose the imposition of government into their lives might consider their feelings about the government's making medical decisions for them. It is inconsistent to express concern about presumed government "death panels' while arguing that government should intercede in other life-and-death matters such as abortion and "death with dignity." Those who hold choice to be valuable should also respect the choices of those with differing beliefs and not attempt to ridicule or belittle such beliefs or the emotions behind them.

Whether one agrees or disagrees with the path just taken, it is an approach that looks at an emotionally charged issue in a nonemotional way, focusing on needs rather than beliefs. Indeed, this was a discussion about the need to preserve individual beliefs rather than impose them on others. Framed this way, a more fruitful discussion can ensue and perhaps lead to a degree of consensus. Instead of ideological and religious stalemate we can focus on rational, unemotional approaches to such issues as the health of the mother, rape and incest, timing, orphans, and other factors. Regardless of one's belief, if we can address the needs of both sides of the abortion issue in pragmatic and unemotional terms, then we can then begin to have a discussion about how to best reconcile those needs. We can also begin to view medical decisions as between medical professionals and their patients, without the unfeeling and blind intervention of government. In that light, few would argue that the state is a better arbiter of care than those trained in medicine and in possession of all of the relevant medical history and indications.

The tragic case of Terri Schaivo illustrated the folly of politicizing medical decisions. Schiavo was repeatedly determined by specialist doctors to have been medically brain-dead (in a "persistent vegetative state") after suffering massive brain damage in 1998. The damage was initially thought to have been caused by cardiac arrest related to bulimia. Although she remained in a coma over the next few years, her husband and physicians made repeated efforts to bring her out of the coma, to no avail. She was kept alive only by means of a feeding tube and had a stimulator implanted in her brain. When her husband finally came to the heartrending decision to petition the Florida court to have the feeding tube removed, Terri's parents intervened. A tug-of-war then ensued that lasted until 2005, when the tube was finally removed. During that intervening seven-year period, there were fourteen appeals and numerous motions, petitions, and hearings in the Florida courts; five suits in federal district court; Florida legislation (Terri's Law) struck down by the Supreme Court of Florida; a subpoena by a congressional committee to qualify Schiavo for witness protection; federal legislation (known as the Palm Sunday Compromise, where President George W. Bush returned to Washington to sign the bill); and four denials of review from the Supreme Court of the United States. This personal tragedy was turned into a public circus, not only with the intervention of state and federal legislatures but also in the form of a memo authored by an aide to Florida Republican Senator Mel Martinez. The memo suggested that the Schiavo case offered "a great political issue" that would appeal to the party's base and could be used against Senator Bill Nelson, a Democrat from Florida, because he had refused to cosponsor the federal bill. The political sideshow included the Rev. Jesse Jackson arguing on behalf of the parents. After her death an autopsy revealed that she had endured on life support with massive and irreversible brain damage that left her body functioning but with no cognitive ability. She was essentially a partially functioning organism with no mind. The Schiavo case involved not only people who saw political advantage in the tragedy and the emotions it provoked, but also well-meaning people who genuinely felt that removal of the feeding tube would have forestalled a possible recovery (albeit a recovery that was repeatedly shown by medical evidence and repeated effort to have been impossible).

The Schiavo case reinforces that emotions lead us astray in ways that poorly serve the best interests of those most directly affected and also poorly serve the larger public. Though it may be hard for those on all sides of issues like abortion and end-of-life matters to acknowledge, passion is a poor basis for sound medical decision making. When government is allowed to intrude into matters that are difficult even for medical professionals, the situation is only made worse. Medical decisions are intensely personal ones and should be left to those most directly affected and their doctors without interference from those removed from the situation, not in possession of all of the facts, and acting solely upon emotion or hidden agendas.

As noted in the quote from Abba Eban at the start of this chapter, consensus is where people agree collectively to something that they individually do not believe. They ultimately do so because compromising meets their needs on balance. People may not believe that war is acceptable, but agree they must fight or their civilization will be destroyed. Individuals may not believe that raising taxes is a good thing, but agree to an increase in order to achieve an objective like providing sewers or police protection. We seem to have lost sight of Eban's point in this country, especially in Congress. Those who demand ideological purity will lose the practical benefits that come from compromise. And we all lose when ideology supplants pragmatism. We need to push aside the emotionalism and dogma that is running rampant is this country in favor of recognizing what our needs are and then doing what it takes to reconcile our individual needs with those of others. *Compromise does not mean that one need must give way to another*, as we seem to think in the emotional terms that are thrown about today. Rather, consensus is about resolving needs in a way that *maximizes* the needs of individuals so that the greater common good can be achieved. With that process in mind, we can begin to make the kinds of wise choices that will move our country forward. Making wise choices, however, also involves being well informed. In a later chapter we will look at those things that are inhibiting our ability to be well-informed. First, we will turn to "The Great Divide."

Chapter Seven

The Great Divide

Government is not a solution to our problem, government is the problem.
—Ronald Reagan

*The legitimate object of government is to do for a community of people,
whatever they need to have done, but cannot do, at all, or cannot, so well
do, for themselves—in their separate, and individual capacities.*
—Abraham Lincoln

The foregoing quotes from two Republicans of vastly different generations reflect fundamentally different views of government's role. They also reflect the central divide in our country that seems to immobilize us in endless debate. On the one side are those who desire a minimalist role for government, while those on the other side perceive a much broader role that includes government programs and regulations to address the needs of various groups within our society. The divide spans both political and economic spheres, with proponents and opponents not necessarily on the same side in both spheres. Thus, one may see a limited role for government in the political arena but a larger role in the economic sphere, such as subsidies and tax breaks for business. Moreover, Americans vacillate from issue to issue as to the appropriateness of government involvement in the respective issue. The Reagan view has become the doctrinaire position of Republicans and most strongly the position of Libertarians, members of the Tea Party, and those often labeled as conservatives. The more expansive view of government's role has largely been the province of Democrats and those labeled as liberals (who now seem to prefer to be called progressives). Yet examined simply as polar positions, these two opposing views of the role of government in America are useful to understanding the intransigence and vitriol that keeps us from reaching agreement about the vast majority of national and local problems we face as citizens of the United States. Such an understanding can then aid us in comprehending the efforts needed to bring us together. If we do not find a path to accommodation here, then the suicidal debacle that was the debt ceiling fiasco in Congress will have been only a harbinger of even worse things to come. The Great Divide simply must be bridged.

In its broadest terms, the Reagan view leans heavily upon self-determination and disdains what is perceived as government interference in business and in certain aspects of people's lives. It asserts that social programs, such as welfare, do more harm than good by discouraging people from acting on their own behalf to solve their own problems. Viewed as such, government programs, such as Social Security and Medicare, are said to be wasteful and frustratingly bureaucratic intrusions into areas of personal choice. As a consequence, government taxation used to support such programs is viewed as an abuse of the role of government, or, at the very least, are areas that should be handled by the private sector, such as insurance and private investment. There are also concerns about the impact these programs have on government finance over the long term. The view argues that people should be allowed to keep more of their own money in order to solve their own problems and not be compelled to underwrite the difficulties of others. At its extreme, efforts to regulate the economy through fiscal and monetary policies are similarly seen as government interference in what is deemed to be a self-regulating economy. That is the view that supports a balanced-budget amendment to the Constitution in order to mechanically limit spending. Underlying the Reagan view is an assumption that the wealth of a nation will automatically be divided equitably. In the words of the eighteenth-century economist Adam Smith,

> The rich ... divide with the poor the produce of all their improvements. They are led by an invisible hand to make nearly the same distribution of the necessaries of life which would have been made, had the earth been divided into equal proportions among all its inhabitants.

The Lincoln view sees an expansionary role for government as a provider of anything that people cannot do well for themselves as individuals. There, however, is the rub. The Reagan view is quite restrictive as to what people cannot do for themselves (i.e., they can do a great deal for themselves) while the Lincoln view, as expanded by subsequent presidents, primarily Democrat, has become rather open-ended as to the role of government. Indeed, Thomas Jefferson is known to have described one of the purposes of government as enabling the people to live in "happiness." At the same time, Jefferson was no fan of intrusive or acquisitive government, declaring that

> A wise and frugal government, which shall leave men free to regulate their own pursuits of industry and improvement, and shall not take from the mouth of labor the bread it has earned—this is the sum of good government.

A modern-day Jefferson would be quite shocked to see just how much government has come to regulate the "pursuits of industry and improvement" and how much it takes "from the mouth of labor." Yet even Jefferson realized that his "frugal government" nevertheless required money to operate. From 1791 to 1802, the United States government was supported by internal taxes on distilled spirits, carriages, refined sugar, tobacco and snuff, property sold at auction (including slaves), and corporate bonds,. The high cost of the War of 1812 brought about the nation's first sales taxes on gold, silverware, jewelry, and watches. And there was that little matter of purchasing the Louisiana Territory. In 1817, however, Congress did away with all internal taxes, relying on tariffs on imported goods to provide sufficient funds for running the government. That subsequently proved inadequate to fund the huge cost of the Civil War, causing Congress to enact the nation's first income tax law in 1862. The Sixteenth Amendment to the Constitution, enacted in 1913, made an income tax upon individuals and corporations a permanent source of revenue for our government.

Just as major crises initiated taxing programs, other crises initiated government-created social programs and regulations. The sometimes horrific working conditions that grew out of the machine age brought government intrusion into the workplace in the form of national labor laws. And the Great Depression fathered a host of financial regulations, and ultimately a series of social programs, under government auspices. Grappling with the perceived excesses and failures of capitalism, President Franklin Roosevelt espoused a dramatically broader role for government:

> Every man has a right to his own property; which means a right to be assured, to the fullest extent attainable, in the safety of his savings. By no other means can men carry the burdens of those parts of life which, in the nature of things, afford no chance of labor; childhood, sickness, old age. In all thought of property, this right is paramount; all other property rights must yield to it. If, in accord with this principle, we must restrict the operations of the speculator, the manipulator, even the financier, I believe we must accept the restriction as needful, not to hamper individualism but to protect it.

Roosevelt did not stop at mere increased regulation. He went on to assert an activist role for government in economic matters that included equitable wealth distribution and the management of production:

> Our task now is not discovery or exploitation of natural resources, or necessarily producing more goods. It is the soberer, less dramatic business of administering resources and plants already in hand, of seeking to re-establish foreign markets for our surplus production, of meeting the problem of underconsumption, of adjusting production to consumption, of distributing wealth and products more equitably, of adapting existing economic organizations to the service of the people. The day of enlightened administration has come.

Roosevelt's views were generally well received by a populace who viewed themselves as victimized by the perceived excesses and failures of capitalism that were reflected in the economic crises of the time, including an unemployment rate of 25 percent. Smith's "invisible hand" had been far too invisible and ineffective in allocating wealth and income. As people watched their savings vanish, banks fail, farms being foreclosed, and jobs disappear, they sought help from their government. It was a seminal turning point in our views about government's role in our lives. What followed were government programs to provide construction and other traditionally nongovernment jobs directly, rather than through private industry, and to aid people in their retirement in the form of the Social Security Act of 1935. One of the regulatory programs enacted during the period was the Glass-Steagall Act of 1933, which limited the role of commercial banks to customary lending and deposit-gathering activities, so that they would not be exposed to the more risky investment banking activities that helped spawn the bank failures of the Great Depression. Glass-Steagall was repealed in 1999 by the Gramm Leach Bliley Act, named after its sponsoring senators. At the time of its repeal, Senator Gramm stated:

> In the 1930's, at the trough of the Depression when Glass-Steagall became law, it was believed that government was the answer. It was believed that stability and growth came from government overriding the functioning of free markets. We are here today to repeal Glass-Steagall because we have learned that government is not the answer.

Only a few years after the repeal, the United States once again faced massive bank failures and another severe economic downturn. The government, so spurned by Gramm in favor of free markets, had to intervene to save the very bank conglomerates created by the repeal because they were deemed "too big to fail." Gramm's support was later critical in the passage of the Commodity Futures

Modernization Act of 2000, which kept derivatives transactions, including those involving credit default swaps, free of government regulation. These derivatives were the very instruments that brought down insurer AIG and various investment banks, necessitating government intervention to save them.

What is useful to understand here is that every expansion of government's role in America has been presaged by one crisis or another, one glaring deficiency or another, where Americans found that they, in Lincoln's words, could not do well for themselves; that government alone could solve the problem at hand. These expansions of the role of government did not come stealthily in the night through the actions of power-mad bureaucrats acting conspiratorially or because of a turn to socialism by our people. They were publicly accepted correctives perceived at the time as achievable only through new federal government programs and regulations. Yet despite the relative dearth of undemocratic government usurpations in America, many Americans fear what they see as "big government." A 2009 Gallup poll in the midst of the financial crisis showed that people saw big government as a greater threat to America's future than big business by a nearly two-to-one margin. This faith in laissez faire and concern about "big government" is broad-based, and was part of the popular support for the very bills passed by Senator Gramm. Other Americans see danger from the expansion of government surveillance and detention powers from things like the euphemistically entitled Patriot Act that authorized increased wiretapping and the holding of people, including American citizens, without trial and without immediate access to court protection. Many fear that nameless, faceless bureaucrats have the power to take things from them unjustly and without recourse. From parking tickets to zoning issues to TSA inspections, people's interactions with government can sometimes be frustrating, intrusive, and even intimidating.

There is much that our government has done right and quite a bit to criticize. Bureaucracies, whether in government or business, are by their nature subject to error and inefficiency. We hear about the government blunders, but seldom do we hear about the successes. When our water flows, we drive on our vast interstate highway system, or our lights work powered by the electricity from federal dams, it doesn't make the news. But two-thousand-dollar toilet seats, excessive pensions, and other deviations from the norm do. Many will find this hard to accept, but the reality is that business bureaucracies are often no more efficient or effective than governmental ones. We just don't normally hear about business blunders in the public way that we hear about government foibles. The ultimate business failure, bankruptcy, is simply accepted as a part of business rather than as proof of business ineptitude in general. The recent financial crisis is a good example of both business and governmental failures and government successes. Whether you agreed with the bailouts or not, the government saved much of the U.S. auto industry from extinction and is being paid back well ahead of schedule, with a profit. And it was only due to federal regulatory power and financing capability that the government was able to intervene in the recent financial crisis in order to avert financial catastrophe. One can argue about the means, but the objective of staving off worldwide financial collapse was achieved.

Another concern about government growth is the sentiment that private investment is preferable to government expenditure. While that is true generally, various economic studies simply do not support that position where broader social needs are concerned. For example, charter schools have not been found *on average* to be superior to public schools. While some private schools of higher education, like Harvard, can claim superiority over their public- and state-supported counterparts, their cost to students is also demonstrably higher, and their ability to retain highly competent educators is therefore greater. Their higher costs and other factors create an exclusivity that bars the broader student population from qualifying. Moreover, there simply is not the economic incentive for private business to build and maintain major airports, highways, sewer systems, and bridges. Instead, the return on these investments comes in the form of jobs and business profits that benefit society at large, both initially and through the commerce these improvements facilitate. Major roads and sewerage treatment systems, for example, facilitate the building of houses, offices, and manufacturing facilities by private enterprise and provide a means of access to and from them. The idea that tax money used for these purposes would be better spent, or even spent at all, by individuals and private industry is simply misguided. These are true investments in growth and productivity that also generate increased tax revenues in addition to the reduced costs provided to the users. But the question as to what is appropriate for government expenditure and what is not is a legitimate one. Unfortunately the dialogue is often negatively fear-based rather than fact-based.

A strong argument can be made that much of what our government does wrong, beyond normal bureaucratic bungling, has grown out of our fears. We have already observed that fear is a poor basis for decision making. Yet fear of "big government," and lobbying and public relations campaigns by various special interests designed to play upon fear, have cost us dearly when it comes to the actions of our government. The repeal of the Glass-Steagall Act, noted previously, is a case in point. Had Glass-Steagall remained in place, with its lessons from the Great Depression, the infection of the mortgage crisis would have been largely limited to the investment banks and their investors, the very organizations and people who created the mess in the first instance. Commercial banks would have been spared and able to continue to provide much-needed funds to feed growth, freed from the crippling losses of investment banking. Not only did the investment banking losses infect the commercial banks who were part of financial colossi, the affected commercial banks then cut back drastically on their lending, resulting in a deep recession from the lack of available credit. The very relaxation of regulations and lending standards that presaged the financial crises was justified under the mantle of more freedom for private enterprise, greater competition, and less government interference. Yet we seem not to have learned from this experience. In 2010 the powerful banking lobby along with Wall Street lobbyists managed to eviscerate attempts at financial reform (the Dodd-Frank legislation) by getting Congress to strip out reinstatement of the provisions of Glass-Steagall at the last minute. This came as the airwaves and the halls of Congress echoed with the very scare tactics about business freedom and "overregulation" that spawned the repeal of Glass-Steagall in the first place.

The unfortunate thing is that there *is* too much government regulation in some areas and not enough in others. The U.S. Tax Code is an abomination; a hodgepodge of poorly crafted complexity piled upon often out-of-date and invalid assumptions. It could be greatly simplified, but it will not be as long as a host of special interests benefit from the myriad of provisions it contains. Every attempt to remove a deduction is met with the fearful cry that it constitutes a "job-killing tax increase." Congress simply has no appetite for the feeding frenzy and constituent alienation that would result from any attempt to enact a simplified tax, the simplest solution of all. By all accounts a simplified tax would save hundreds of billions of dollars in legal and accounting expense, not to mention eliminating all of the lost productivity now spent navigating the twists and turns of the current tax code and the massive bureaucracy needed to administer it. Yet we are deterred by our fears from even attempting something that is so obviously and simply correct. We are afraid that the net effect will be to increase our taxes. We are afraid that the beneficiaries of current deductions like charities and the homebuilding industry will suffer. We are afraid of the unknown that would ensue. And our legislators are afraid of alienating the sources of the campaign contributions upon which they depend for reelection.

There is ample room for discussion about *specific* regulation and *specific* examples of government waste. But when we hear generalities about big government, we are simply once again watching politicians do a "sweep around the wide step, cut a little swathe and lead the people on." The expansion of government programs, so dramatically espoused by Roosevelt and significantly furthered by Lyndon Johnson, did not grow solely out of humanitarian concern. The underlying basis for these programs was economic benefit for the country as a whole. Ensuring minimal financial well-being for our seniors through Social Security helps guarantee that they will be purchasers of shelter, food, and clothing, thereby continuing to contribute to our economy rather than being a drag upon it in their old age. Medicare and Medicaid help to reduce the societal burden of medical costs by facilitating preventative care and reducing the exorbitant cost of emergency room crises. We pay a much higher cost for people who have not had preventative care who then show up at emergency rooms with chronic severe illnesses. The hidden cost of uncovered emergency care shows up in more expensive care for us all and higher insurance premiums for those with insurance. While Medicare can be made more efficient, attacks against it as big government and arguing for substituting insurance companies who would then be subsidized by taxpayer-provided vouchers are poorly veiled attempts to line the pockets of health insurers. The central problem is not with Medicare, but with health *costs*. These opponents of big government are the very same people who frustrated attempts in Congress to grant the government the ability to negotiate drug prices and change the way we pay for medical services. Individual citizens have no economic leverage and must pay whatever drug companies want to charge for drugs that they often cannot do without. Similarly, most people now pay medical providers for services rather than results, encouraging unnecessary and costly procedures that could otherwise be avoided as part of results-oriented care. This isn't about lawyers and tort reform. It's about what we pay for when we seek medical care. Paying for results would put the burden on the provider instead of forcing the patient to play Russian roulette with treatments while doctors try to avoid malpractice exposure. What self-proclaimed opponents of big government currently see as a solution, under the mantle of reducing the federal deficit, is in reality the gradual elimination of Medicare in favor of an insurance voucher system that would do nothing to reduce medical costs and simply transfer uncontrolled rising costs back to the public, many of whom would then be unable to afford the insurance. A rather startling fact attesting to the foolishness of this approach is that in recent years health insurance costs have actually risen much faster than the health-care costs they are supposed to pay for.

The point here is that too often we, as Americans, are not being discriminating enough. We allow politicians to "dance a little sidestep" when they supplant fact-based economic arguments in favor of bogeymen like "death panels," "overregulation," and "big government." Fear tactics like these allowed the insurance industry to turn health-care reform from a simpler, cost-effective single payer approach into a several-thousand-page legislative boondoggle, where taxpayers will now underwrite millions of new customers for insurance companies without any offsetting device to control premium costs in exchange. Many Americans have been sold a bill of goods when it comes to taxes as well. Broad-based tax cuts can have a stimulative effect by putting more spendable dollars in the hands of people most likely to buy a new car or furniture or just eat out more often. But tax cuts for the wealthiest one or two percent of the population are like pushing on a rope. Granting a few thousand more dollars to someone with a huge income and millions of dollars in net worth is more likely to go into an investment in stocks and bonds or the purchase of a luxury item than it is to stimulate direct new job creation. We have also seen too often that with such tax breaks, if they do lead to job growth, the investment and growth occurs outside the United States. The false premise of job creation through tax cuts for the wealthy, which found its greatest expression during the George W. Bush presidency, resulted in ever-larger deficits, an actual loss of jobs, a worsening decline in the standard of living for the middle class, and a widening gap between rich and poor.

For what the labels are worth, lest you think that I am some "wide-eyed, bleeding-heart liberal," I am not. I am a former banker and an entrepreneur. I did not found successful companies, including a bank, and hire people because I got a tax cut. I did these things because I saw opportunity in doing so, irrespective of taxes. The simple fact is that the majority of new job creation comes from small business, not mega-corporations. Small businesses are formed based on filling a need, not on tax cuts. And they grow from broad-based demand, the kind that comes from lots of people, not merely the wealthiest, having a willingness to spend,. Similarly, capital flows to ideas and the people capable of executing them. It does not originate because of a tax cut. I have watched with astonishment as many Americans have swallowed the nonsense about tax cuts for the wealthy, apparently with the belief that they too will be rich some day or out of some misplaced belief that only the wealthy know what is best or only the wealthy create jobs. The benevolent "invisible hand" of Adam Smith is not only invisible, it is nonexistent.

So-called supply-side and trickle-down economics have repeatedly demonstrated that they are failed theories, yet many in the public continue to believe in them, persuaded by those politicians and economists whose real constituency is the affluent and big business. The supply-side theory emphasizes incentives to those who supply capital and supply goods rather than a focus more directly upon creating the underlying demand for capital and goods. Here is a succinct explanation of "supply side economics" from Pennsylvania Republican Senator Patrick Toomey:

> There's a huge difference between lower taxes and increased spending. Lower taxes generate growth through the supply side. It makes it less expensive to launch a venture, to expand a venture, to hire workers and so it's an incentive to increase production and ultimately it's production that's the source of wealth of a society. So my focus has always been on the supply side.

The central problem with this focus on supply is that supply is created to meet demand, not the other way around. It puts the cart before the horse. People start and build businesses and expand them to meet demand, not because of a tax break. In addition, it does not follow that "lower taxes generate growth through the supply side." Instead, lower taxes can simply lead to nonproductive investment or luxury goods purchases that have minimal if any effect on jobs. That is especially true in a downturn because demand is already soft and therefore the impetus to expand and hire is not there regardless of lowered business taxes. There is also no guarantee that the funds made available through business tax cuts will even be spent in the United States.

During economic downturns people collectively have less money to spend. That is why government expenditures can be useful to put money broadly in the hands of millions of people, as opposed to only a wealthy few, so that they can buy more goods and services they would not have otherwise purchased when the economy is down. Government projects increase the need for workers who then buy things with their earnings. That additional demand then leads to hiring and capital investment, thus creating more jobs and spurring the economy.

Despite its backward and disproven approach, supply-side economics has been the primary justification by Republicans for tax cuts and subsidies for the wealthiest citizens and business. The theory has been that the benefits of these incentives to the wealthiest citizens will "trickle down" to the rest of the citizens. As we have noted in various references to the widening income and wealth gaps, precisely the opposite has occurred. Whatever gains might have trickled down have been far exceeded by gains at the top. In addition, much of the extreme wealth creation has come not through the employment of people, but through nonproductive (for the general economy) financial activities available to the superrich like trading futures in commodities and currencies. Hedge funds and high frequency trading not only distort market swings, they take capital out of the hands of already-wealthy sources and apply it, not to job-creating investments, but to financial products. When people put money in the bank, it provides funds to lend to growing businesses. Money put into hedge funds does not.

Incentives, whether tax or otherwise, facilitate, but they do not create, opportunities that were not there in the first instance. Taxes have only a marginal effect on economic decision making by businesses and investors; they do not drive fundamental decisions. Thus, for example, the decision to build an additional manufacturing plant is driven solely by demand for the product, although the place where the plant is sited may be influenced by favorable tax treatment. Giving a business or a wealthy individual a tax cut will not create new investment where the demand is lacking for the product or service. That is why businesses are sitting on hordes of cash as of this writing, because the demand is lacking for their products to the extent of needing new production capability. Economic uncertainty is also a major factor. If a machine shop has no customer growth, or is worried about future demand, a tax cut for the owner will not create new customers or result in the hiring of more employees. It simply puts more money in the pocket of the owner. That may have a small stimulative effect on his or her purchasing, but it is too limited. That is why we have seen one of the effects of the Bush tax cuts being to exacerbate the wealthy getting wealthier, while job growth and the middle class withered, and our national debt soared. In contrast, putting money in the hands of large numbers of the public, not just the uber-rich, though broad-based tax cuts or broad-based government expenditure stimulates broad-based demand. And that results in broad-based job creation.

Tax incentives are offsets against taxable income. If something isn't going to generate income in the first place, then the incentive is useless unless there is some larger societal benefit like the reduction of pollution. But even here, if the product or business is viable, then private investment should not need additional impetus through tax abeyance or reduction. We long ago started down the road to taxation as a tool of economic policy, and that road has led to a variety of distortions in our economy. Such incentives can create artificial allocations of capital, such as the subsidy for ethanol, which has proven to be a gross waster of energy in order to produce it. The home interest deduction has helped spur housing growth, but now only worsens the situation for those who depended upon it to lessen the net effect of their mortgage payment; that effect is lost without a job or other income.

A major caveat here is that these government-related economic decisions about spending and taxes are complex and interrelated and cannot be viewed in the abstract. Despite the objection of some, the active intervention of the government, through fiscal policies (expenditure) and monetary policies (regulating interest rates and the supply of money in circulation), has smoothened the otherwise damaging swings of the business cycle over the period since the Great Depression. Yet when administrations and Congresses fail to eliminate or dramatically reduce deficits during good economic periods it takes away, or makes politically difficult, a major tool to stimulate economic expansion when times are not good. The failure to adhere to fiscal discipline (and candor about the true costs of tax cuts and of our military actions and their effect on our national debt) by most administrations and Congresses, Republican and Democrat, has painted our economy into a corner. The problem with all of the talk about paying down the debt during periods of severe downturn is that it favors bondholders of U.S. debt, like the Chinese, at the expense of our economy.

If we are to move forward as a country to best address the challenges we face, then we need to dispense with the misleading, fear-based arguments about abstractions like "big government." The discussions need to be about where government is required, regardless of economics, and where government can assist our national well-being in an economically beneficial way. Matters of national defense and foreign relations are appropriate provinces of central government while subsidies, tax incentives, and social programs should be viewed in terms of economic benefit and fiscal soundness. The terms *waste*, *big government*, *massive deficits*, *class warfare* and the like are nothing more than simplistic, vacuous, fearmongering labels that lead us astray instead of in directions by which we can improve life in our country. That does not mean that we should undertake national security programs without regard to their cost any more than it means we should ignore inefficiency in government just because the particular program or operation is economically beneficial. Nor does it mean that we should stand aside when government oversteps or a program outlives its usefulness. But anecdotal reference to this inefficiency or that excess obscures the larger picture and our need for facts rather than emotional stories concerning aberrations. Unfortunately, profit-driven media and special interests find anecdotes about government missteps far more entertaining and diverting. Moreover, such easy prey also obscure the structural issues such as the decline in higher wage manufacturing jobs, increased foreign competition, and the increasing gap between rich and poor in America. There are many factors at work that are leading to a lessened standard of living for many Americans. We need to be addressing those factors instead of engaging in vapid attacks on big government and foolish quarrels about tax cuts as if tax cuts are a panacea.

At its heart the Great Divide in America really addresses whether this nation will continue to concern itself with the individual needs of our citizenry for relative economic and personal security through the collective action of government, or whether we all will fend solely for ourselves; whether we should be our brother's and sister's keeper or indifferent to their needs and the lessons of history. History is replete with examples of what happens to societies that disregard the health and welfare of the general populace in favor of the interests of a wealthy few: such societies are wracked by revolution, repression, and aggressive redistribution. Those who express concerns about socialism ought to also consider the peril imposed by masses who feel unjustly and inequitably treated. In the words of author John Steinbeck in *The Grapes of Wrath*, echoing from a not-dissimilar time,

> …when property accumulates in too few hands it is taken away—and that companion fact: when a majority of the people are hungry and cold, they will take by force what they need. And, the little screaming fact that sounds through all history: repression works only to strengthen and knit the repressed.

As commented earlier, the social programs that have been enacted in the United States have far more than moral concern or sympathy behind them. They are based in pragmatism and sound economics, and that is how such programs should be viewed going forward, rather than with knee-jerk emotional reactions and labeling. Issues about unemployment, retirement security, cost-effective medical care, and the like should be concerns for all Americans, not just Republicans or Democrats or any other partisans. Solutions should not arise out of party dogma or ideology. Instead, these are issues that cross party lines and defy labels. We all have a stake in seeing people gainfully employed, and ought to be willing and able to join together in finding ways to best accomplish that. This country grew from the development of a burgeoning middle class, not on the backs of the poor and elderly. We all have an interest in a healthy populace that is productive and not a drag on medical resources and health costs. We ought to be able to join together, regardless of party, to find ways to provide for the health of all citizens in the most economical way possible, all factors considered. These are just examples of the point throughout this book that labels, dogma, party affiliation, and fear are serving us poorly as a nation and as individuals.

The ability of government to meet the needs of the larger populace is inextricably tied to government's role when it comes to business. Issues of business taxation, regulation and even foreign affairs often compete with the needs of the larger public in terms of resources and priorities. There is a balance point of political power in that competition whereby the needs of both business and the public can be accommodated. In recent years, however, that balance point has shifted dramatically in favor of business at the expense of the public and our democracy. While there is much to criticize in Roosevelt's expansionist views, he made an interesting observation in 1933 that has relevance today to the issue of government and big business:

> If the process of concentration goes on at the same rate, at the end of another century we shall have all American industry controlled by a dozen corporations, and run by perhaps a hundred men. Put plainly, we are steering a steady course toward economic oligarchy, if we are not there already.

When Roosevelt expressed his concern, the top 5 percent of the population was receiving 25.5 percent of the income. In recent times, according to the Census Bureau, the percentage of aggregate income going to the top 5 percent of people in the U.S. went from 16.6 percent in 1980 to 21.5 percent in 2008 in constant (2008 deflated) dollars. At the same time, the power and influence of certain industries, notably energy, healthcare (drugs, treatment, and insurance), and finance, has risen dramatically. The direct and indirect consequences of these trends, along with the impact of the Supreme Court decision known as Citizens United, will prove far more disastrous for our democratic self-determination and freedom than any concerns about big government. That will be the subject of the next chapter.

Chapter Eight

The Quiet Overthrow of American Democracy

...the essence of plutocracy, fulfilled by [the year] 2000, has been the determination and ability of wealth to reach beyond its own realm of money and control politics and government as well.
—Kevin Phillips, former Nixon speechwriter and author, Wealth and Democracy

Democracy's a very fragile thing. You have to take care of democracy. As soon as you stop being responsible to it and allow it to turn into scare tactics, it's no longer democracy, is it?
— Sam Shepard

Let the people think they govern, and they will be govern'd
—William Penn

William Penn's comment quoted above has proven to be very prescient. Most Americans believe that we live in a democracy and that "we the people" govern. Yet that phrase, enshrined in the Preamble to our Constitution, rings increasingly hollow these days. The inordinate influence of wealth, both corporate and individual, in the United States has insidiously turned our country into a plutocracy, a society ruled by the wealthy. Substantive democracy in

America is being stolen, not through force of arms or in the dead of night, but by an insidious assault that not only lets the people think they still govern, it has the diehard support of many who stand to lose the most from that assault.

What our Founding Fathers set in place in our Constitution was a system whereby wealth could become a vastly disproportionate influence upon governance. The majority of the Founders themselves were wealthy aristocrats. Although they were leery of the concentration of power in the hands of one or a few, they were also concerned about too much power in the hands of the masses. While we often focus romantically and patriotically on their lofty pronouncements about freedom and liberty and "government of the people, by the people," there was also much concern about the protection of property, including property in the form of slaves, on the part of some of these founding aristocrats. For purposes of apportioning voters for the House of Representatives, for example, it was determined that a slave should count as three-fifths of a person. A preponderance of the delegates to the Constitutional Convention, including one of the authors of the Declaration of Independence, Roger Sherman, even felt that the national legislature should be elected by state legislatures, not directly "by the people." Although subsequently amended, Article Three of the original Constitution prescribes exactly that form of election, one that is twice removed from popular vote. That concern about the "middling class" resulted in a representative, rather than a direct, form of democracy. Citizens do not vote on federal legislation; they only elect others to do so. There is no national referendum process either.

The Founders provided for the election of presidents, not by popular vote, but indirectly by electors from each state. And the initial form of our Constitution discussed primarily the form and allocation of government power, not the rights of citizens. The latter was only addressed significantly in the subsequent amendments known as The Bill of Rights—amendments that were slow to be adopted by all of the states. Initially there wasn't even one man, one vote. Qualification to vote in our formative years was tied to religious criteria or the possession of a minimum amount of wealth. Such restrictions in Pennsylvania and Maryland, for example, gave the right to vote only to a small fraction of the public: those with wealth. Ordinary workers, sharecroppers, teachers, and others could not vote. The resentment of aristocratic governance so vividly espoused by the Founders was, more often than not, antipathy toward those in power by virtue of birthright. At the same time, those whose wealth came from their investments of money and effort were seen as more appropriately entitled to suffrage than were those of the "middling class." Even the first Chief Justice of the Supreme Court echoed the belief that wealth equated to governance in America when he announced in 1787, "The people who own the country ought to govern it." Little did he know that several hundred years later that would begin to become a reality.

Despite the early influence of wealth upon the formation of our government, the common man was not to be denied. From the armed uprising of Shays Rebellion in 1787 onward, with due accord given to the informative impact of the printing press, the "middling class" began to assert their right to participate in governance. Over time voting restrictions were withdrawn and the right to vote was extended to nearly all citizens. America became the "land of opportunity" with its inexpensive real estate, burgeoning population, and growing need for products and services. Immigrants flocked to the country to become farmers and shopkeepers, professionals, laborers, and millworkers. Politics was largely a local affair for most Americans, with simmering differences between northern and southern states contained largely beneath the surface until those differences erupted into the Civil War. The wealth of the nation that was being created was also being shared broadly with those willing to put their back to it. There were excesses of course, what with robber barons and sweatshops in the so-called Gilded Age, but the public was otherwise quite pleased with this engine of prosperity known as America; at least until a Tuesday in October of 1929.

The stock market crash of Black Tuesday and the Great Depression that followed shattered the confidence of many in our economic system, but did little to shake the confidence of the vast majority of Americans in their form of government (as opposed to confidence in those elected). There was rioting and unrest for sure, but no revolution, despite the dire conditions at the time. One quarter of all workers had no job (there were pockets of unemployment even greater), farm prices plunged 60 percent, major and minor banks failed, and economic devastation spread throughout the world. While many theories have been offered as to the causes of the Great Depression, there is broad agreement that lax regulation of Wall Street speculation and the refusal to prevent major bank failures by the federal government (primarily the

Federal Reserve) were contributing factors to the ultimate lack of credit and the resultant plunge deeper into economic calamity. Full recovery didn't really occur until after the major mobilization that supported World War II. Through it all most Americans never lost hope in the land of opportunity, despite the intervening nightmare they were enduring.

Following the war, sanguinity about the promise of America continued. Returning soldiers were provided for by the Serviceman's Readjustment Act of 1944, more commonly known as the GI Bill. It provided unemployment compensation, college and vocational training, and low-interest home loans for millions of veterans. These massive and broad-based government expenditures that found their way into housing and education helped kick-start the postwar economy. Another bill in 1952 provided similar benefits to veterans of the Korean War. There were intervening recessions, but, once again, Americans were experiencing an ever-increasing standard of living as these returning veterans entered the workforce to build homes, work in factories, and provide services. There was upward mobility and a higher standard of living for most Americans throughout this period. Even the Wall Street scandals of the 1980s, the savings and loan crisis, and the stock market crash that followed the dot-com bubble in the 1990s did not shake Americans' faith in the system that was overall providing a better life for most of them. Or so they believed. Despite populist burbles here and there, Americans remained wedded to their economic system and its oft-demonstrated promise of opportunity whereby the poorest could become wealthy. Yet all the while, the relationship between government and the wealthy, both individual and corporate, was changing in ways that would move our country from representative democracy in name and deed to a plutocracy in fact. In a most perverse and ironic way this change began to intensify with the philosophical shift toward less government articulated during the Reagan presidency. In his debate in 1980 with then President Jimmy Carter, Reagan announced,

> I'm not running for the presidency because I believe that I can solve the problems we've discussed tonight. I believe the people of this country can.

It was one of those quiet watershed moments. It reaffirmed a belief in self-reliance and suggested that people should regard government as best when it governs the least. He made this point quite explicit in his inaugural address by stating that government was the problem, not the solution. Implicit in that view was a separation of the people from their government. For in a true democracy the people *are* the government ("government of the people, by the people, and for the people"). But in the Reagan view, government was now a separate antagonist, a problem-creating colossus to be cut down to size by its stakeholders. The focus was no longer to be upon government efforts to curb the seeming excesses of capitalism through regulation and legislation. These were stifling growth and competition, it was argued. Nor was government's role to provide programs to address perceived societal ills. Such programs were too intrusive, costly, and stifled initiative. Rather, the focus was upon reducing government's footprint on both business and individuals,, thereby letting a self-correcting economic system and individual initiative prevail. It was economic Darwinism at its finest hour.

This view of government as the adversary, government as the problem, was an emboldening concept for many Americans. It implied power in the hands of voters and a target against which to apply that power: big government. Coming on the heels of the Iran hostage embarrassment that stained the Carter presidency, Reagan's cowboy personae and forthrightness appealed to many. He stood up to Moammar Gaddafi and stared down the Soviet Union, contributing with Russia's Gorbachev to the beginning of an end to the Cold War. On the economic front, Carter had presided over a period of high unemployment and even higher interest rates. But by the end of Reagan's presidency, interest rates and unemployment were down substantially. Reaganomics, with its avowed emphasis on deregulation, tax cuts for the wealthiest individuals and businesses, and the cutting of government expenditures (despite doing the opposite), was seen as validation by advocates of supply-side economics along with what was thought to be the resultant "trickle down" of benefits to the middle class. Despite the adulation, Reagan was no pure supply-sider. He presided over several significant tax increases and tripled the deficit over what was left by Carter to a then-whopping $2.8 trillion. Nevertheless, Reagan became a conservative icon, enshrined in Republican Party thinking and later by Tea Party supporters. There was a growing affinity for business and an increasing antagonism toward unions and federal programs such as Medicaid, the EPA, food stamps, and federal support for education. There are many myths and crosscurrents surrounding the Reagan legacy, but one thing is very clear. His presidency began the rift in the country previously referred to in Chapter Seven as "The Great Divide." The Reagan legacy also unknowingly laid the groundwork for our government to surreptitiously become the handmaiden of wealth with the full, if unknowing, support of many Americans.

In the years following World War II and up to the Reagan years, family income growth was fairly evenly distributed across the spectrum. Thereafter income growth was actually negative for the lower three-fifths of American income earners, while it soared for the wealthiest segment, according to the Congressional Budget Office, which keeps such statistics. In 1980, the last pre-Reagan year the top 1% took home an average of $5.4 million. By 2006 the superrich had average incomes over five times that much at $29.6 million. They also controlled over half of the stock and mutual-fund ownership as of 2007. Yet while the superrich got richer, for everyone else real average earnings (expressed in 2008 dollars) had not increased in fifty years! After the Reagan tax cuts the wealthiest 1% averaged 156 times the wealth of the median household. After the Bush tax cuts that disparity had grown to 190 times the wealth of the median household. The gap between the rich and poor had not been that great since the period that presaged the Great Depression, and all the while the middle class languished. The benefits of rising productivity, stock market gains, and soaring executive salaries and bonuses had flowed largely to the already wealthy, while declining union influence and increasing foreign competition eroded real wages for average Americans.

For many, however, the American dream seemed to remain alive and well, despite their stagnating income in real terms. That is because many were able to acquire more and more things by taking on increasing debt, withdrawing the equity in their appreciating homes, and by becoming two-wage-earner families. Americans were simply working harder and borrowing more. Home equity gains and increased leverage substituted for real earnings growth. Yet the very engine of affordable home ownership and increasing home values over the past decade, low interest rates, was also fueling the underpinnings of a collapse. As the disparity between average Americans and the wealthiest grew to pre–Great Depression levels, it again presaged a calamity brought on by economic excess and greed. The chimerical American dream finally turned into a nightmare for many Americans as the housing market collapsed and the financial crisis in banking began.

Why then, despite this reality, do so many Americans continue to support policies that favor the wealthy at the expense of the rest of American society? Why have these supply-side, trickle-down policies become so entrenched at the grass roots when they have hurt or done little for most Americans? The answer most often advanced is that America is still the land of opportunity where anyone can become rich. So, it is argued, people don't want to gore the ox that may someday pull their wagon. Yet as we have seen, America as the land of opportunity has largely become a myth. The chances of moving up or down economically was about equal (around 2 percent moving up and 2 percent of the population moving down) in 2005. That relative immobility in 2005 was part of a fairly steady downward trend in mobility that occurred during the postwar period. We know, from the extremely high unemployment figures that grew out of the financial markets' meltdown so evident in 2009, that downward mobility can only be presumed to have vastly increased, while upward mobility declined even further since 2005, except of course for the superrich. At the same time that average workers' salaries have turned stagnant, CEO pay has skyrocketed along with Wall Street income and bonuses, despite the gross mismanagement displayed by the beneficiaries of this largesse. Even when CEOs had destroyed shareholder value during their tenure, many left their companies with rich severance and retirement packages, as if to reward their incompetence. Efforts to deal with ridiculous levels of executive compensation have been virtually nonexistent, thanks to boards filled with fellow travelers.

Another argument for supporting policies that benefit the wealthy has been that the rich and superrich are the job creators. If that were true, then the trend of stagnating real income would have been reversed during the Reagan years, and we would have seen substantial job growth as a result of the tax cuts and regulatory relaxation that occurred during the Bush years. Just the opposite has occurred, to the point that there are now a reported fourteen million Americans out of work. The reality is that most job *growth* comes from small business, not from billionaires, Wall Street, or large corporations. Corporations, in fact, have been moving jobs and operations overseas, while Wall Street laid off staff following the financial meltdown they helped create. Small businesses are not generally owned by the superrich, but rather by middle-class Americans who are currently suffering the most as a result of the severe economic downturn spurred by the financial crisis.

So in the face of real unemployment as high as 22 percent, where was the concern being focused by 2011? Republicans turned the focus toward the federal deficit and a compliant president went along with them. Governors pointed to the need to cut the wages and numbers of state workers, including firemen, police, and teachers, and to reductions in programs for education and Medicaid. Republicans and a few Democrats in Congress refused to consider tax increases for the wealthy or abatement of subsidies and other tax breaks for corporations, while arguing instead for cuts to the EPA, Medicare, Medicaid, and Social Security in order to reduce the federal deficit. That was the same kind of wrongheaded thinking that snatched defeat out of the jaws of victory during the initial recovery from the Great Depression. Then, a focus on cutting government spending, along with rising interest rates (that now may result from deficit gamesmanship), cut the legs out from under a nascent recovery in the late 1930s. Why would our current elected representatives, armed with the lessons of history, act in a manner so contrary to the welfare of the country as a whole? Why would they refuse shared sacrifice in favor of placing the burden of the deficit upon the backs solely of the poor, the elderly, and social services, when the deficit was created principally from bailing out wealthy investment banks, and speculators, from two wars, from an unfunded prescription program, and from what were to have been temporary income tax reductions for the very wealthy? The answer is that the real constituency of the vast majority in Congress from either party is not the American people. It is the powerful interests that support these politicians in exchange for tax breaks, government contracts, competitive advantage, and relief from regulation. It suggests that our government is now of the wealthy, by the wealthy, and for the wealthy. That state of affairs is perpetuated and furthered by nuanced appeals to the hopes and dreams of Americans who are led to believe that their path to a good life is inextricably tied to increasing the wealth of the already wealthy. These nuanced appeals take the form of carefully crafted public relations campaigns, position papers, lobbying, issue advertising, and political spin from politicians themselves and from conglomerate-controlled media. To better understand how wealth has crowded out the public interest and solidified its power over our democracy, it is useful to look back at the early underpinnings of the financial crises that became widespread in 2009. It is there that we will find a shining example of the efforts on the part of powerful, wealthy interests to gain even more power and wealth by manipulating public opinion, public servants, and legislation.

The previously discussed Depression-era law known as Glass-Steagall, which barred banks from being engaged "principally" in the securities business, was designed to shield commercial banks from the risks of underwriting or trading third-party securities (investment banking activities) and thereby protect the public and depositors from commercial bank failures. In 1986 the Federal Reserve reinterpreted *principally* in the law to allow banks to generate up to 5 percent of their gross revenues from certain investment banking activities. Parenthetically, it is important to understand that the Federal Reserve Board is made up of presidential appointees and that the individual overseeing Federal Reserve District Bank boards are filled two-thirds by bankers from the very banks they are supposed to regulate in their district. As the Fed loosened the reins of Glass-Steagall, Alan Greenspan, a former director of J.P. Morgan Bank and staunch proponent of bank deregulation, became chairman of the Federal Reserve Board. Then in 1989 the Fed further broadened the loophole to include not merely the issuance of commercial paper, but also debt and equity securities, and raised the limit to 10 percent of gross income. The camel's nose was now firmly in the tent. Which bank became the first one to issue securities under the relaxed authority? It was none other than Greenspan's J.P. Morgan. Then in 1996 Greenspan's Fed expanded the limit to 25 percent of gross (not net) income, virtually making the Glass-Steagall prohibition completely ineffective. That allowed commercial banks to engage in highly profitable, albeit highly risky, securities activities.

Then in 1998 Travelers Insurance Group (that included the investment banking house Salomon Smith Barney), headed by Sanford Weil, entered into a $70 billion merger agreement with the then commercial bank, Citi Bank, headed by John Reed. There was just one problem: such a combination was prohibited by Glass-Steagall, even with the liberalized interpretation. It would have meant divestiture of Travelers' investment banking operations within two years of the merger. They had to get rid of Glass-Steagall. So they commenced *both* a lobbying *and* a public relations campaign. The threefold arguments made in support of repeal were that since 1933, there was an effective Securities and Exchange Commission to guard against fraud, investors were more astute, and that there were sophisticated rating agencies overseeing securities issuance. Subsequent events would forcefully prove the arguments to have been wrong on all counts.

In the 1997–98 election cycle the finance, insurance, and real estate lobbies (known collectively as FIRE) spent more than two hundred million dollars on lobbying and made more than one hundred fifty million dollars in political contributions. Campaign contributions were targeted directly at members of congressional banking committees and other committees with jurisdiction over financial services legislation. The money got results in the form of the repeal of Glass-Steagall through the Gramm Leach Bliley Act. Gramm Leach was passed in the Senate 90–8 (1 not voting) and in the House: 362–57 (15 not voting). With majorities large enough to override any possible presidential veto, the legislation was signed into law by President **Bill Clinton** on November 12, 1999. When Weill told Clinton's treasury secretary, Robert Rubin (who had endorsed passage of the repeal and who was a former co-chair of Wall Street investment bank Goldman Sachs) that he had important news at the time of the merger with Travelers, Rubin is alleged to have quipped, "You're buying the government?" Within days of the repeal's passage, Rubin left the Treasury to become Weill's chief lieutenant at none other than Citigroup, the new megabank. Rubin reportedly thereafter made over one hundred million dollars while Citigroup nearly collapsed; a collapse that required three separate federal bailouts totaling billions in taxpayer money. As to Senator Gramm himself, immediately after his departure from the Senate in 2002 he became vice-chairman of the investment bank division of UBS AG, an integrated banking colossus of the kind permitted by the repeal. UBS subsequently became one of the major banks hit most severely by the mortgage crisis, writing off over fifty billion dollars in losses and laying off over eleven thousand employees. Senator Gramm had also shepherded another law that weakened the Commodity Futures Trading Commission (CFTC) that oversaw trading of the very kind of derivative instruments, like credit default swaps, that precipitated the bailout of insurer AIG. And who sat upon the board of the CFTC from 1985 to 1993, chairing it the last four years? It was none other than Phil Gramm's wife, Wendy Gramm. Since 1991 the CFTC quietly gave exemptions from hedging regulations to nineteen major banks and market participants, allowing them to accumulate essentially unlimited positions. These exemptions were originally given in secret, coming to light only as the 2008 financial crisis unfolded and Congress requested information on market participants. A trader or bank granted an exemption as a bona fide hedger can affect the price of a commodity without being either its producer or consumer through the manipulation of massive dollar amounts of futures contracts. Such trading can then affect consumer markets in the form of gas and heating oil prices and electricity rates charged to hapless consumers.

While there were many factors behind the mortgage crisis and resultant financial meltdown, including profit-conflicted rating agencies and an era of lax regulation, most would agree that the weakening and ultimate repeal of Glass-Steagall not only allowed the contagion to affect commercial banking (as distinct from investment banking), but also created the "too big to fail" issue by allowing the creation of mega-banks like Citigroup to be created. So when Congress began to consider financial reform, surely they would deal with "too big to fail" and reinstate something akin to Glass-Steagall. That didn't happen, despite the near economic Armageddon that had resulted. The two thousand or so lobbyists who registered to lobby on behalf of the financial industry carefully steered the legislation so that those financial institutions, the same ones given billions of dollars in taxpayer bailout money only a year or two before, would remain just as big, dangerous, and powerful as ever. The final bill weighed in at 2,319 pages. On almost every page there were dozens of phrases—typically framed in near unintelligible legalese—whose wording could mean millions or billions to some company or industry, according to a *Time* magazine analysis. Of those two thousand lobbyists working on financial reform, more than fourteen hundred had been congressional staffers or worked in the executive branch, and seventy-three had been members of Congress. With that kind of career path (the typical tenure of a congressional staffer is only two years), it would be very hard to resist the entreaties of your potential future employers, the lobbyists, while you were in government. It is not surprising then that young, impressionable, and inexperienced staffers can become willing recipients of the points of view offered by lobbyists. They then pass on the "wisdom," given to them by lobbyists in the form of position papers and assurance of reelection support, to their congressional bosses. Even after passage of the reform legislation, weak as it was, banking lobbyists were hard at work to weaken it further. According to the *New York Times*, some fifty-two million dollars was spent through July of 2011 on lobbying Congress to produce a slew of bills aimed at gutting the reforms. In addition, congressional Republicans have signaled their intention to block the appointments of any administrators called for in the legislation, including blocking the appointment of the head of the federal agency created to oversee financial consumer protection. Even the administration has failed to give the legislation support. A year after its passage, only thirty-eight of the expected four hundred rules stemming from the bill had been crafted. And President Obama passed up an opportunity to sidestep Congressional approval with a recess appointment of the person he proposed to lead the agency. Such actions are rather astonishing, given the litany of abuses committed by banks in the run-up to the mortgage meltdown. One of those abuses, robo signing, where the bank executes documents without reviewing their accuracy, is reported to still be going on at major banks. The failure to verify documentation was one of the major reasons for the large number of failed mortgages executed by homeowners who either did not understand what they were signing or who were defrauded.

One might argue that lobbyists offset one another, thereby protecting the public interest. Yet there were only a handful of lobbyists representing consumer interests during the financial reform hearings. They were arrayed against the several thousand representing powerful financial interests. Lobbyists not only draft legislative proposals, which are then submitted by a compliant congressman, they become the initiators of billions of dollars in campaign contributions. These contributions take the form of not only direct payments from the particular lobbyist, but also from their corporate clients and the corporate employees. It is quite common for corporations to give "bonuses" to their employees that are (wink, wink) to then be contributed to a key senator or representative on a committee whose legislation they stand to benefit from. All of these payments have huge payoffs. For example, the White House sought to bar banks who received Federal Reserve support from trading for their own gain. Three of the megabanks—JP Morgan Chase, Morgan Stanley, and Goldman Sachs—stood to lose up to $4.5 billion in potential profits, according to *Time* magazine. After $15.4 million in 2009 to lobbyists and $2.6 million in campaign contributions, the prohibition was watered down to allow up to 3 percent of their capital to be invested in risky private equity and hedge funds. It was estimated that this thereby protected $2.9 billion in profits and billions more in risky trading. That's quite a return on investment. A cursory look at the Web site of the public interest group Center for Responsive Politics, which tracks congressional lobbying records, shows a continuous pattern of relatively small contributions resulting in enormous monetary benefits in the form of government contracts, tax breaks, regulatory relief, and favorable legislation. The year 2009 was a watershed year for the tidal wave that is lobbying. Some $3.4 billion was spent that year on lobbyists alone. Ordinary citizens have no lobbyists, nor could most afford one. Even public interest groups that have lobbyists are far outweighed by corporate and trade lobbyists. The only meaningful offset has been union organizations, but as we shall see there is a concerted effort to vilify and remove unions from the landscape.

In addition to finance, another pillar of the American plutocracy is the health-care industry. In the first six months of 2009, the drug industry alone spent more than $110 million on lobbying during efforts to reform health care. That equated to about $609,000 per day to protect their interests. They also provided $2.6 million from 2006 to the middle of 2009 directly to members of the House Energy and Commerce Committee who worked on the legislation. According to congressional records, the American Medical Association, the Pharmaceutical Research and Manufacturers of America, the American Hospital Association, and health insurer Blue Cross/Blue Shield spent a combined $811 million dollars on lobbying since 1998. During the health-care debate, health insurance giant United Heath Group marshaled its thousands of employees in a letter-writing campaign and funded media placements designed to deter aspects of support for health-care reform. Is it then any wonder that health insurance rates are outstripping health-care costs; that health insurers were granted an exemption from the antitrust laws that apply to most other businesses (who are prohibited from price-fixing);

and that drug prices in America are often so much higher than in other countries that do not permit drug advertising or collusion and that use government purchasing power? The American Chamber of Commerce almost equaled the health-care industry with lobbying expense of nearly $776 million during this period. All of these amounts were spent directly on lobbyists. They do not account for campaign contributions, officer contributions, or political action committee (PAC) money. The health-care industry, for example, spent $54.6 million in 2010 for PAC contributions to federal election candidates. The split was 55 percent to Democrats and 45 percent to Republicans. These numbers do not reflect amounts less than the lobbying reporting threshold, which was ten thousand dollars per contribution pre-2008 and five thousand dollars thereafter. Individual contributions less than these levels, no matter how numerous, are not reported.

Most Americans understand the corrosive impact of lobbying, if not its extent. But while lobbying is subject to a degree of reporting and scrutiny, a more insidious form of the corruption of our democracy is not. Thanks to a series of Supreme Court cases, based upon the faulty premise put into a summary (headnote) of a prior Supreme Court case, corporations have been deemed to come within the protection of the Fourteenth Amendment's equal protection clause and thus to have a right to free speech as guaranteed by the First Amendment. Not only is there no such provision in the Constitution, many of the Founders, most notably Thomas Jefferson, railed against the evils of corporate power and would be aghast at the idea of corporations being protected by the Fourteenth Amendment, much less granted the ancillary protections of the Bill of Rights. That notwithstanding, and leapfrogging upon a leapfrog by overturning prior cases, the Roberts Supreme Court ruled recently in a case called *Citizens United v. Federal Election Commission* that there are essentially no limits to the money that can be spent by corporations and unions to influence elections, effectively making them a vastly disproportionate voice to that of living, breathing American citizens. The five-to-four majority of the Court knowingly took this position even though they realized that this unlimited influence money could come indirectly from corporations controlled by governments and others outside of the United States. Any attempt to regulate such monetary contributions in campaign finance laws was contorted by the Court to be a violation of corporate and union free speech. Never mind that actual citizen individuals are limited in what they can contribute. What the Court incredibly said, in effect, with no tongue in cheek, was that money was speech.

It was now official: money talks in America, and loudly enough to drown out all other voices. These horrific Supreme Court decisions were the effective nail in the coffin of American democracy as we knew it. Not only had the tide of lobbyist influence upon legislators reached epic proportion, now carefully crafted public relations campaigns, underwritten by virtually no limits on spending, could mold voters' opinions and actions without any effective mirror of truth or accountability being applied as an offset. Certain political action committees, those espousing so-called issue ads, like those of the populist-sounding PAC Citizens United, do not even have to disclose the source or amount of their funding. Unnamed corporate and wealthy contributors, with specific agendas, can throw vast resources behind campaigns to get voters to do their bidding by framing issues in ways that mislead and galvanize citizen support. Typically, the method is to instill fear. The voter is led to believe that very bad things will happen to them if they don't support the position being advocated. Or a politician's voting record is distorted. There is no requirement of truth, no disclosure of purpose, only an unwitting public being exposed to what is in reality pure, uncontrolled propaganda. One of the most egregious of these, the distortion of John Kerry's Vietnam military record, set the label for such propaganda now known as swiftboating. A similar PR campaign was aired to distort George W. Bush's service record.

Then there are the leadership PACs. These are political action committees of elected officials designed to raise money to dispense to their colleagues and thereby to have clout over these colleagues, rewarding those who support and cooperate with their legislative agenda. The largest among these in 2010 belonged not surprisingly to Republicans Eric Cantor and John Boehner and Democrats Steny Hoyer, James Clyburn, and Nancy Pelosi.

The quiet takeover of American democracy by wealth is now virtually complete. Most shocking of all is that there has been little alarm and virtually no meaningful attempt to counter it. There have been feeble suggestions about amending the Constitution to deny free speech rights to corporations, but the barriers to doing so are almost insurmountable, especially when the state legislatures that must ratify any such amendment (even assuming a two-thirds vote of each federal house) are also beneficiaries of the status quo. Add to all of this the monumental sums required to gain and hold political office, and the average citizen effectively has no say in the influence game. The temptations and monetary demands are so great that even the most well-intentioned politicians soon learn to bend their principles, or they will become the target of a privately funded campaign of negative ads against them or lose needed campaign funds. Sadly, there has been no Paul Revere to alarm us. There has been no Thomas Paine to inspire us. There has only been the ever-increasing flow of money drowning our democracy.

Chapter Nine

Will We Ever Learn

Education in America

Education's purpose is to replace an empty mind with an open one
—Malcolm Forbes

If a nation expects to be ignorant and free, in a state of civilization, it expects what never was and never will be.
—Thomas Jefferson

The increasing willingness of Americans to accept revisionist history, blatant untruths, and political obfuscation is the canary in the coal mine of education in America. Besieged by budget cuts and arguments about curriculum and taxes, the canary is gasping for breath. Why should this be the case when nothing is more critical to a democracy than an educated, informed electorate? Education, even more than raw intelligence, is crucial to making good life choices. Education is the software that runs on our intelligence. Good software can make even a lesser computer function quite well. But with bad software (a bad education), even the best of computers (the most intelligent people) will come to erroneous conclusions. If our formal and informal education does not provide us with the tools to think independently and deal with the challenges of life, it will foster poor decisions for our personal lives and for our country as well, regardless of our level of reasonable intelligence. If our education fills us with fear-based imperatives, dogma, and emotional approaches to issues or fails to equip us with the tools we need to rationally analyze problems, then our decision making will be suspicious of complexity and anything else that makes us fearful or violates unquestioned imperatives and doctrinaire beliefs. We will also be more likely respond to our gut feeling and to manipulation than to divine the truth of the matter.

This is not to suggest that one needs a college education to be a voter in a democracy, although more education is certainly better than less. Rather, we need to come equipped with certain tools that basic education in America should provide. Sadly, however, too many Americans lack important context, such as a fundamental understanding of our basic Constitutional framework, or a grasp of the core elements that drive our economic system. That educational deficit allows them to rely, often unknowingly, on false or incomplete interpretations and populist slogans, believing them to be well-founded. Supposedly intelligent pundits in America frequently confuse and mingle socialism and capitalism, which are economic systems, with democracy, despotism, and monarchy, which are political systems, as if one begets the other. Other pundits, either out of ignorance or pandering, misinterpret the Constitution and re-write history to their liking or simply make up "facts" that they ask their audience to believe on the basis of feeling that they are true; "you know it in your heart." This now growing propensity to disregard science, objective history, and facts in general in favor of gut-level belief has contributed to the rise of what best-selling author Charles F. Pierce has called "Idiot America." If something is repeated often enough, sells books, creates ratings, is said with enough conviction, or flows from respect for the effort to promulgate it, the theory will be believed; no logic, facts, or scientific evidence required. In fact, such an approach can actively disregard known facts, just as so-called birthers disregarded a host of factual evidence attesting to the state of Hawaii birth of President Obama. They just "knew" he was born in Kenya despite a state-issued Certificate of Live Birth, the existence of contemporary birth announcements in two Honolulu newspapers, the independent validation by both Republican and Democratic governors of Hawaii and the people responsible for maintaining the birth records. For some it simply boiled down to an inability to accept a biracial person as a legitimate president. But these were not just outliers. The erroneous belief was held by a large percentage of the populace at one time or another and even furthered by respected individuals such as Donald Trump (for whom respect declined significantly as a result). Conspiracy theories are made of such stuff. The willingness to accept conspiracy theories and other dubious premises relates directly to the level of our formal *and informal* education. Education is not the sole province of the classroom, but our formal education has a determinative effect upon how we interpret the world and therefore upon our informal, or cultural, education.

Despite its pivotal role for each of us personally, and collectively as a democratic country, ultimately formal education in America is the recipient of much heat but little light. There is schizophrenia in this country when it comes to education. Schizophrenia connotes a detachment from reality and a term for a state of mind characterized by contradictory or conflicting attitudes, behavior, or qualities. That fits our approach to education in America quite well. At the same time that we laud its importance we repeatedly divert resources from it and accord it lesser status than other spending priorities that we say have far less importance. A review of the statistical evidence from nearly every source indicates that, despite our supposed high valuation, education is being given short shrift. It is often the first to feel the knife of budget cuts and is continually mired in controversy about curriculum, teachers, and funding. As a result, by nearly every metric our system of education is failing us. In early March of 2011 the Department of Education announced that as many as 82 percent of the schools in the United States could be labeled as "failing" under the No Child Left Behind Act. The critical job of teaching in America is full of obstacles to success. Fully 25 percent of all public school teachers quit within their first three years. According to *The Economist,* something approaching 42 percent of tenth-graders in the United States are functionally illiterate. We are also falling behind other countries such as India and China in future international competitiveness. While the number of college graduates in the U.S. is increasing, these other countries are graduating far more engineers and scientists. The dropout rate for American students in science and engineering is alarming. At the same time, a study undertaken by the Business–Higher Education Forum found that fifteen-year-old Americans were behind their peers in twenty-five other countries in terms of their problem-solving ability. All of this is occurring as our place in the world economy is shrinking. For the first time, third world countries are producing more than half of the world's output. There is serious consideration being given to removing the U.S. dollar as the world currency standard, and the venerable New York Stock Exchange has recently passed to foreign ownership. Also ominous is the fact that China's GDP is expected to surpass that of the United States by 2016.

The situation at the high school level is dire. A recent report by ABC News, and confirmed by other sources, disclosed that nearly one-third of all public high school students do not graduate, with roughly twenty-five hundred per day dropping out due to poverty, pregnancy, or disinterest. While the average percentage of students who graduate high school nationally, on time and with a diploma, is 66 percent, the completion rate for black and Hispanic students drops to half that percentage. A startling one out of every ten schools in the United States graduates less than 60 percent of its initial enrollment. Some of the consequences are shorter life spans, increased crime, and lowered productivity. Dropouts live years less than gradu-ates, earn nine thousand dollars per year less, and make up 68 percent of state prison populations. These are shocking statistics for a country as wealthy as the United States.

Education suffers in the United States for a variety of reasons related to both our attitudes about education and our conflicting views about curriculum. With respect to curriculum, a strong argument can be made that there is too much emphasis on reading and math and not enough on broader subjects needed for the requirements of daily living. The basic tools needed to make a living and function in a capitalistic economy are seldom taught at the pre-college level, making many Americans who do not go on to college poor consumers and ill-equipped in the job market. A recent Associated Press-Viacom poll found that 60 percent of students who did not go on to college felt that school did only a fair to poor job of preparing them for work. Too many of today's students cannot balance a checkbook, maintain a budget, or prepare a proper resume. A greater emphasis on basic finance in school, for example, might have minimized the number of Americans victimized by the mortgage crisis in terms of agreeing to borrowings they should have known they could not support. On the broader worldly front, a surprisingly large number of students today cannot identify all fifty states or most of their capitals, let alone the location of significant countries outside the United States. In this increasingly interconnected world, the importance of history and geography, as well as related cultural studies such as language and comparative religion, cannot be overstated. As the ultimate decision makers in our democratic society, it is vital that we have the tools to make informed decisions about our foreign policies. We cannot evaluate the so-called experts or judge the information we receive as news without a context and background. To the extent we do not provide a well-rounded education, it becomes a vicious cycle where we produce citizens who then provide a lesser education for the next generation.

With respect to our attitudes about education, our words about primacy are not matched by deeds. Education is often the first place where the axe falls when budgets are strained in America. As this book is being written, budgets savaged by deep recession have legislators looking for ways to balance the shortfall. Schools, teacher numbers, and pay are high on the list. In Detroit serious consideration is even being given to shuttering a shocking one-half of the city's schools. There is considerable resentment, as well, where costly gains made by teachers' unions have burdened school districts across the country with high pension and health-care costs, even though teacher salaries are often uncompetitive with private industry. Insistence by teacher groups and unions upon seniority rather than competency is not helpful. And despite the importance of education to our democracy, our national security, and national competitiveness, there has been a resurgence of anti-intellectualism, with some labeling those with advanced educations as elitist and out of touch. At the same time, those with extensive formal educations sometimes lack understanding of, and sensitivity to, the views and conditions of those with lesser educations and differing circumstances. Professor-speak and talking down to people does not resonate well with much of America and reinforces the elitist label. Whether you agreed with much of what George W. Bush said or not, his manner of saying it resonated with many because he conveyed a folksy, trustworthy appearance. Some intellectually gifted individuals have spent too much time with books rather than people and too little time learning how to communicate.

As a result their lesser communication skills can portray them as cold, out of touch, aloof, or even undecipherable. When we do not understand what someone is saying, or it is over our head, we will be less likely to trust them. Not all is communication issues, however. Some of the anti-intellectualism we are witnessing flows from the debate between those advocating solely science-based education and those urging teachings more consistent with certain Christian spiritual beliefs. These latter individuals see the heavy hand of government in our public schools trampling upon their freedom of belief and disregarding their moral imperatives.

At its heart our educational failings are a product of our priorities in America. While we pay athletes and movie stars exorbitant sums to entertain us, we often underpay and disparage teachers and scientists and repeatedly cut education and research budgets. Too often we provide little incentive for people to get the education required to be effective teachers, scientists, engineers, and doctors who could find cures for diseases like cancer and help solve our nation's other pressing problems. This is not just a matter of our relative valuation of entertainment. Other needs, public and private, often crowd out education when it comes to the allocation of resources. Our politicians talk a good story but fail us when it comes to substance. Appeals to banning certain books, generic charges of waste, and empty grandstanding about the importance of education by politicians do not aid us. When we engage in debates about specific religious views filtering curriculum, we are being treated to a diversion. When politicians pit education against other pressing social needs, without mention of corporate welfare or other sacred cows, we are witnessing selective argument that again blurs the issue.

In the late 1950s, Russia's ability to place objects and people into space ahead of us served as a wake-up call that shook our complacency about our assumed educational and technological superiority. What followed was not only an increased outlay for NASA, but a renewed commitment to better education in this country. Sadly, that period was the apogee of not merely our spoken support but also our deeds in terms of improving the quality of education in the United States relative to other countries. That brief spurt of action was driven by the fear of Russian superiority and died out as that perceived threat disappeared. A national complacency, coupled with long lead times, has cost us dearly in educational achievement. We do not lack discussion and debate about education. Its value is not seriously disputed, but solutions are.

The problem is that the debate is misplaced, and thus so are the resources. The bulk of our local and national discussions about education are not about the achievement of identified *and meaningful* national goals but narrowly about what should be taught and how to allocate limited resources. And so we debate prayer in the schools, the teaching of intelligent design, government waste, and issues of taxation, while the quality of education in the United States continues to suffer and our competitive position in the world declines. Legitimate discussions about core competencies, class size, charter schools, and other issues of greater impact take the back row. We have again allowed our politicians to "do a little sidestep," and failed to hold them accountable for our educational failures. Instead we allow them to point fingers everywhere but at themselves and the inappropriate priorities they have put in place as they favor special-interest needs over public need.

Here again the politics of fear has had disastrous consequences. So much of our discussion about education is fear based. Politicians and certain interest groups love to talk about waste in education, citing anecdotal evidence but without any comprehensive fact-based analysis. These negative appeals make headlines, frighten those on fixed incomes, and sell air time, but the rhetoric is less about solutions and more about empty condemnation. The negative appeals demean all educators and waste resources that could be applied to actual teaching. They also do much to defeat local and national funding efforts and little to shed light on solutions to cost-effective education. Where the political appeal is not negative, it is more often empty platitudes of support for education without specifics. We see the smiling politician surrounded by young children in a classroom, while the voice-over declares the candidate's pious support of education; all without the slightest mention of specifics. Then there is the discussion about local control. Apparently we do not trust our fellow Americans, even those in the next county, to share our values and concern for education. So we demand local control over educational policy. Sometimes heartfelt, and sometimes a stalking horse for religious influence at the local level, the end result is to create gross disparities in educational quality at every level, right down to individual districts within cities themselves.

All of these polemics by our politicians and interest groups divert our attention to emotion-charged issues that divide us rather than offer solutions to the needs that could bring us together. In my home state, we became locked in a funding debate not dissimilar to debates in other states. A property tax limitation initiative that played to fear rather than educational need was passed by the voters several years ago. It forced state educational funding to be made up more out of the state General Fund and less from dedicated property taxes. On the surface it sounded reasonable. Property tax growth limitations had already restricted educational funding to the point that schools were fairing very badly. And those on fixed incomes were suffering from special levies and other property tax increases. Backers assured voters that education would benefit by moving the funding source from property taxes to the General Fund whose source was state income taxes. But education then had to compete with other demands on the state's undedicated income tax revenues in order to replace the funding lost to the property tax limitation. This pitted education funding against funding for state police, infrastructure, health-care for the elderly and mentally ill, prisons, and other emotionally charged needs. Further, the income tax–based General Fund rose and fell with the economy, so school funding rose and fell, irrespective of need. In the end education funding did not keep up with need. The solution for many was to argue for a state sales tax (the state has none), an approach repeatedly rejected by the voters of my home state. But all of this debate simply diverted the discussion from education to taxation. The result has been a stalemate where classrooms continue to deteriorate, good teachers leave, and overall educational quality continues to decline relative to other states and countries. We argue about the mortgage while the house burns down.

It is not that we do not know what to do. Educational successes abound throughout our country. Creative approaches that produce exceptional results are available and proven. What is lacking is a commitment to our future and to the preeminent role education should play in our democratic society—the ability to match our words with our deeds. The result has been a discouraging fatalism that has gripped many of the children in our country. The system has failed them not only in the quality of their education, but in convincing them of the value of education to their own efficacy. Some of the highest dropout rates are in areas where young people once could get jobs without a high school education, such as in the textile mills, but those and other manufacturing jobs are no longer available. The system has also failed to lessen the economic and social hurdles that many teens face in our throwaway society. The shortsighted failure to elevate the importance of education in terms of *meaningful* actions, rather than mere words, has enormous societal costs, including higher crime rates, increased teen pregnancies, and the creation of a segment of society that depletes human and monetary resources, rather than generates them. Finally, the lost productivity and lack of competitiveness are immeasurable. We seem to not realize that the very real long-term costs of not educating our citizens properly far outweighs any short-term savings from budget cuts to education. Funds expended for education should be viewed in investment terms, not as irretrievable expenses.

This isn't just about money, though. Teaching is an intensely interpersonal endeavor. Smaller classes and more teachers of themselves do not address educational quality. For that reason the debate about these approaches becomes circular. Each side can cite statistics to support their position, and so progress toward educational improvement falters. What is at the heart of the issue at the local level is *quality teachers*, not just more teachers. Quality teachers and administrators create and maintain learning environments that stimulate and inspire students to *want* to learn. After all of the studies and debate, at the end of the day it is the quality of the teacher in the classroom that determines whether a child's interest is turned on or is turned off, whether the child learns or is merely passed on. That point does not denigrate the important role that parents play in motivating their children, but for some children such motivation from their parents is lacking. Even where parental support and encouragement exists, if the milk is sour it won't be consumed. If children are not inspired and stimulated by their experience in the classroom, they will not want to continue nor will they be motivated to excel, no matter how small the class or well-paid the teacher.

Apart from its importance to us personally, education is such a profound determinant of our place in the world that we simply cannot vacillate further. Even if we were to find the national resolve tomorrow, it would take decades for the changes to take full effect. The average educational cycle for a child, including college or vocational training, begins at age five (in most public systems) and can continue to twenty-two and beyond. A world-class education would take seventeen years to produce a college graduate even if commenced today. But we are nowhere near providing world-class education to our children. We cannot even agree on the proper place of education in our national and local priorities, much less the goals of education that we wish to achieve.

The No Child Left Behind Act was an attempt to attain national goals for education, but it was poorly thought out and underfunded. President Bush said in January of 2001, regarding the NCLB Act:

> These reforms express my deep belief in our public schools and their mission to *build the mind and character* of every child, from every background, in every part of America. (emphasis added)

What do we do to "build the mind"? Do we truly see as coequal a national mission of education to build character? We might agree on certain values, but character in this context, and mind-building, are quite subject to interpretation and disagreement. Moreover, countries like China and India are not so much in the character-building business as they are in the business of producing first-rate graduates to foster and administer the growth of their countries. This kind of ambiguous direction in the United States is at the heart of the problem. It is where religious and other extraneous issues divert us from what ought to be the principal goals of primary education: teaching children basic life skills to cope with an interconnected world (reading, English language skills, math, basic science, geography, basic economics, and history), and in the process teaching children to think independently and to value further education. Building upon those basic life skills should be exposure to the arts and physical and health education. Sadly, the arts and athletics have fared poorly in many school districts where funding cuts have eliminated team sports, bands, and other enriching activities. Such activities are not frivolous. They have been shown repeatedly to reinforce and enhance classroom performance.

It is a common refrain that the No Child Left Behind Act has also encouraged "teaching to the test." Schools and teachers know they will now be evaluated based on the test scores for the specific areas defined by the Act (principally reading, writing, and math). Some children simply do not do well on standardized tests. More importantly, the standards and related tests do not emphasize the broader subjects needed for an understanding of our world such as geography, history, and language. Some districts have simply lowered the test levels (each state writes its own tests), rather than raise the educational levels, in order to meet federal mandates. Additionally, many teachers feel the NCLB Act has forced them to disregard brighter students in order to concentrate on lifting up the slow learners. Finally, the NCLB Act is seen to have a negative effect on graduation levels. Linda McSpadden McNeil, director of the Center for Education at Rice University had this to say:

High-stakes, test-based accountability doesn't lead to school improvement or equitable educational possibilities. It leads to avoidable losses of students. Inherently the system creates a dilemma for principals: comply or educate. Unfortunately we found that compliance means losing students.

Teaching ought not to be about teaching to standardized tests or filling heads with dogma or data but about teaching students to understand, work with, and be discriminating about the information they receive throughout life. This is not "building a mind," but about providing specific tools to live a full and productive life. An independent-thinking and informed electorate is also critical to the long-term survival of a democracy. Successfully taught children become inspired adults, eager to make learning an ongoing part of their lives. They become knowledgeable voters capable of informed decision making as well as creative participants in the political process. And they are less susceptible to manipulation by political agendas and entertaining misinformation passed off as news or fact.

Our country's failure to have a clear, *meaningful* national policy toward education—embodied in a clear set of goals and specific strategies to attain those goals, which are echoed and implemented at the local level—is reflected not just in the statistics, but in the character of the lives of working Americans. Education has relevance to our ability to obtain meaningful and rewarding work, to compete in the world and to enhance our standard of living. What we are witnessing, however, is a continuing decline in these very areas. Individuals are working longer, more stressful hours while many families need to have both partners employed in order to make ends meet; this despite the fact that the individual workweek has actually declined over time (leveling out in the last few years), thanks to wage and hour laws and union efforts. Many are working for less compensation than in previous jobs, are working multiple jobs or part time or not at all. While the "official" Bureau of Labor Statistics (BLS) unemployment number for August of 2011 was 9.6% the "real" unemployment level was estimated to be as high as 22% using the BLS pre-1994 method of calculation.

The entire dynamic of the employment relationship has changed. We will have more to say about this later, but for now it is important to note that there are significant social consequences that flow from an increasingly competitive global economy where education is a paramount determinant of success. Those social consequences include the prospect of a declining standard of living and increasing personal stress in the United States when the competitive challenge from workers in other countries is unmet. Unless we wish to compete with foreign wage levels by drastically lowering our standard of living, we must compete in the knowledge and innovation arena. For America to remain competitive in the arena of higher-wage jobs, it will require a massive shift in our national priorities for education and research. And yet just the opposite is occurring. Intel's former chairman, Andrew Grove, asserted that our premier research universities are losing their edge and that our scientific infrastructure spending is inadequate. The president of MIT, Susan Hockfield, stated, "We're underfunding research in the physical sciences and lagging seriously on publications in these sciences." As this is being written, Congress, as part of the debt limit extension, has ripped a billion dollars from federal funding for research rather than ask our wealthiest Americans to part with a paltry few extra dollars in taxes. We cannot keep making these kinds of wrongheaded choices and expect to provide future jobs and remain competitive with other nations that put a priority on education and research.

We are also making it harder for people to afford higher education in general. Like health costs, the cost of a college education has been far outstripping inflation. In 1988, the average tuition and fees for a four-year public university was about twenty-eight hundred dollars, adjusted for inflation. By 2008, that number had climbed about 130 percent to roughly sixty-five hundred dollars a year— and that doesn't include books or room and board. To make matters worse, the ability of the middle class to afford educating their children has declined. If incomes had kept up with surging college costs, the typical American would be earning seventy-seven thousand dollars a year. But in reality it's nowhere near that. In 2008—the latest data available—the median income was thirty-three thousand dollars. That means if you adjust for inflation, Americans in the middle actually earned four hundred dollars less than they did in 1988. As a result of rising costs and decreasing ability to pay, those seeking to finance their education are often confronted with a mountain of debt after graduation and before they have even begun their careers. Many state legislatures, facing growing pressure to fund other priorities such as Medicaid, prisons, and primary and secondary education, have in recent years reduced their appropriations for higher education on a per-student basis. In my home state one of the state universities now receives less than ten percent of its funding from the state, hardly qualifying it anymore as a "state" school. Yet it still must struggle with restrictions placed on it by the state legislature.

Until we can achieve a national consensus about the importance of education and funding basic and advanced research (relative to other demands upon our local and national financial resources), and reach agreement on a set of national goals with a plan to achieve those goals, education will continue to suffer in this country, and our competitiveness and viability in the world economy will continue to deteriorate. The meaningfulness of our lives will also continue to be compromised as the economic demands on our time crowd out other more fulfilling endeavors. Finally, our ability to have the best informed and educated electorate and competent elected officials is at risk. Effective solutions to increasingly complex societal and world problems hinge upon leading education and research. Global warming, curing diseases, maintaining economic stability and prosperity, as well as solutions to world conflict, all call for our best educated approaches. Instead, we are going backward, locked in debates about science versus intelligent design, fiscal priorities, and local control. Until we recognize the value of teaching in our society, the turnover rate will be high and the performance largely substandard. At the same time, teacher unions need to abandon their insistence upon seniority over performance. This again is a misplaced debate that does harm to the ultimate goal of providing the best education. The debate should be about what the performance criteria should be for evaluating teachers. In most locales, however, the only criterion is longevity (and certain mandated credentialing standards) that bears no direct relationship to the quality of teaching. When people feel they are getting something better for their money, they will feel better about paying for it. Good teachers should be well paid and bad ones released, regardless of years on the job. We also need to face the huge amount of deferred maintenance in our school systems. Like our roads and bridges, our misplaced priorities and failure to take a long-term view have diverted funds from needed infrastructure maintenance, repair, and new construction. Children are hard-pressed to learn in places where ceiling tiles fall, heat is intermittent or sweltering, and the facilities are otherwise inadequate for learning.

Education is just one of the areas where America is adrift. Referring again to one of my favorite sayings, "If you don't know where you're going, you will get there," we don't know where we are going with education in the United States, and we are getting there. It will not be a place we want to be in this increasingly interconnected, challenging, and competitive world. And for a democracy, which depends upon the education of its citizens to determine its direction, we have sorely misplaced our values and misspent our dollars. What we can do about all of this will be the topic of further discussion later in this book. For now it is important to recognize that the disturbing trends in education in the United States, which are exacerbated by priorities that direct resources elsewhere, are contributing to the dumbing down of America and to the poisonous usurpation of our democracy by special interests.

Chapter Ten

Leadership and the Big Con

Men make history, and not the other way around. In periods where there is
no leadership, society stands still. Progress occurs when courageous, skillful
leaders seize the opportunity to change things for the better.
—President Harry S. Truman

Abraham Lincoln did not go to Gettysburg having commissioned a poll to
find out what would sell in Gettysburg. There were no people with percent-
ages for him, cautioning him about this group or that group or what they
found in exit polls a year earlier. When will we have the courage of Lincoln?
—Robert Coles

Advocates of capitalism are very apt to appeal to the sacred principles
of liberty, which are embodied in one maxim: The fortunate must not be
restrained in the exercise of tyranny over the unfortunate.
—Bertrand Russell

There are so many elements of greatness in
America, so many decent people quietly striving to
achieve good, that the corrosive divisions, negativity,
and drift that have increasingly gripped our country
are all the more disconcerting. Many of the guiding
principles that girded the founding and growth of
this country lie in shambles. Not only has there been

a failure of leadership, those in power have misled. A significant number of patriotic, well-meaning Americans have been conned into being warriors for actions and policies where victory will leave them the losers. There has also been a failure of our leaders to act on behalf of the people's interests, as opposed to primarily for the special interests. The result has been bloated, ineffective legislation and misguided regulation. In the context of geopolitics, our failure to adequately address crucial issues of fiscal responsibility, economic growth, national security, environment, health care, education, and other critical needs for present and future generations is even more ominous. These are not the failures of one political party or of only certain leaders. The lack of positive direction and creative solutions is endemic to too many aspects of American life: political, economic, and social. We have succumbed to a malaise where getting by is the vision of many, and getting all you can is the vision of others.

We are better than this. The sooner we acknowledge where we are, the sooner we can take the steps needed to effect *positive* change. We are a great nation, but our leaders and our political systems have let us down. More importantly we have let ourselves down. Too many of us have been willing to accept superficial sloganeering over substance; too many willing to relinquish America to those with narrow, self-aggrandizing agendas. We have become hostage to the exigencies of daily existence and the complexity of our problems. And we have acquiesced to the fears cynically implanted by those imbued with the sense of their own power and driven solely by their own self-interest.

What we lack is true leadership: a vision of greatness that empowers rather than inhibits, that coalesces rather than divides, that expresses that vision and then honors it in deed rather than sacrifices it to expediency. We need courageous individuals to step forward with integrity and conviction and, most of all, the strength of character to *act* in the best interests of our communities and our nation rather than for special interests or their personal benefit. Asking for leadership's presence, however, is far easier than understanding its absence.

Truman was right in implying that history does not make leaders. Rather, leaders see in their times a compelling need for change and have the vision and the conviction to inspire that change. But the need for change must be great enough to compel leaders, for good or ill, to come forward. In periods of relative complacency, agents of change are not induced to brave the tide of opposition and the human and monetary cost that they will surely face. In contemporary America we devour those who seek to lead. In the aftermath of Watergate, reverence for the office of the president of the United States declined dramatically. Subsequent disclosures, including the sexual misadventures of several of our presidents in recent years, have done little to restore luster to the office. The advent of entertainment-style reportage has exposed the peccadilloes and foibles of our former heroes and other public figures everywhere without adding to meaningful debate of the issues. With cameras ubiquitous, including in cell phones, no one is safe from the glare of public exposure.

Few individuals lack skeletons in their closet, although one might question the life experience and fitness of one lacking any skeletons at all. The end result is that public service has become a gauntlet that few wish to run, especially in what are perceived to be less than critical times. The price of public service is no longer just the high emotional and monetary costs of campaigning, as well as the extreme stress of leadership, but can also include the added personal costs to the leader and his or her family. Sensationalist journalism and attack ad politics, which demean rather than inform, create strong disincentives for the best and the brightest to forsake the private sector in favor of public service. Unless we make some dramatic changes, we will resign ourselves to mediocrity and grave risk to our lives, our liberties, and our pursuit of happiness.

The changes that we must make relate to both of our major political parties, the political system itself, and our attitudes. We must become more discerning about what is appropriate for political discourse and what is not by focusing on issues rather than on personalities. To do that we need media that educate us rather than pander to our preconceptions, fears, and preferences. That will occur only when we vote with the channel selector for enlightenment over entertainment and exercise selectivity in the material we support, whether through outright purchase of the media or the advertisers whose products we choose to buy. We must take the time to become informed from *multiple* sources, not merely one perspective that reinforces our prejudices—and we all have prejudices of one form or another. How many of us take the time to read our voters' pamphlets? How many of us do independent research of the issues? How many of us vote in each election? And how many of us simply accept what we see and hear from very limited media choices as the correct and complete story?

In a democracy the people are supposed to be the ultimate decision makers, yet in America we have one of the lowest levels of voter participation of all the world's democracies. Being vested with the right to vote carries with it the obligation to exercise that right, a right that can be sullied by disuse. The pressures of life in America relegate politics to a low priority, a status that politicians have done little to improve. But if we are to interdict this vicious cycle, we need to inspire and vote for better people. That means taking the time to learn about, encourage, and support qualified individuals so they will take up public service. We should also focus on the person, not the party. There are usually good people and bad in each of the major parties. We don't elect parties. We elect people. We need to elect people who will act in the public interest, not in response to ideological or special interest pressure or who are focused only on one or two issues. Zealots of any kind make poor legislators. We need leaders who are guided by achieving what is in the best interest of the country over the long term, and who recognize that a compromise that achieves an objective is better than a dogmatic approach that achieves nothing. We also need to restore vigor and participation to our local political processes, so they involve a variety of viewpoints and not merely those of an entrenched clique of party regulars who support the same tired candidates.

The only way to deal with the influence of PAC money, in the absence of legislation, is to hold candidates accountable for the truth of their claims. Use independent sources like factcheck.org to independently verify claims. As long as we are gullible enough to be swayed by attack ads, they will continue to be seen as effective by the PACs and their PR machines that gin them up. We can end this use of the fear card by demanding that candidates tell us what they will do rather than what they allege is wrong with their opponent. When enough candidates whose campaigns are negative lose, the negative campaigning will end. We not only get the candidates we deserve, we also get the kind of campaigns we deserve. Until we insist upon factual, informative campaigning we will get platitudes, evasion, and diversion.

Will Rogers, a pundit and humorist from the 1930s, once said, "I don't belong to any organized political party. I'm a Democrat." Some eighty years later that statement is as true as it was then. The Democratic Party today has become more a party of people who are not Republicans than a party with a clear idea of what it stands for anymore. Some history is useful here. Until the mid-term elections of 2006, as the party out of power, it had become a party of complainers, often rightly accused of having no clearly defined programs of its own. The tendency of Democrats to complain, rather than congeal, has been their Achilles heel. This has been compounded by a propensity to run from their ideals. The label *liberal* has often been attached derisively with great effect to Democrats, and they have run from it as if it were a highly contagious disease. The preferred appellation now is *progressive*. *Liberal* used to mean support of the powerless, working people, the poor, and the aged. It used to mean the wise application of government to redress ills and inequities and to address the general well-being of the populace. It used to mean something noble. Ironically, most Americans support so-called liberal programs such as Social Security, Medicare, and environmental protection. Yet Democratic leaders often do a poor job of justifying and explaining the programs they advocate, opening themselves up to demagoguery from Republicans and others. And too often the programs then enacted are replete with so much special-interest accommodation, or layered in so much complexity, that achievement of the original objectives becomes problematic, leaving Democrats open to charges of supporting excessive regulation, special interests, and overbearing government.

As the oldest political party in the United States, the Democratic Party has had a long and varied history. It grew out of a group of Thomas Jefferson's supporters who called themselves "Democratic Republicans" because of their opposition to strong central government, their support for the small farmer, and their suspicion of urban commercial interests. The party, which did not take on its present name until 1828, espoused many of the ideals of the French Revolution and its faith in the common man. By 1800 it had become a nationwide party, uniting a coalition of Southern farmers with Northern city dwellers. It remained the sole national party until the 1850s, when the anti-slavery Republican Party began to emerge. The issue of slavery began to divide the Democratic Party into those advocating popular sovereignty (each territory should decide for itself whether to endorse slavery or its absence), those who felt slavery should be protected, and those completely opposed to slavery. This split in the party led to the election of Abraham Lincoln as president, the candidate of the antislavery Republican Party. For many in the South, the Republican Party was seen as the source of the defeat of the Old South and as the architects of Reconstruction. Thus, the states of the old Confederacy remained solidly Democrat, and anti-Republican, until the 1960s. The election of Franklin Roosevelt in 1932, out of the distress of the economic depression that began in 1929 on the watch of Republican Herbert Hoover, took the Democratic Party in a dramatically reformist direction. The widespread and entrenched unemployment that existed called for dramatic new expansions of government into the lives of Americans, despite a Democrat tradition to the contrary. The government became the employer of last resort as it funded construction of massive public works projects such as dams, roads, and bridges. Under the Works Progress Administration, it even put artists to work decorating public buildings. The party of Jefferson and limited government had become the party of active government involvement through the creation of safety nets to ease societal burdens and the regulation of what were deemed monopolistic big businesses. It began to solidify itself as the party of unions and working people. By 1948 many Southern Democrats were becoming disillusioned with the party and they nominated J. Strom Thurmond, an avowed racist, as their candidate for president. Southern dissatisfaction reached a crescendo with the third-party candidacy of George Wallace in the 1968 presidential election. Wallace was the governor of Alabama who had earlier openly defied federal desegregation efforts. Through his divisive candidacy, he helped bring about the defeat of Democrat Hubert Humphrey by Republican Richard Nixon. Despite the prior efforts of Republican President Dwight Eisenhower to implement desegregation by sending federal troops to Little Rock, and the Voting Rights Act passed during his presidency, the once "Solid South" felt even more betrayed by the civil rights efforts of Democratic Presidents John F. Kennedy and Lyndon Johnson during the 1960s. Increasingly disaffected by a party that was perceived to be an alliance of intellectuals, middle-class reformers, and ethnic minorities, the South began to shift its support to the Republican Party. This shift was not lost on Richard Nixon or Ronald Reagan, who began and continued an appeal by Republicans to these Southern voters. Reagan's alliance with the Reverend Jerry Falwell began to cement a connection that has endured to this day between the evangelicals and religious fundamentalists, primarily in the South, and the Republican Party. The shift gained ground in the 1994 midterm loss of control of both houses of Congress by the Democrats. Although there were four Southern Democratic presidents in the second half of the of the twentieth century, three were Southern Baptists (Truman, Carter, and Clinton) and one was a Disciple of Christ (Johnson); the Democratic Party policies they pursued in the areas of desegregation, states' rights issues, and cultural and foreign affairs were anathema to historical Southern perspectives. In one of American politics' great ironies, the largely Northern-directed Democratic Party had utilized Southern-born presidents to effect what the Republican Party of Abraham Lincoln had attempted to do one hundred years prior in creating biracial coalitions and Southern reconstruction. At the same time, shrewd political strategists in the Republican Party began capitalizing on the traditional moral values and religious fervency most prevalent in the South. The critical element that the South provides to the idiosyncratic and archaic electoral college was not lost on these Republican strategists, culminating in Al Gore's loss in the election of 2000, despite his having won the popular vote. The Midwest and South had essentially been lost to the Democrats by the 2004 election. Republican efforts to portray the Democratic Party as latte-drinking East Coast elitists had begun to erode the party's traditional support from working people. The party, by aligning more with the growing middle class, Hollywood, and wealthy scions of big business, did little to help itself in that regard. The midterm election of 2006, restoring Democrat majorities to both houses of Congress, can be viewed more as a repudiation of the Iraq War policies of the Republicans and George W. Bush than a shift away from the underlying sentiments that propelled earlier Republican successes. A Pew Research Poll taken in March of 2006 found that people moved away from Republican affiliation, but not significantly toward Democrat registration. This fact was not aided by the fretful performance of the Democrats in terms of failing to alter the course of the Iraq War and their acquiescing to the erosion of civil liberties by the Bush administration.

This admittedly notational history illustrates that the Democratic Party has evolved far from its roots but in the process has lost its identity and significant support. Democrats cannot afford to write off the entire center of the nation and the South, thereby forcing critical contests for the presidency to rest upon the remaining states, and making retention of control of either the House or Senate extremely difficult. Democrat weakness, rather than Republican strength, cost the Democrats control of the House in 2010. The party needs to find the courage of its convictions and achieve legislative and tactical results. And it must stop being disorganized. Time was when a big turnout favored the Democrats because of their once mass appeal and union support. But the Republicans, as we shall see, have been able to create a well-organized political machine that galvanizes their base into getting out the vote and raises substantial money. Until the most recent elections, the Republicans have been able to outspend the Democrats in most contests, thanks in part to the centralized efforts of the Republican National Committee. That Republican machine maintained control of both houses of Congress for over a decade. It is a sad commentary on the Democratic Party that its gains in the midterm election of 2006 came largely because of Republican scandals and opposition to the Iraq War rather than because of inherent Democratic attractiveness. Even on the issue of the Iraq war, the Democrats were late to the party and inconsistent in their positions. For the Democrats to regain relevancy, they need to coalesce around a platform that resonates with their traditional base and the broader mass of Americans. That means standing united for the interests of middle America—the disadvantaged and the middle class—in clear, concrete terms. Instead of advocating government solutions to every problem, the appeal should be to programs that embody smart government. Instead of abandoning those with legitimate concern for morality and faith, the party needs to reach out to the pious in ways that do not trample on the rights of others but give expression to integrity, honesty, charity, and faith. This can be accomplished without accepting extremist views or endorsing the views of a particular religion in public life. A focus on the indigent, education, drug rehabilitation, and other programs that embody a charitable outreach, and even the environment (for example, that God's work should not be destroyed by man), will resonate with many of the faithful who honor the adage that "I am my brother's keeper." It must become a party that champions fiscal responsibility as opposed to being viewed as one that merely throws money at problems. And the party must define intelligent economic and foreign policy strategies that address globalism and the dire threats we face from an increasingly restive third world in bold, comprehensible terms. There is incredible opportunity for the Democratic Party to reassume a leadership role in America if it can find a way to stop the endless internal debate it tolerates, choose a path, and stay on it to achievement. That opportunity involves dispelling the negativity and division in America with positive approaches to our problems in ways that bring us together as a nation. Critical issues of education, the environment, health care, Social Security, economic growth, and national security cry out for constructive solutions. America is tired of diversions—such as the Republican-proposed flag-burning amendment to the Constitution, or the attempt to resurrect condemnation of Turks for long-ago atrocities against Armenians, as was proposed by certain Democrats—in the face of critical and substantive needs in the areas just noted.

In a battle between a professor and a street fighter, the professor will lose. The Democratic Party needs to find a way to incorporate the strategic thinking of its intellectuals and others into hardnosed, fiscally sound, and practical solutions that can be understood by, and are acceptable to, the majority of Americans, without appearing imperiously elitist. There is no question that Democrats have heart, an expressed empathy for the less fortunate and the underdog. But heart without a backbone won't carry the day. Once they have adopted their core positions, the Democrats must have the strength of their convictions and be consistent and resolute in their advocacy. That does not mean whining or retreat from attack. It means positive assertion and factual defense. In business terms it means doing a better job of marketing itself. The Republicans have capitalized on Democratic disarray not only by playing the fear card on carefully chosen issues in recent years, but also by casting Democrats as weak and ineffective. More importantly, they have tarred the Democrats with being elitist and on the wrong side of the social issues that matter to many former Democrats. The midterm elections of 2006 afforded the Democrats an opportunity, which they squandered badly, to demonstrate leadership. Leadership begins with conviction and succeeds with fortitude. Democratic Party ideals have great value to the character of America. However, unless the party can unite to translate those ideals into positive solutions that are effectively communicated to, and resonate with, the majority of

Americans in ways that energize them to vote Democrat, the party will remain a largely irrelevant backdrop and sparring partner to the Republicans and open the door further to attempts to create third parties. Its strength, a spectrum of views on subjects from abortion to social programs, will be its undoing if it cannot find a coalescing path along which to unite. It simply cannot continue to wither in timid disarray as the Republicans convert traditional working-class Americans, who used to be the focus of the party, into staunch and angry Republicans. Just as the Republican Party has abandoned traditional Republicans, the Democrats have abandoned the working class in favor of the management class. Their unholy alliance with Wall Street, in an effort to increase financial support, has also not been helpful.

As noted, the Republican Party has also evolved considerably over its existence. The party of Lincoln that so alienated the old Confederacy for decades after the Civil War has now become the favored party of the South. Its traditional support for big business has remained intact, but has been overshadowed by the party's appeal to fundamentalist Christians over the last few decades and its embrace of hard-line stands on reducing or eliminating social programs in its advocacy of corporations and the wealthy. The Supreme Court's 1973 decision in *Roe v Wade* became the first harsh alarm bell for those concerned about what came to be known as family values. The alarm only intensified as issues of school prayer, gay rights, pornography, the right to die, and the equal rights amendment took a prominent place in American politics. In an effort to combat what they saw as a tide of godlessness flowing over America, groups such as the Southern Baptist Convention and the major Pentecostal denomination, the Assemblies of God, began to mobilize their congregations, encouraging them to put forth and support candidates that met their litmus test of faith-based issues. These groups found little support in the pro-choice, secular-leaning platforms of the Democrats, but did meet with receptivity from out-of-power Republicans running for House and Senate seats in the late 1960s onward and in local elections where the faithful worked the precincts and caucuses. Astute Republican strategists saw in these fundamentalists not only individual voters, but a cadre of inspired workers and organizations who would contribute time and money to get their candidates elected. White conservative evangelical Christians, among others, became the grassroots engine of organization that labor unions had previously been for the Democrats. Christians do not, of course, think or vote in a block. Christians are comprised of many denominations and variations, and their beliefs span a broad spectrum on a variety of issues, from separation of church and state (some, such as Jerry Falwell, the Reverend Sun Myung Moon, and Pat Robertson appeared to openly advocate a Christian theocracy in the United States) to views toward women in the clergy and homosexuality. But for those Christians with fundamentalist evangelical leanings, who see in the Bible more literal meanings—the approach of Armageddon and the second coming of Christ—a call to arms had clearly been sounded. This awakening was not lost on a host of evangelist preachers and authors who have fed the insecurities and beliefs of evangelicals with books and sermons that, not incidentally, generated substantial revenues and turned scores of charismatic fundamentalist preachers and operatives into multimillionaires.

Religious fervency was such a potent motivator that the Republicans under George W. Bush, with the astute guidance of Karl Rove, turned it into an art form. But the artwork was a particularly cynical one, according to one of the White House's inside operatives. In his book *Tempting Faith*, David Kuo, who served in the Bush White House for two-and-a-half years as a special assistant to the president, and eventually as deputy director of the Faith-Based Initiative, asserted that "National Christian leaders received hugs and smiles in person and then were dismissed behind their backs and described as 'ridiculous,' 'out of control,' and just plain 'goofy,'" by Karl Rove and other senior Bush administration officials. Kuo, a self-confessed "compassionate conservative," was stung by what he felt was a betrayal of the Faith-Based Initiative program to the point that some twenty million dollars less were spent under Bush than Clinton for such faith initiatives. And while the Democrats have not shown themselves free of corruption and missteps, the sheer number of Republicans involved in scandals during the G. W. Bush years, including one congressman preying sexually on House pages while his Republican leadership colleagues looked askance, and another refusing to leave office after conviction for acts involving alleged solicitation of homosexual sex in the Minneapolis Airport men's room, set the bar as low as ever. The sheer hypocrisy and outright cynicism with which the Republican leadership engaged its most-religious supporters caused anger among many of the Republican faithful. It was a most sorry state of affairs for the Grand Old Party of equality and liberty.

The Republican Party discovered, however, that in its appeal to the pious, it could erode the traditional base of Democrats by seizing upon cultural values issues. Issues such as prayer in the schools, opposition to abortion, and gay marriage and defense of freedom resonated with those who had formerly cast their lot with Democrats or who had remained independent. These were small-town folks, working men and women, patriotic Americans, all who felt abandoned by the Democratic Party. In their eyes the Democrats had become big-city liberals, latte-drinking effetes who aligned with godless gays and destroyers of life in the womb. A new breed of moral, God-fearing Republican leaders were able to characterize Democrats as godless elitists and socialists whose policies were destroying the real America. Yet, in focusing on social issues and patriotism, the Republicans were able to attack and eat away at the very things that benefited these new converts: unions, Social Security, a rising middle class, progressive taxation, and even morality. Republican leaders talked values but walked corporate. The values of God, fiscal conservatism, and freedom were so strongly held that these converts have remained with the party despite a complete failure to deliver on the promises. Abortion was not abolished, freedom has been impinged by such things as the Patriot Act and domestic spying, several key Republicans were found to have committed immoral behavior, Wall Street was deregulated and allowed to run amok, and faith-based programs were given minimal support. Republicans have given the decent, God-fearing people of middle America and elsewhere the sleeves off their silk corporate vest. Yet in the face of all of that, Republicans have successfully laid the destruction of small-town America and the inability to deliver on the social agenda not at the feet of government-strangling tax reductions or the lessened government regulation that led to the mortgage meltdown, but at the feet of big-spending, liberal Democrats.

The Republican Party was once the party of fiscal conservatism, protection of civil liberties, and pragmatic and engaging foreign policy. This was, after all, the party of Nixon, who reached out to Communist China, and the party of Ronald Reagan, who helped end the Cold War and railed against government growth. In recent years traditional Republicans sat on their hands as they allowed their party to veer away from pragmatism in foreign policy and toward a messianic go-it-alone vision that engendered enmity in many parts of the world and allowed tyranny to fester in the absence of face-to-face negotiation and diplomacy. On the economic front, we watched the largest federal deficit in our history accrue on the watch of G. W. Bush and the Republican-controlled Congress, coupled with ballooning trade deficits of historic proportion. The true costs of the Iraq War were withheld from scrutiny through accounting gimmickry and with the admonition of Republican Vice President Dick Cheney that "deficits don't matter." All other wars were fought without incurring deficits of such magnitude, including even World War II. While some have argued that the Bush tax cuts spurred the economy, that reduction in taxes contributed mightily to the deficit without achieving their stated objective of job creation. Some six hundred thousand jobs were lost during the Bush presidency. Huge foreign capital inflows over the prior decade helped lower interest rates, which in turn caused a boom in housing and consumer spending as many Americans spent the rising equity of their homes and became two-wage-earner families. But then the housing bubble collapsed, and the financial meltdown followed. What seemed on the surface as a continuation of the American dream all came crashing down. The financial bailouts initiated under the Bush administration, carried forward under President Obama, along with passage of the stimulus bill, fueled even more anger against government on the part of more-doctrinaire Republicans and independents, and finally spawned a populist revolt in 2009 known as the Tea Party movement. Without an identified leader, but finding expression through individuals such as Ron Paul, Sarah Palin, and Dick Armey, it has had a profound impact upon the Republican Party. Members of the movement have demanded achievement of more traditional Republican values: fiscal conservatism, lower taxes, less government, and a more literal interpretation of the Constitution. It is a truism of politics that zealotry trumps numbers. Demonstrating their zeal, Tea Partiers made it clear that they would work to unseat any who did not share their values. They flexed their might in the 2010 elections, when a number of Tea Party supporters won seats as frustration with "politics as usual" reached a new level. The result was Tea Party caucuses in both houses of Congress, and a further shift in the Republican Party towards hardline Tea Party objectives, even by more moderate Republicans, including the Republican leadership itself. Having previously aligned itself with Christian fundamentalists and evangelicals, the party was now seeking a broadened base in the form of a group dedicated to tax reduction, the elimination of union influence, lessened government size, reduced spending and regulation, and the reduction or elimination of government support for social programs such as Medicare. At its margins, Tea Party enthusiasts would prefer privatization of many current government functions, including prisons and Social Security. The Tea Party is comprised of a multitude of viewpoints, however, like any organization. Polls have indicated that a large majority of its members favor strong immigration laws like the one recently passed in Arizona; support equal opportunity, but don't feel it is the government's place to enforce it; and oppose gay marriage.

Because of its impact, it is useful to understand some of the financial support behind the Tea Party Movement. A number of nonprofit (IRS 501(c)(4)) organizations provide leadership and support to the Tea Party. The organization named Tea Party Patriots claims more than one thousand affiliate groups across the country, but refuses to disclose the source of its funding. Significant Tea Party support has also come from Americans for Prosperity, the group founded by billionaire Robert Koch. Freedom Works is a supporting organization, whose predecessor was allegedly also founded by Koch (the Koch brothers deny ties to, and funding of, Freedom Works). It claims over one million members and five hundred affiliates and is headed by former House Majority Leader Dick Armey. Freedom Works has also made local and national Tea Party candidate endorsements. The Tea Party Express is a national bus tour reportedly run by a PAC created by the Sacramento-based Republican consulting firm Russo, Marsh and Associates. Legitimate questions have been raised regarding the major sources of funding for the movement, with the suggestion that it is primarily funded by enormously wealthy individuals who are desirous of seeing lower taxes and lessened regulation. It has been derisively called an Astroturf movement rather than a grassroots movement on that account. But that is largely speculation, since some of the most significant supporting PACs do not have to disclose their contributors.

There are several things relevant to our overall discussion here about democracy that relate to the Tea Party Movement. First, economic and fiscal issues are paramount with members, more so than ethnic issues, according to most polls of the membership. Second, many Tea Party themes resonate with a number of non–Tea Party Americans to varying degrees: limited government, lower and simplified taxes, a balanced federal budget, reduction of earmarks, and repeal of health-care legislation passed in March of 2010. From all appearances, most Tea Party adherents are sincere in their efforts, and their objectives deserve consideration. As always, however, the devil is in the details and the tactics.

Those details became abundantly clear during the debate over raising the debt ceiling in July of 2011. Largely at the urging of Tea Party-supporters and Tea-Party-backed freshmen legislators, the Republicans in the House took the position that they would not support a raise in the debt ceiling without drastic cuts in federal programs and the enactment of a "balanced budget" amendment to the

Constitution. Some of the programs that were suggested for deep cuts were Social Security, Medicare, and the EPA. Yet despite the recommendations of a previous bipartisan commission on the deficit, most Republicans and virtually all Tea-Party-committed Congressmen vowed that they would not support deficit reduction if that included any attempts to raise revenue such as through elimination of any tax breaks or by allowing the Bush tax cuts to expire. Taxes were off the table, they said. Some Tea-Party-leaning Republicans, including 2012 presidential candidate Michelle Bachman, argued that a failure to raise the debt ceiling would not create any problem at all with the borrowing capability of the United States if the default were handled properly. All that was necessary, they asserted, was to assure the holders of our debt that they would be paid. Not only had the rating agencies indicated that would result in a downgrading of U.S. debt and a consequent rise in all interest rates in the United States (including for consumers whose credit card, mortgage, and installment loan rates are tied to U.S. Treasury rates), the shortfall would then result in a lack of funds to honor such payments as those for people on Social Security, Medicare, and military wages, to name just a few. Economists and other finance professionals were essentially unanimous in these views and in their prognostication of worldwide financial problems that would result.

Despite stated goals that many Americans would agree with, the Tea Party legislators have advanced legislative changes and tactics that would greatly injure average Americans, including many of the Tea Party supporters themselves. We have already discussed the fallacies inherent in supply-side economics that focuses on tax cuts for the wealthy and illustrated its historic failure to create jobs while creating even greater disparity between the wealthiest Americans and the rest of the populace. Taxes were raised during the Clinton years when some twenty million new jobs were created. Taxes were significantly cut while roughly six hundred thousand net jobs were lost during the eight-year G. W. Bush presidency. Senate Minority Leader Mitch McConnell tried to argue the opposite by referring to job growth during the Reagan years as an example that tax cuts worked. As we have noted, however, Reagan approved a number of tax increases and oversaw the largest federal deficit at that time on his watch, tripling it in size, with Republican support. Such a deficit increase was very expansionary. Yet, during the debt ceiling press conferences, Republicans continually justified their refusal to consider the revenue side of the equation by repeating the talking point that the wealthy were the "job creators" who should not share the burden of deficit reduction lest it result in job losses. Once again the fear card was being played: tax the rich and you will worsen unemployment. The word *wealthy* was avoided altogether in favor of referring to the uberrich obliquely and often as job creators. Although couched in terms of a populist appeal, the result was to justify a continuing special exemption for the most wealthy and major corporations from bearing the burden of the deficit—the very deficit whose creation benefited so many of them through tax cuts, defense contracts, and lax enforcement of regulations. Even supporters of Reaganomics, such as Reagan's budget director David Stockman, pointed out that in a deep recession tax increases on wealthy individuals have a lesser negative impact on the economy than do budget cuts, because budget cuts directly reduce consumption dollar for dollar, while tax cuts to wealthy people do not. In other words, tax increases are preferable to budget cuts in a recession. We have also discussed the Great Divide that is driving a wedge into the heart of America. The Tea-Party-urged Republicans' insistence on dismantling social programs and eliminating government regulation is damaging to most Americans, including those in middle America. It establishes a priority for government largesse in favor of business and the wealthy while taking money and security from the rest of America, including middle class seniors. At the local level, Republican-enacted tax cuts are decimating state budgets that are now incapable of surviving a severe downturn. And what are we to make of the so-called balanced budget amendment? The answer is that it is another of those shiny toys that looks good but have fatal defects. Under the current state of our deficit, it would mandate massive cuts in federal spending (or massive tax hikes) that would be ruinous to an already fragile economy. It is also a charade that substitutes for the hard work of identifying just what programs would have to be cut and thereby avoids immediately antagonizing constituents. It is an attractive-appearing device whose pain will be noticed and felt only later. Once in place its implementation would decimate Social Security, Medicare, and a host of popular federal programs, not to mention enforcement of environmental, consumer protection, and health and safety laws, not to mention the loss of federal money to already desperate state governments. It would also significantly reduce military spending and a host of other federal programs that even Tea Party members support. A balanced budget requirement would tie the fiscal hands of the government and prevent its ability to deal with extraordinary circumstances, such as wars, natural disasters, and economic crises. It is a tacit admission by its supporting legislators that they are incapable of governing their own actions and need a brick wall to stop them. Taking a drug away from an addict does not thereby make him more reliable. The fact that our legislators, Republican and Democrat, have acted irresponsibly in the past is also not a reason to accept a cannon to shoot an ant. The answer is to elect legislators who understand finance and micro and macro economics and who are committed to sound solutions to the deficit rather than simplistic bludgeons.

As to "less government," it was lessened regulation during the Clinton and Bush years that contributed mightily to the mortgage crisis and economic meltdown. Moreover, the dismantling of the social safety net could ultimately lead to civil unrest by people without sufficient food, medical care, or shelter during harsh economic times. Additionally, the cost of emergency and chronic care we pay for in hospital and insurance rates to cover the costs of dealing with indigent people with chronic illness is far greater than the cost of preventative programs. Those who argue that people should simply take care of themselves without government intervention are ignoring the realities of life, such as illness and layoffs and the inadequacies of charitable organizations. These realities create often insurmountable hardships despite the supreme efforts of the people affected. As we have observed, government programs serve practical purposes, not merely the need for society, especially a wealthy one, to be charitable. Virtually all other Western democracies provide for their unemployed, infirm, and elderly through government-provided unemployment assistance, health care, and pensions.

It is therefore useful to inquire if the major backers of the Tea Party have in reality created a cynical appeal to the legitimate concerns of many Americans while instead only furthering the goals of certain people at the expense of the broader public. Are the Tea Party and the Republican agenda now really vehicles to further the interests of a few very wealthy individuals, corporations, and leaders? The signs are ominous in that regard, and not merely from the actual ends being pursued. Despite their denials, there is substantial evidence that the multibillionaire Koch brothers are significant players in the movement. According to an article by Jane Mayer in the *New Yorker,* "by giving money to 'educate,' fund, and organize Tea Party protesters, they (the Koch brothers) have helped turn their private agenda into a mass movement." Charles Lewis, the founder of the Center for Public Integrity, a nonpartisan watchdog group, said, "The Kochs are on a whole different level. There's no one else who has spent this much money. The sheer dimension of it is what sets them apart. They have a pattern of lawbreaking, political manipulation, and obfuscation. I've been in Washington since Watergate, and I've never seen anything like it. They are the Standard Oil of our times." Others admonish the Kochs for being one of the largest contributors to the denial of global climate change. Koch Industries is reported to be the largest privately held energy company in the country. In a study released in the spring of 2010, the University of Massachusetts at Amherst's Political Economy Research Institute named Koch Industries one of the top ten air polluters in the United States. Bruce Bartlett, a conservative economist and a historian, who once worked at the National Center for Policy Analysis, a Dallas-based think tank that the Kochs funded, said the Kochs are "trying to shape and control and channel the populist uprising into their own policies." An April 9, 2009 article by Lee Fang reported that the principal organizers of Tea Party events are Americans for Prosperity and Freedom Works, and referred to them as two "lobbyist-run think tanks" that are "well funded" and that provide the logistics and organizing for the Tea Party movement from coast to coast. It should be noted that Fang's allegations are often disputed by Tea Party leaders.

Other significant contributors supporting Tea Party efforts include the Sarah Scaife Foundation, which has given as much as $2.9 million to Freedom Works, according to Media Matters. The foundation is financed by the Mellon industrial, banking, and oil fortune. Also according to Media Matters, in 2010 the Claude R. Lambe Foundation, also controlled by the Koch family, has donated more than three million dollars to Americans for Prosperity. At what served as a training session, in part, for Tea Party activists in Texas sponsored by Americans for Prosperity (founded by David Koch in 2004), an advertisement cast the event as a populist uprising against vested corporate power. "Today, the voices of average Americans are being drowned out by lobbyists and special interests," it said. "But you can do something about it." Yet it would appear that it was corporate power and lobbyist guidance that was ultimately behind the event in whole or in part. But thanks to the veil of secrecy legitimized by the Supreme Court in its recent rulings, the true extent of corporate and wealthy individual monetary contribution and other support to what are billed as populist organizations is impossible to ascertain with certainty. One of the founders of Tea Party Patriots, Mark Meckler, was a star performer with the multilevel marketing (MLM) company Herbalife. In 2004, the company paid six million dollars to settle a class action suit filed by eighty-seven hundred Herbalife distributors who alleged the company was a pyramid scheme. MLM is a scheme where the real money is not in selling the product. The real money is in selling distributorships to people who pay fees to acquire the right to sell distributorships to others, hence the term multilevel marketing. It is an economic chain letter. According to an article in *Mother Jones*, in late September of 2010 Tea Party Patriots' top organizers met with a secretive group of far-right movers and shakers to make a fund-raising pitch for the group's multimillion-dollar "40-year plan" to change the country. The group, the Council for National Policy, is funded heavily by the DeVos family, the owners of Amway, one of the largest MLM companies in the country. With over a thousand affiliates, Tea Party Patriots has the earmarks of MLM organizationally. It is also a rich source of committed, politically active people. After leaving Herbalife Meckler went on to join a firm that provides leads to groups like Herbalife and possibly to political groups. Tea Party Patriots' privacy policy provided for the third-party use of member names.

The Republican Party's 21-page 2010 blueprint, "Pledge to America," was put together with involvement by a House staffer, Brian Wild, who, up until April 2010, served as a lobbyist for some of the nation's most powerful oil, pharmaceutical, and insurance companies. Wild had served as a lobbyist for the U.S. Chamber of Commerce, where he reportedly helped steer more than thirty-four million dollars' worth of lobbying activity for the business interest group. In cynically describing the pledge, which was short on detail as to how it would achieve its goals, then Minority Leader John Boehner said, "This new governing agenda, built by listening to the people, offers plans to create jobs, cut spending, and put power where it belongs: in the hands of the people." After reading the document one is compelled to wonder just which of "the people" they were listening to. Once again, corporate and wealth objectives were couched in a populist appeal, with the participation of one of Washington's significant power brokers for major corporate interests.

No discussion of the Republican Party would be complete without a reference to Grover Norquist's influence and the Americans for Tax Reform Taxpayer Protection Pledge that he provided members of Congress. The pledge states:

> I, _____, pledge to the taxpayers of the (_____ district of the) state of _____ and to the American people that I will: ONE, oppose any and all efforts to increase the marginal income tax rate for individuals

and business; and TWO, oppose any net reduction or elimination of deductions and credits, unless matched dollar for dollar by further reducing tax rates.

Norquist has amazingly gotten 236 Representatives (all Republican) and 41 Senators (all Republican) to sign the pledge. Here again is something that might seem fiscally responsible and enticing to those who value fiscal responsibility. It is the exact opposite. While disproportionately protecting the wealthy from tax hikes, this kind of ideological sandbagging takes away a major fiscal tool of government to regulate the economy for the benefit of the larger populace. The Congressional sheep who signed this cynical chicanery abrogated their responsibility as elected representatives. They did so by giving up their responsibility to exercise their legislative judgment as circumstances demand, tying their own hands with this mindless pledge. There is no dispensation here for the needs of a war or other national emergency, no wiggle room for runaway inflation or for any other fiscally responsible action. Arguably, this is even a violation of their sworn duty to uphold the Constitution and the legislative power they are thereby granted. The Norquist pledge brought the country to the brink of economic disaster as Republicans, painting themselves into a corner, became unable to work out a legislative compromise on the debt ceiling in the name of ideological purity during July of 2011. One has to wonder, what is the source of the power Norquist wields over so many Republicans that they would sign such a pledge?

Ronald Reagan, a Republican icon, raised taxes and raised the deficit multiple times during his presidency. In fact, Congress raised the debt ceiling during the Reagan presidency eighteen times. He and Republicans and Democrats of his era understood the need for compromise in a democracy: that no one party or individual has a lock on what is best for all Americans; that compromise is at the heart of democracy, as opposed to the self-righteous tyranny of a few ideologues. Too many modern-day Republicans seem to have forgotten that as they are driven further into the darkness that is ideological purity. That is the mind-set of true believers, of religious and other fanatics who think theirs is the only way. And that is anathema to democracy because it rides roughshod over the evolving will of the people and the protections afforded the rights of those without substantial power in this country. Yet all of this is couched in populist appeals to liberty and freedom. Where is the freedom and liberty when one group abuses the legislative process by holding it hostage to their demands and theirs alone? That is not democracy, it is dictatorship.

What we are witnessing in this country is a great con job, whereby reasoned Americans with legitimate concerns are being manipulated into being the populist tools of the powerful. These powerful interests do not want a smaller, more efficient government that better serves the populace; they want government to give them free reign to overcharge, pollute, collude, maintain unsafe workplaces, and be otherwise unregulated so they, like the Wall Street investment bankers, can game the system with the taxpayer to backstop them. It is known as privatizing the gains and socializing the losses. Under the guise of reducing taxes, what these wealthy individual and corporate interests want is to have the benefits of government support and protection, in the form of trade agreements, security, services, subsidies, and tax and other incentives, without paying for the privilege. Instead they want to place the cost of their largesse upon the general population, while they continue to push jobs and revenues offshore. In so doing, under the guise of calls for a balanced budget and tax and debt reduction, they are forcing a continuing redistribution of wealth from the middle class and poor to the wealthiest in our country. In one of the great ironies, *opposition* to their schemes has been labeled as introducing class warfare and socialist wealth redistribution. Their cynical efforts are becoming virtual thefts of the monies Americans have paid into programs for Social Security and Medicare, in order to continue to subsidize the corporate welfare these special interests seek to expand and maintain. That is why they, and the politicians they support, so vehemently oppose the elimination of tax breaks and subsidies and resist any other redirection of the tax-supported payments that flow into their coffers, all under the rubric of protecting the job creators and trickle-down supply-side economic nonsense. And as a consequence of this duping of conscientious, patriotic Americans into clamoring for smaller government, we are watching schools close, police and fire protection diminish, our climate worsen, libraries limit hours or close altogether, and our roads and bridges crumble. The same corporations that the Supreme Court has deigned to anoint with the benefits of equal protection contemptuously argue that they have no coequal obligation to support the country that shelters them. Instead they play one community against another, seeking the state which gives the most and gets the least when they build new facilities or re-locate from one state to another.

How could so many Americans be duped into supporting policies that are so antithetical to their and their country's best interests? How could they be coaxed into being vehement advocates and ideologues for positions that will leave them poorer, in decaying communities with lessened opportunity, and less secure? For the answer we need only hearken back to one of our basic assumptions, that perception is relative reality. For many of our citizens the American dream and the promise of our democracy are still alive and well. That is their perception, despite staggering unemployment, nearly a half century of real wage stagnation, the near collapse of our economy in 2009 from Wall Street excesses (that are as yet largely unchecked), and lax regulation and the virtual takeover of our democracy by special interests. Add that to that the fact that upward mobility has also become a myth for all but the very smallest segment of our country, with far more people moving downward. For those who have been casualties of the destruction of the American dream, they have been persuaded that it has come at the hands of "liberal socialists," thus buying the label rather than the reality. Their embrace of the destroyers has come from acceptance of carefully crafted, empty sloganeering: that we need only to "take back our country"; that "government is the problem"; that "fascists," "socialists," and "liberals" are the problem; that by sending single-issue ideologues to Congress, rather than reforming the political system itself, that will solve all of our problems. This wrong-headed embrace has been furthered by Democrats who have managed to alienate a large portion of their former supporters through hubris and disregard as much as from policy. Hope springs eternal, especially when clothed in simplicity. But our problems will not be solved by slogans or simplistic appeals to fiscal responsibility, a balanced budget amendment, or protecting the job creators. Nor will our difficulties be surmounted by massive legislation that is self-defeating and rewards the malefactors, lofty speeches, or unarticulated goals. Our political system is badly broken. Until it becomes again the servant of the people it is supposed to serve, nothing positive can be accomplished. Until people separate the rhetoric from the reality, they will continue to support and follow false gods. Until we can remove the poisonous influence of special interests *at every level* and restore a balance between economic and political needs, there will be only the gut-wrenching sound of our country foundering upon the rocks of lost opportunity and decline.

The single most important change we can make to our democracy, so that it is truly representative, is to level the political playing field financially. Votes should count, not dollars to *buy* votes. Several states and localities have enacted so-called "Clean Money, Clean Elections" laws. These provide equal public funding for candidates who can demonstrate that they are indeed viable candidates by obtaining a certain number of qualifying small donations. In turn such candidates cannot accept further outside money or spend their own. This latter aspect would prevent wealthy individuals from buying their way into office with their massive personal campaign spending ability. There is even a glimmer of hope here with respect to the Roberts Supreme Court. In a more recent case that struck down a piece of spending limitation in an Arizona campaign financing law, Justice Roberts said, "We do not today call into question the wisdom of public financing as a means of funding political candidacy. That is not our business." That suggests strongly that even the Roberts court would support public campaign financing laws.

Opponents argue that public money should not finance partisan individuals. They also suggest that it encourages pork-barrel politics and professional politicians. These arguments are specious. The level playing field that public campaign finance creates means equal access to all viewpoints that can demonstrate minimum viability, and puts the focus on content rather than sideshows. It is then up to us to select the best person for the job. Secondly, pork-barrel approaches will hold less sway, not more, when the force of sound positions in the public interest is determined to be more relevant to voters than offerings of pork. A level field encourages that. It is after all the office, and not the office holder, that affords the opportunity to channel public money into one's community. A level field also exposes those who seek personal wealth through the influence of their office. The failure to perform in public office will be far easier to discern with a level playing field than one where an entrenched incumbent's fund-raising ability can buy cover for his deficiencies. There will still, however, be unlimited, unaccountable PAC money to sway voters. Ways must be found to at least identify the source of the influence peddlers. Without public pressure upon Congress this will not happen, because the powerful interests who benefit from the stealth influence will strongly resist attempts to "sunlight" them. The best solution, which will be discussed later, is a constitutional amendment.

Opposition to campaign finance reform efforts creates the strangest of bedfellows as various special interest groups feel threatened by equal access. Thus, environmental groups have joined with polluters, and civil liberties groups with Christian theocrats, to oppose various efforts at reform. Yet underlying such attempts to limit or inhibit reform is a lack of conviction about the solidity of their own causes on the part of those opposed to reform. If their causes are truly sound, then a level field will be to their advantage, not their detriment. It is ultimately up to all of us to insist upon equal access for ideas in our democratic process. It is estimated that public funding of federal elections would cost about five dollars per citizen: a small price indeed for truer representative democracy. There have also been suggestions to obtain funding from a small tax on the recipients of government contracts or payments to lobbying firms. The point here is simply that there are a variety of funding options. Initiatives like California's Proposition 89 and similar laws that provide public funding in other jurisdictions should become the law of all elections in this country. Only then will we truly have a democracy in the United States where the fullest expression of ideas and the best candidates will all have equal ability to influence our thinking and actions at the voting booth. In addition, elected officials can focus on meeting the needs of their constituents and the country as a whole without being forced to constantly seek huge amounts of campaign funds. Accomplishing this will not be easy. The vast array of public relations firms, lobbyists, pollsters, and consultants who feed at the trough of the status quo will bitterly oppose public financing. But corporations still do not vote; citizens do.

As we continue to witness the diminishment of our rights, our right to vote is also threatened by technology and other means. After the debacle of the 2000 presidential election that gave the ultimate determination of who was to be president to the Supreme Court, we are now confronted with the presence of electronic voting machines and a host of efforts to adjust voting boundaries and add requirements to eligibility. Without the requirement of a paper receipt, these voting machines can turn your vote into nothing more than an electronic impulse, easily altered or erased. That is the current state of affairs in the land of the free. Most people have some concept of the havoc that computer hackers can cause. There are a multitude of computer experts who have concluded that tampering with electronic voting machines as they are presently configured is child's play. Yet several states have now moved ahead with electronic voting, without ensuring adequate safeguards. There are times when electronic wizardry can be carried too far. The need for a paper trail for each vote is a case in point. In other states attempts to require a driver's license or special picture IDs disadvantages poorer or senior citizens who may not drive or for whom the cost of a picture ID is intimidating enough for them to not bother. In Texas and elsewhere, partisan gerrymandering (the drawing of voting district boundaries to favor a party's demographics) has tipped the balance in state legislatures and had consequent effects on U.S. House races. Boundaries can be drawn to favor one party and disadvantage the other so as to ensure a majority in the state house. With that in hand, congressional districting can be adjusted. An incumbent can solidify his reelection chances by creating a district that maximizes his supporters and minimizes his opposition. It can also be employed to divide, and thereby reduce the influence of, ethnic minorities, the poor, and other voting blocs. And it can accomplish the opposite by consolidating one group or another into a voting district, but that may result in lessened clout for their limited district as opposed to others. The point is that districting needs to be judiciously done in order to fairly distribute voting power within each state.

It has been recently suggested that a new third party should be formed using social media. While sounding promising, such an effort faces the tide of history against it. Not only have third-party efforts failed in the past, but also they have more often than not thrown elections toward the minority candidate by taking away the more centrist vote. Even where successful, the candidates are ultimately forced to side with one or the other of the major parties legislatively. That can create both power and legislative gridlock. We witnessed just that during the crucial debt ceiling debate of 2011.

At the end of the day, I do not know how to put this in stronger terms. We are diminishing our freedoms and debasing our rights to a frightening degree in America as we stand sheep-like and leaderless. This is not about evildoers. This is not about subversives in our midst, or

Republicans or Democrats, right or left, religious or atheist. It is about the misleading of the well intentioned, the fear-based appeals embraced by the unsuspecting, and the silence and complacency of the rest. These are times that call for courage. If we do not alter the current state of politics in the United States, then we have doomed ourselves to a continuation of gridlock, opportunism, and timidity. Our problems and shortcomings will not wait or cure themselves. They will worsen from inattention and raise the very real specter of civil disobedience. People who are unemployed and without food or shelter are not interested in grand speeches or the political blame game. These are times that call for true leadership that advances a bold vision and the ability to carry it off. That will be best found not by looking to others, but by looking to ourselves to initiate and propel much-needed change in our political processes, so that leadership can arise and function in the public interest.

It has been estimated that the 2012 presidential election will cost candidates a combined three billion dollars! Abuse of the gaping loophole for corporate influence of elections has now moved beyond mere sponsorship of so-called issue ads. Candidate Mitt Romney became the recipient of a one million dollar contribution from a corporation that came into being immediately before, and ceased to exist immediately after, that contribution. One individual, who could not have made that contribution as an individual citizen, was found to have been the source. By creating the corporation for the sole purpose of making a political con-tribution, wealthy individuals can exert their influence far beyond that of ordinary individuals and in contravention of contribution limitations. Until we substitute the power of the vote for the power of the dollar, the viability of our American democracy is in grave jeopardy. We will discuss strategies for reclaiming our democracy in Chapter Seventeen. Those changes will involve removing the corrupting influence of money at all stages of the political process so that true leadership in the public interest can be obtained and encouraged. For now, let us turn to another significant issue of our times, the scourge of terrorism

Chapter Eleven

The Tree of Terror

Roots of Despair, Branches of Isolation, Leaves of Hatred

"This is not jihad. This is strictly business."
—Essan al Ridi, quoting his superior, Osama bin Laden, at a trial of terrorists

Every gun that is made, every warship launched, every rocket fired signifies in the final sense, a theft from those who hunger and are not fed, those who are cold and are not clothed. This world in arms is not spending money alone. It is spending the sweat of its laborers, the genius of its scientists, the hopes of its children. This is not a way of life at all in any true sense. Under the clouds of war, it is humanity hanging on a cross of iron."
—Dwight Eisenhower, U.S. president and supreme Allied commander, WWII, 1953 speech

As a nation we have been deeply scarred by the brutality that was brought to our shores on September 11, 2001, and inflicted upon our brave young soldiers abroad in the years that have followed. It brought the whole subject of terrorism to the forefront of our thinking, and became the pretext for engaging in wars on two fronts. One front was abstract: the so-called War on Terror. The other front involved overt and covert military actions in a number of countries, in particular Iraq and Afghanistan.

The cost of all of this in terms of blood and treasure has been both immense and ongoing. It has become a major contributor to our national debt and stolen the lives, limbs, and mental well-being of courageous Americans as well as those of adversaries and innocent noncombatants alike. It is therefore useful to delve a bit into a topic that looms so large in our country in order to understand both its genesis and to divine a path forward that avoids repeating the mistakes of the past.

One of our cherished beliefs is that at our core we are a caring and generous nation. We wage war to support democracy, donate vast sums to eradicate illness, and we endeavor to feed the starving in other countries. We believe that our actions are honorable and humane. How can it then be that so many people in these other countries revile the United States and take comfort when we are attacked or held up to ridicule, or are willing to die in order to cause us harm? Using labels to call such people terrorists or extremists or evildoers does not advance the cause of understanding nor aid us in changing the paradigm we face. It is a mark of just how mindless we have become when leaders like former Vice President Dick Chaney can make the visceral appeal that we can "hunt down and kill" every person so labeled. It is also an indication of how anxious for answers we have become that some take comfort in such simplistic, jingoist rhetoric. One of the lessons of the Arab-Israeli conflict is that violence becomes an unending cycle when leaders do not address underlying issues.

While it will always be true that we cannot please everyone in the world, to the extent that we are reviled or disrespected, our leadership, and consequent ability to martial support for security and constructive change in the world, is thereby diminished. We do not have the luxury of disregarding world opinion, nor of retreating into isolationism, even as a reaction to terrorism. If we are blind to the hatred, anger, and disrespect, or think we can just kill the haters, then we doom ourselves to deal with even greater consequences. The argument that we need to merely export democracy to areas of turmoil ignores cultural and political realities in these areas and flies in the face of why people commit terrorist acts to begin with. We need to follow a different path that fosters national security while keeping us true to our ideals as a nation. That begins with an understanding of the forces that spawn terrorism. To accomplish that it is critical to return to our basic assumptions, and do away with simplistic labels, in order to begin to understand the complexity of the horrors and vitriol we are witnessing in the Middle East, Central and South Asia, Africa, and elsewhere throughout the world. It will also be important to understand why our leadership in the world has diminished as our actions have diverged from our traditionally espoused aspirations and beliefs as a country.

At the outset it should be noted that much of the broader-based support for the indiscriminate violence and terrorism we are witnessing festers in the poorest countries or within pockets of poverty in more developed countries. While the specific issues differ from country to country, hatred finds fertile reception among the illiterate, isolated, and poor of the world. These are people whose formal governments have failed to adequately provide them with the necessities of life and just social structures.

The illiterate, the impoverished, the hungry, and the down-trodden are smoldering embers easily ignited by those who offer food, education, health care, money, and esteem. Appeals that place blame on wealthier people and countries give outlet to the frustration and resentment of the forgotten. Individuals whose dignity has been denied are also receptive to appeals that suggest they are superior, not inferior. A religion or movement that rewards zeal by glorifying the zealot has great appeal to the oppressed and those with low self-esteem. Many people in the downtrodden and humiliated nation of post–World War I Germany succumbed to such appeals that glorified the supposed superiority of the Aryan race. Despair is easily turned into exploitable hatred. When the cause of the despair is poverty, the object of hatred becomes the wealthy. But this does not explain the seemingly irrational nature of the hatred we are witnessing from acts of terror that are perpetrated indiscriminately. It also does not explain why well-educated individuals, including doctors trained to heal, can become involved in an ideology that sanctions the death of innocents. Support for extremism has its primary genesis in hatred, and hatred is not a respecter of education or intelligence. It will be useful then to look at hatred and its origins.

Hatred takes two forms, rational and irrational. Rational hatred flows from some perceived unjust act or situation imposed upon the hater that creates a sense of helplessness. Lacking the ability to rectify the situation, the helpless victim despises or pities the creator of the situation. Thus, the relative of a murdered family member may feel pity toward the attacker or hate him. We often see such responses in courtrooms across the country during sentencing, where the victim's family is either forgiving or outraged. The hatred in this circumstance may be said to be a rational response to the wrong. Hatred may also be irrational in the sense that it occurs where no wrong may have been done, but grows instead out of the insecurity of the hater. It is an offensive reaction to their insecurity. Racial prejudice is one form of irrational hatred growing out of insecurity. Not all people are haters, but all irrational haters are insecure people.

Irrational haters seldom keep their hatred to themselves. Instead they seek to enhance their sense of self-worth by enlisting others to their cause. This allows them to focus their energy on their cause rather than acknowledge their insecurity or the heinous results of their actions. Their sense of ineffectiveness is alleviated by being a part of a group that acts out, and thereby enables them to lessen personal responsibility for their actions. The group reinforces their beliefs and implies that the hater is justified in inflicting harm. This situation can build upon itself, whereby irrational hatred fuels rational hatred as we have seen repeatedly in the cycle of violence occurring in the Middle East. An irrational hater commits an act of violence, an indiscriminate bombing of innocent civilians, which sparks rational hate and retaliation by the innocents and their brethren. Invariably, innocents suffer and become drawn into a widening circle of hatred. So often it is the poor and defenseless who are drawn into the conflict and become its victims.

But the poor and the haters are powerless to act without leadership, money, and materiel to fuel action.

Here the agendas of countries and demagogues come into play. The messianic role of Iran in supporting the hate mongers of Hezbollah and Hamas is becoming more widely understood. It is also becoming clear that Iran continues to supply weapons and money to the so-called insurgency in Iraq and the Taliban in Afghanistan and Pakistan. Weapons found among captured insurgents bear the same labels as those found in the possession of Iranian-supplied Hamas fighters captured in Lebanon by the Israelis. Saudi Wahabism is reaping the whirlwind of its support for madrasas (Muslim religious schools) that offer extreme teachings and hateful inculcations to generations of young Arabs and others in Pakistan, Egypt, Indonesia, and beyond. Saudi Arabia is also one of only three Arab countries to recognize the Taliban. Pakistan, which has lavished its scarce resources on its military, shockingly has no effective public education system, thus providing an open door for hate-mongering madrasas to "educate" many of its impoverished children, including those of eastern Pakistan. Its military and ISI (its equivalent of our CIA) have long-standing ties to terrorists who were generally seen to further Pakistan's aims in the dispute with India over Kashmir. The genesis of al Qaeda arose from the type of religious extremism found in the Wahabist madrasas, and from the Mujahedeen movement originally supported by the United States to fight the Soviets in Afghanistan. Osama bin Laden's earliest appeals were tied to Wahabist outrage over the presence of U.S. troops on the holy ground of Saudi Arabia. Our military presence, ostensibly to protect Saudi Arabia, in actuality served to protect the Royal Saudi family government and safeguard the oil reserves upon which we relied. But that military presence was bitterly resented by fundamentalists who saw us as infidels and defilers of places holy to Islam.

Religious antipathy and intolerance are at the heart of much of the atrocities we are witnessing, especially from those leaders whose followers feel their brand of religion authorizes and even glorifies "harassing, torturing, and killing" nonbelievers, to paraphrase a particular interpretation of a passage in the Qur'an. Religion has been the tool, but not the ultimate problem. The poor and the powerless are the sustenance in which the bacteria of hatred can germinate and grow. If we want further proof of this, we need look no further than the resurgence of the Taliban in Afghanistan. Government corruption and rampant unemployment have taken hope from the poor and disaffected. The failure of the Kharzi government to deal with corruption and extend government services and support throughout the country, despite billions of dollars in U.S. aid, has driven impoverished and frightened Afghans back into the arms of the Taliban and other autocratic groups. Attempts to trace the billions in foreign aid to Afghanistan have resulted in a denial of access by the Karzai government to any airport screening by U.S. officials necessary to detect the absconding of those funds. Terrorism becomes a lucrative business for people on both sides of the conflict; those in government and without. Al Qaeda in Somalia is estimated to take in seventy million dollars a year from taxes, control of ports, and just plain extortion from the struggling Somali populace.

In Iraq, where al Qaeda was kept out by Saddam Hussein, al Qaeda subsequently joined forces with Sunnis and tribal leaders to fuel the insurgency that grew out of the Bush administration's failure to have any effective plan for Iraq in the vacuum created by Saddam's departure. One of President Bush's shifting justifications for invading Iraq was to pursue an alleged al Qaeda connection. Now there is one, and far greater and more ominous. The conflict and death in Iraq that has come at the hands of American soldiers and State-Department-contracted personnel, whether justified or not, have created new hatreds and recruitment for extremists. And it is reinforced because of our failure, and that of the new Iraqi government, to provide stability, work, and adequate basic services in the region in a timely fashion. Further frustrating the situation is an Iraqi government, created Western style, composed of historically opposed factions lacking a history of democratic functioning and incapable of achieving the most fundamental of accomplishments. Efforts to instill Western-style democracy are doomed to fail where the cultural underpinnings are lacking and where there are shortages of life's necessities.

Messianic, demagogic leaders know that security and food are strong attractions to new converts. But demagogic leaders are not alone driving the instability and violence. It is no coincidence that continuing instability in the Middle East has generated ever greater revenue for oil-rich countries and companies who stand to profit from the uncertainties that reverberate in the oil market. The price of oil vacillates ever upward with every Middle East crisis. Instability in the Middle East has also perversely served the interests of the United States in terms of controlling and influencing the region's vast oil reserves.

Instead of protection money, Arab rulers paid with oil to maintain their power, although there are those who claim the Saudi royal family made a sub rosa deal with al Qaeda for backdoor support in exchange for being left alone. For a well-documented analysis of the history and hegemony of oil, see Kevin Phillips' book *American Theocracy*. Phillips cannot be labeled a wide-eyed liberal. He is a best- selling author and former Republican strategist. He points out that Iraq has vast untapped oil reserves as a result of embargoes and lack of development, and makes the convincing argument that the Iraq war had its genesis in the politics of oil rather than in our immediate security. The continually changing justifications for that war, from weapons of mass destruction, to support for democracy, to the war on terror all suggest that the real justification was elsewhere, as Phillips suggests.

The point here is not to debate various aspects of the Iraq War, but to point out the consequences of the values and beliefs that led us into that war, and the war in Afghanistan. Those consequences include the lives of many innocent men, women, and children whom we tend to either forget or dismiss as "collateral damage." Such a sanitized term brushes over what is at the very least the collateral *death* of many innocent noncombatants. Our military presence in Iraq and Afghanistan has also been the ill-founded intrusion into worlds that we were ill-prepared to comprehend, much less deal with effectively. For a fuller discussion of this point, see Thomas E. Ricks's excellently researched and well-thought-out book *Fiasco: The American Military Adventure in Iraq*. Yet even Ricks, in a postscript written in April of 2007, saw a glimmer of hope that Congress was beginning to get it and reverse the failed policies and strategies that were outlined in his book. Unfortunately subsequent reality dimmed that hope as a timid, Democrat-controlled House and Senate repeatedly failed to summon the courage to alter the progress and horrific costs of the Iraq War in any substantive way whatsoever. That Congress was more intent on scoring public relations points by succumbing to presidential vetoes of their tepid measures than having the courage to wield their power of the purse to negotiate meaningful compromise. Only when the horrific cost of both wars, human and economic, finally began to exhaust the American public, and a new president promised withdrawal, did we begin to reassess and withdraw. Yet even that did not occur promptly in Afghanistan, where we actually increased our involvement until a limited reduction was finally commenced in late 2011.

Incongruously calling itself the Democratic People's Republic of Korea, North Korea is a severely impoverished nation that seeks revenue from it exploitation of nuclear and munitions technologies. Many North Korean citizens have died of starvation and the rest kept in isolation from the rest of the world by a brutal, repressive regime. Power was maintained through a cult of personality enforced by its dictator, Kim Il-sung, and then perpetuated by his son Kim Jong-il, all supported by patronage to the Korean military. Isolated from the more progressive nations of the world, Kim Jong-il has been only too willing to ally with those who seek ever more powerful weapons to achieve their goals. The presence of Iranian officials at North Korean long-range missile tests was disturbing, to say the least.

Here there has occurred the confluence of poverty, isolation, and hatred. North Korea has found a source of wealth for its leaders in the export of weapons and weapons technology.

This profiteering from conflict, and the threat of conflict, is not limited to repressive regimes. Major progressive nations, including the United States, Russia, China, and many European countries, have significant arms industries and are major suppliers of the technology and implements of war. One of our greatest generals, who then became president, Dwight Eisenhower, warned of the perils of the growing alliances between our military and the corporations who supply them. His concern was that this would produce distortion of our foreign and domestic policies by those who stood to profit from the results. Eisenhower was no dogmatic pacifist, but a man who had been supreme allied commander during World War II. He knew well the origins and horrors of war, the consequences of weakness, and what was needed to maintain freedom. He was no advocate of a weak military. But he could not support needless, counterproductive diversions of limited government resources. Frustrated at his inability to control wasteful military spending during his presidency, he witnessed the growth of alliances between military bureaucracies and their corporate suppliers of planes, armament, and other materiel. Perhaps he also knew that the bulwark of our freedoms, our senators and representatives, would find it in their constituents' (as well as their own) interest to drink from the fountain of military appropriations. It was no coincidence that the B-2 Bomber had parts made in practically every state in the Union. This intertwining of government, the military, and the industries that supply them reached its zenith with the election of a former CEO of a major government contractor to the office of vice president of the United States and the son of an oil man to the presidency. I do not question the patriotism of Dick Cheney or George W. Bush. What I question is their frame of reference and how much we lost our national ideals as a result of their worldview, or lack thereof. Yet their view is still shared by many in Congress and elsewhere in government and out.

The legacy of the Bush years, with a continuation of the Afghan and Iraq involvement by President Obama, has not stood us in good stead. Rather than a shining beacon of democracy, integrity, and freedom, a compassionate nation reaching out to the disadvantaged of the world with our strength, we project an image of belief in might over understanding and pragmatic persuasion. We have supported brutal dictators and denied support to legitimate attempts at self-determination, all the while with lofty pronouncements that have many times rung hollow and cynical. At the same time it would be naive to suggest that foreign policy should be conducted in a moral vacuum. The foreign policies of all nations serve their own domestic economic needs and have done so since time immemorial. There is, however, a way to reconcile principle with pragmatic self-interest. A look back is useful.

Whether to show up his father, or from conviction about the neoconservatives' simplistic view of the world, or as part of a global oil strategy, George W. Bush took us down a path that ousted the very Iraq dictator prior administrations had helped bring to power. Saddam Hussein maintained a balance of power between Iran and Iraq and held Shia and Sunni antipathies in check through brutal repression. Our heavy-handed approach to secure his removal ignored political realities, cultural differences, and partnerships with other nations in this world. The strategy of the neoconservatives of the Bush administration ignored a truth as old as the Roman Empire: that occupiers are never regarded as liberators. Even in post–World War II Japan and Germany, Allied troops were recognized as occupiers, especially in Berlin. But exhausted from years of war, and lacking the kind of internal civil strife that existed in Vietnam, and that now exists in Iraq and Afghanistan, there was an element of acquiescence to the occupation of Germany and Japan. The cultural underpinnings were also far different in Europe and Japan than in the Middle East and Asia. The grand irony is that Bush, who campaigned to win election by arguing in rebuttal to his rival John Kerry that we should not be the world's policeman, assumed that very role for us. A further irony was that he was driven by a messianic religious fervor of righteousness that intractably had to stay the course to victory no matter what the facts on the ground were, and no matter how lacking any clear concept of victory. Our enemies possess a messianic religious fervor of their own, creating the recipe for endless bloodshed. Where ideology is involved, pragmatic reason becomes largely irrelevant.

President Bush was not alone in the setting the direction we took as a country, although the buck is supposed to stop there. Our press, our representatives of both parties, and many of us individually stood silent as we drifted into militancy and away from informed pragmatism in our foreign policy. In his June 29, 2006, speech before the House of Representatives, Republican Congressman Ron Paul of Texas noted:

> The military-industrial complex we were warned about has been transformed into a military-media-industrial-government complex that is capable of silencing the dissenters and cheer-leading for war. The cost of war since 1945, and our military presence in over 100 countries, exceeds two trillion dollars in today's dollars. The cost in higher taxes, debt, and persistent inflation is immeasurable. Likewise, the economic opportunities lost by diverting trillions of dollars into war is impossible to measure, but it is huge. Yet our presidents persist in picking fights with countries that pose no threat to us, refusing to participate in true diplomacy to resolve differences. Congress over the decades has never resisted the political pressures to send our troops abroad on missions that defy imagination. Our undeclared wars since 1945 have been very costly, to put it mildly. We have suffered over one hundred thousand military deaths, and even more serious casualties. Tens of thousands have suffered from serious war-related illnesses. Sadly, we as a nation express essentially no concern for the millions of civilian casualties in the countries where we fought. The 2002 resolution allowing the president to decide when and if to invade Iraq is an embarrassment. The Constitution

authorizes only Congress to declare war. Our refusal to declare war transferred power to the president illegally, without a constitutional amendment. Congress did this with a simple resolution, passed by majority vote. This means Congress reneged on its responsibility as a separate branch of government, and should be held accountable for the bad policy in Iraq that the majority of Americans are now upset about. Congress is every bit as much at fault as the president.

We allowed the politics of fear and diversion to silence our better judgment. We succumbed to challenges that label as weak and naive those who would dissent and question to find better answers. And we failed to look beyond simplistic arguments that people hate us because we love freedom, or that these are evildoers and simply terrorists. Such rhetoric appeals to our emotions but does nothing to provide meaningful action and direction for our foreign policy. It gives the impression of toughness, but is devoid of effective strategy. Even the expression "war on terror," that most seem to have accepted without question and use repeatedly in their discussion of our actions, indicates how vacuous and ill-defined we have become in response to the events of 9/11. Terror is neither an enemy nor a condition like poverty; it is a tactic. You cannot wage war against a tactic. When we can't describe the target it becomes all the harder to hit the mark. The Iraq and Afghanistan wars diverted our attention away from strategically pursuing terrorists like bin Laden, sapped precious resources (human and economic), and weakened us throughout the world. While we pursued bin Laden in Afghanistan, he was living comfortably in Pakistan under the nose, and perhaps with the support, of its military.

In Iraq, Afghanistan, and other conflicts, anger and fear clouded our ability to perceive the reality as our leaders of both parties led us from our principles with rhetoric, misinformation, and inappropriate action. As Iraq became a visible chess piece to demonstrate strength and action by our president in the face of 9/11, and a veiled stratagem to maintain influence over oil reserves, few of our representatives questioned the shifting rationales, and even fewer members of the press asked penetrating questions or sought information beyond that fed to them by our bureaucrats and elected officials. It was a time and lesson from which we should learn. When you are wrapped too tightly in the flag it is hard to see beyond the stars and stripes. Patriotism is laudable, but it has often been misused by our leaders. "Patriotic" exhortations to freedom and democracy do not substitute for a pragmatic and reality-based foreign policy.

Understand clearly that this is not an argument for pacifism; quite the opposite. There are real and dire threats in this world, and they have all too painfully been laid at our doorstep. There are also significant pragmatic issues that affect our national security and interests. It is not the purpose here to explore in detail the many and complex issues that contribute to specific violence in differing parts of the world. There is a plethora of books and studies about area after area. But the commonality of illiteracy, poverty, religious extremism, and hatred cannot be ignored. Attempts to impose Western-style democracy do nothing to feed or educate people or take them out of their isolation. As noted by President Eisenhower in a far different time, the diversion of resources on all sides to bombs and bullets robs food from mouths and education from minds. Buying favor with corrupt leaders through "foreign aid" and weapons sales is also a failed approach. When our aid fails to help educate and feed a country's populace, and instead is diverted into the Swiss bank accounts of its leaders, we are the worse off for the effort—both here and in that country. Buying the support of a despot is short-lived. Earning the admiration of a people is long lasting.

As Americans we are an impatient lot. We want quick solutions and simple answers. But the anarchy and terrorism we face took many years to develop and spread. They involve complex relationships and interests with disparate objectives. Poverty, illiteracy, and religious extremism cannot be resolved with a shooting war. Indeed, the more we interject violence, the more we play to the objectives of the terrorists: the more we expand the cycle of violence and hatred.

What if the billions of dollars spent fomenting hatred and maintaining a state of war in the Middle East had been spent instead to educate, feed, and house dislocated Palestinians and other misbegotten people of the Middle East, not to mention address pressing needs at home? What if Fatah had not been corrupt and actually helped to elevate its people so they were not then receptive to a more radical Hamas? What if the money spent on guns and instruments of brutality in Darfur had gone instead to sustenance, AIDS and other health concerns, and education? Those who argue against foreign aid as wasteful ignore the monumental costs of wars. The problem is not the aid, but the manner in which it used to support heads of state rather than the needs of their people. Just as with the Holocaust, we are squandering lives and the gifts those lives could offer to society by bettering mankind. We have missed too many opportunities to give the misbegotten a stake in peace rather than extremism. Israel's own sense of isolation, betrayal, and persecution has inhibited more fruitful attempts to connect with those who have become its enemies as violence fuels more violence. Israel's effort to trade "land for peace," while a step forward, did not address the indignities of the vanquished people just beyond its original borders. Instead the simmering hatred, poverty, and inability to find work has persisted for Palestinians and continues to be co-opted by those with political agendas. Israeli Arabs continue to be second-class citizens in their own country, hardly creating loyalty or understanding. Our projection of ourselves as the world superpower with God-given direction only fueled the resentment of those who wanted our help, not our moralizing, and certainly not our bombs and bullets raining down on their country. We ended the Cold War with China and Russia by reaching out and initiating dialogue based on mutual benefit. Isolation and threats had only perpetuated the antipathies. Communication dissolved them. At the same time, there are fanatics with whom communication is pointless. But communication can be fruitful with the people the fanatics seek to exploit.

A pragmatic approach to foreign policy understands the cultural differences and needs of people in other countries. It understands that extreme behavior germinates in extreme circumstances, and strives to eliminate or at least reduce the burden of those circumstances. A pragmatic approach to foreign policy projects strength and compassion, not ignorance and arrogance. The actions that need to occur are proactive in a positive way, not reactive in a destructive fashion. Once the bombs detonate and the bullets fly, once the frustration has reached the boiling point where the fire is fueled by demagogues, it is difficult to stop the cycle of violence. By definition the extremists are in the minority. We need to support the majority of more moderate people, as we are learning with Lebanon and Iran. The human and monetary cost of our misguided policies in the major affected countries is too great to disregard, and growing. The solution begins with recognition that the silent poor of the world can no longer be ignored by their relatively wealthier fellow citizens in their own and other countries. Like climate change, poverty, poor medical care, and illiteracy are worldwide issues that call for the concerted commitment of all of the advanced countries of the world. I am not speaking merely of "food for peace" programs or other giveaways. These are short-term fixes to specific famines, and often poorly handled. I am speaking of a fundamental change in our approach to international relations. That change is to an approach that sees force as a last resort, not as part of a global chess game of bending peoples to our will. It is an approach that recognizes the cultural, historic, and ethnic differences that abound in this world and takes into account the unique expectations and needs of different people. Finally, it is an approach that moves us back to a place that respects and holds our military to an appropriate role in our democracy. Quoting again from Representative Ron Paul in his June 29, 2006 address to the House of Representatives:

> We must move quickly toward a more traditional American foreign policy of peace, friendship, and trade with all nations; entangling alliances with none. We must reject the notion that we can or should make the world safe for democracy. We must forget about being the world's policeman. We should disengage from the unworkable and unforgiving task of nation building. We must reject the notion that our military should be used to protect natural resources, private investments, or serve the interest of any foreign government or the United Nations. Our military should be designed for one purpose: defending our national security.

Wars are most often the result of failed policies. The human and other costs of such failure are staggering, demanding that we not acquiesce to policies without having penetrating and demanding debate. That is the highest calling of our elected representatives, and is the most meaningful thing we can do as citizens. There are times when there is no alternative to war. But it should be the last instrument of resort, not one of the first.

Democracy is a form of government and an ideal. Food, water, and shelter are tangible realities. Trying to impose Western-style democracy in countries that have neither the cultural nor the historical prerequisites for democracy is the errand of a fool. The poor and illiterate of the world have more immediate needs. Organizations like Hezbollah and Hamas win converts by providing food, medicine, and other necessaries, along with indoctrination, in the poorest communities, where the legitimate government has defaulted in its obligations to its people. So dire is the need of the misbegotten that they will willingly surrender their freedom and even safety to those who offer food and caring to their children in exchange for poisonous indoctrination. The greatest tragedy of all this is that it is ultimately the poor who become the cannon fodder when violence occurs. It is their children who become suicide bombers and their neighborhoods where the bombs and missiles explode. And it is the innocent who suffer the most. If we want a more peaceful and secure world, then we must take a greater interest in all the people of the world, and not wait until the unrest of the forgotten becomes exploitable. We must be vigilant to the abuse of our own freedoms at home in the name of national security, so that truth and dissent are not stifled. And we must strive to recognize that patriotism is not blind adherence to authority, but the very act of questioning it. President Roosevelt's admonition to "Walk softly, but carry a big stick" has been ignored. We have the big stick but have forgotten how to smartly walk softly.

Chapter Twelve

The Divisive Impact of Our Profit-Conflicted Media

A flawed media, I suggest, leads to a flawed democracy. Ill-informed citizens cannot make proper judgments about their leaders' actions, about the actions that take place in their names, about the laws that govern them.
—Michael Buerk, former BBC news anchor and journalist

The media can facilitate the conversations [about serious issues] or shut them down. They can open up or constrain our beliefs about what is possible, what is desirable, who is deserving, and which perspectives are legitimate.
—Sarah Ruth van Gelder, executive editor, Yes magazine

Global media will be and is fast becoming the predominant business of the 21st century...more important than government. It's more important than educational institutions and non-profits.
—Gerald Levin, former CEO of Time Warner

Any discussion about our disunity and our difficulty in finding common ground must consider the primary source of information for most Americans; our media. By providing information and commentary, the media shape our thoughts and actions. The media in this context refers to all forms of media, from television and movies to books, newspapers, magazines, and the Internet. To the extent our media misguide and misinform us, it contributes to the misunderstandings and divisions among us. While many complain of media bias, more often than not such claims simply reflect the bias of the complainer. This is especially true when the charge of bias concerns perceived political bias. None of us are without bias, and neither are the media. It is a given and varies only in degree. Even where great pains are taken to present purely factual information, the information so presented is still a product of the choices made by the authors, producers, and presenters, and reflects their particular perspective. An outward attempt to appear balanced by giving equal weight to both sides of an issue in so-called point-counterpoint also creates distortion because few if any issues have equally valid opposing arguments. Then there is the whole issue as to who is chosen. Placing a weak proponent against a stronger one for the opposition creates its own form of bias. But charges of political bias distract us from a focus on a deeper problem with our media: the quality and character of the information they provide or fail to provide.

The level of public support that once existed for the Iraq war is illustrative of how our mainstream media misinform or fail to inform at all, even at crucially important times. In the weeks immediately after 9/11, few Americans identified Iraqis as being among the attackers who planned and executed the terrorist acts. Yet more than a year later, a January 7, 2003, Knight Ridder/Princeton Research poll showed that 44 percent of respondents said they thought "most" or "some" of the Sept. 11, 2001, hijackers were Iraqi citizens. Only 17 percent of those polled offered the correct answer that none of the attackers were Iraqis. The misperception about the lack of Iraqi personnel in the 9/11 attack had actually grown worse over time. Where was the public getting this misinformation, and why was it being perpetuated? While the Bush administration was alluding to such a connection, clearly the reporting of the events subsequent to 9/11 and the information being offered in the media were not aiding the truth. In the same poll sample, 41 percent said that Iraq already possessed nuclear weapons, which not even the Bush administration claimed (it did claim they were seeking fissionable materials and seeking to *develop* nuclear weapons). A Pew Research Center/Council on Foreign Relations survey released Feb. 20, 2003, found that nearly two-thirds of those polled believed that U.N. weapons inspectors had "found proof that Iraq is trying to hide weapons of mass destruction." Neither Hans Blix nor Mohamed El Baradei ever said they found proof of this. The same survey found that 57 percent of those polled believed Saddam Hussein helped terrorists involved with the 9/11 attacks. Today most Americans know better what the facts were relating to Iraq and 9/11, weapons of mass destruction, and terrorist sponsorship. But it should not take the mainstream media years to get it right. They should have been in the forefront of debunking the myths that perpetuated support for the war, not late to the truth.

The public airwaves were determined long ago to be a matter of public trust, requiring a certain amount of public service programming in exchange for the broadcast license. An outgrowth of that philosophy became known as the fairness doctrine, which required broadcasters to give equal time to advocates of the major political parties. There were also curbs in place to guard against too much media concentration. The concern about concentration grew out of the media control that was observed in Nazi Germany during WWII and later in communist countries. The fairness doctrine was ended in 1984, during the Reagan administration, as part of a move to reduce government regulation. What followed was a period of media concentration, culminating in domination of our mainstream media by a small number of providers. Efforts to restore the fairness doctrine over time in Congress were not successful. There are now six enormous conglomerates that control the vast majority of what we see, read, and hear in the mainstream media. For a variety of reasons we will discuss, this consolidation does not serve us well. The major players are:

General Electric:

2009 revenues: $157 billion

General Electric media-related holdings include a minority share in television networks NBC and Telemundo, Universal Pictures, Focus Features, 26 television stations in the United States, and cable networks MSNBC, Bravo, and the Syfy Channel. GE also owns 80 percent of NBC Universal. On January 18, 2011, the Federal

Communications Commission approved Comcast's takeover of a majority share of NBC-Universal from General Electric. However, General Electric still has a 49 percent ownership stake in NBC-Universal.

Walt Disney:

2009 revenues: $36.1 billion

The Walt Disney Company owns the ABC Television Network, cable networks including ESPN, the Disney Channel, SOAPnet, A&E ,and Lifetime; 277 radio stations, music and book publishing companies, production companies Touchstone, Miramax, and Walt Disney Pictures, Pixar Animation Studios, the cellular service Disney Mobile, and theme parks around the world.

News Corp:

2009 revenues: $30.4 billion

News Corporation's media holdings include: the Fox Broadcasting Company; television and cable networks such as Fox, Fox Business Channel, National Geographic, and FX; print publications including the *Wall Street Journal*, the *New York Post,* and *TVGuide*; the magazines *Barron's* and *SmartMoney*; book publisher HarperCollins; film production companies

20th Century Fox, Fox Searchlight Pictures, and Blue Sky Studios; numerous Web sites including MarketWatch.com; and non-media holdings including the National Rugby League.

Time Warner:

2009 revenues: $25.8 billion

Time Warner is the largest media conglomerate in the world, with holdings including: CNN, the CW (a joint venture with CBS), HBO, Cinemax, Cartoon Network, TBS, TNT, America Online, MapQuest, Moviefone, Warner Bros. Pictures, Castle Rock and New Line Cinema, and more than 150 magazines including *Time*, *Sports Illustrated*, *Fortune*, *Marie Claire*, and *People*.

Viacom:

2009 revenues: $13.6 billion

Viacom holdings include: MTV, Nickelodeon/Nick-at-Nite, VH1, BET, Comedy Central, Paramount Pictures, Paramount Home Entertainment, Atom Entertainment, and music game developer Harmonix. Viacom 18 is a joint venture with the Indian media company Global Broadcast news.

CBS:

2009 revenues: $13 billion

CBS Corporation owns the CBS Television Network, CBS Television Distribution Group, the CW (a joint venture with Time Warner), Showtime, book publisher Simon & Schuster, 30 television stations, and CBS Radio, Inc, which has 130 stations. CBS is now the leading supplier of video to Google's new Video Marketplace.

As is obvious from this listing, some of these conglomerates control the movies and television you watch, the books you read, and even the Internet providers and theme parks you visit. These aren't your great grandfather's local newspaper, with roots in the community, reporting local and some national events. Their reach and ownership are global. Governed by the overarching goal of profitability, these corporations are inherently interested in maximizing revenue and minimizing costs above all else. That is the nature of for profit companies. With the disappearance of the fairness doctrine and any requirement of public service for cable operations, the sole determinant of programming is profitability. But the goal of profitability is often at odds with the goal of presenting truth and full disclosure. In their efforts to cut costs, many media empires closed their foreign bureaus to save money. They rely, instead, on freelance reporters and foreign news services. In so doing they lose the direct connection to coverage of events abroad. Now they must rely on the perspective and initiative of foreign sources that are dependent upon maintaining a business relationship with them. Cost and marketing pressures have also resulted in an emphasis on personality rather than journalistic integrity or thoroughness. News organizations are constantly shuffling people to find the ones who attract the most viewers and readers. That is typically more about personality rather than competence. Some networks even use focus groups to evaluate and determine programming rather than provide risky leadership. This also applies to the same network operating in different markets. Anyone who travels the world will notice decidedly different presentations of the same issues as broadcast on CNN in the United States and the version aired abroad. Typically, the foreign presentation is more critical of U.S. actions in terms of what it discloses.

These media conglomerates also have important constituencies besides their readers, viewers, and listeners to account for. Those constituencies include advertisers, shareholders, and even the governments to whom they are beholden for access to news makers and for other favors. They are also constrained by related businesses that are a part of the conglomerate and by the personalities and needs of their senior management or major owner. The malfeasance of an affiliate is unlikely to be presented as vigorously, if at all, as would be the case with a disinterested source. And the political and economic beliefs of senior managers and owners are reflected in the choice of people they hire and the type of programming they encourage. The result is a sanitized product designed to avoid antagonizing, and even to support, these constituencies while still appealing to their chosen audience demographic. What we then receive is the kind of sensationalist, entertaining pap that passes for news today. That is usually conjoined and sometimes blurred with opinion from often utterly unqualified talking heads, valued more for their repartee, connections, and appearance rather than for their knowledge of the subject at hand. Fancy graphics and computer-generated maps are brought into play but do not substitute for missing detail or knowledgeable presenters. It has become so silly that often one reporter will look to another for validating commentary rather than to an appropriate expert or do the hard work to develop supporting facts. The piercing questions, the investigative effort, and the complete picture are lost to the exigencies of the sound bite, cost, and time constraints. Things that are important, but boring or potentially offensive to a client, are left out altogether. Truth and the complete picture are the loser for all of this.

The efforts to address the political and economic beliefs of the heads of these corporate behemoths, and to satisfy the desires of their other constituencies, can take many subtle forms. A major drug advertiser, for example, may wind up providing an expert to comment on pending drug issues and legislation, likely in a manner favorable to his or her employer, without the connection being disclosed. Economists routinely comment on matters when they may be on the payroll of those with an economic interest in the conclusion. The use of "political strategists" has become epidemic. Yet the expertise and background of these strategists is never disclosed as they opine freely and present an appearance of honest debate. Then there is the manner in which a story is presented. The omission of critical detail can alter our perception of an issue or person dramatically. With respect to political matters, the individual legislators chosen to comment are generally those with the highest profile or the most entertaining (extreme) views. That reduces our perspective on complex issues to mere sound bites, and does not give us a clear picture of the range of opinions that may actually be involved or necessarily give us access to the most key players behind the scenes.

Then there is simply the issue of the quality level of what is often being reported. In a sad display of the level journalism has fallen to, MSNBC's Andrea Mitchell asked one of the congressmen involved in the contentious debt ceiling voting of July, 2011, if he was given a piece of pizza for his vote? In the zeal to present "important" information regarding this critical national issue, it had earlier been reported that his caucus had sent out for pizza during its deliberations. A crucial issue had been reduced to the inane. An opportunity for insight had been lost to pizza! There was no probing questioning, no search for the heart of the matter, no challenging of assumptions. Even where a probing question is asked, there is seldom any follow-up. Too often the incomplete or evasive answer is simply left as the end point, as if just asking is sufficient. Politicians know that American journalists will not challenge them, and act accordingly. This softball approach by our media was satirized in *The Best Little Whorehouse in Texas,* a play and later a movie that humorously provides us with an example of the kind of political doublespeak that sounds good but lacks substance that American reporters don't challenge. In the movie, with a later-to-be ironic portrayal of a Texas governor (long before George W. Bush took office as Texas governor), Charles Durning spoke and sang the following in response to probing questions from reporters in the movie:

> Fellow Texans, I am proudly standing here for you to humbly see. / I assure you, and I mean it—now, who says I don't speak out as plain as day? / And, fellow Texans, I'm for progress and the flag—long may it fly. / I'm a poor boy, come to greatness. So, it follows that I cannot tell a lie.

> (Aside to himself) Ooh I love to dance a little side-step / Now they see me now they don't—I've come and gone / And, ooh, I love to sweep around the wide step / Cut a little swathe and lead the people on.

> Now my good friends, it behooves me to be solemn and declare / I'm for goodness and for profit and for living clean and saying daily prayer. / And now, my good friends, you can sleep nights, I'll continue to stand tall. / You can trust me, for I promise, I shall keep a watchful eye upon y'all...

> (Aside) Ooh I love to dance a little sidestep, / Now they see me now they don't—I've come and gone And, ooh I love to sweep around the wide step / Cut a little swathe and lead the people on.

Our politicians lead the people on because our press allows them to. Even the most novice reporters know that one does not antagonize your sources. Embarrass or call one out and you will never have access to that person again, or perhaps even to their colleagues. You will rapidly acquire a reputation as a troublemaker. Thus, if you want to be called on at White House press briefings you better not get too aggressive or you will not be allowed to ask questions next time. There is an unwritten decorum of soft balling in play there. Aggressive questioning is even frowned upon by fellow journalists. Politicians gravitate to members of the press who elevate them and show them in a good light, and shy away from the reporters who do not. Any reporter willing to sacrifice a source must then deal with his producer and the network's senior management. You go along to get along, as the saying goes. Then there is just plain sloppiness. Opening his newscast on CBS one evening Scott Pelley announced that the President had just signed into law an "increase in the debt," instead of an increase in the debt *ceiling*. His omission simply fueled the mistaken belief of those who thought the debt ceiling crisis was about allowing more debt, instead of being about authorization to pay debts already incurred. Pelley is an honorable individual, but sloppiness like that perpetuates misunderstandings. And he is far from alone. The media not only fail to give a complete picture, they often inadvertently give the wrong one—just like with Iraq.

A good example of how incomplete and sloppy coverage conveys a totally different picture can be found in the network coverage of the recent failure to timely reauthorize funding for the FAA by Congress. NBC reported about the airport construction projects that had been halted, the seventy thousand construction jobs suspended, and the hundreds of millions in lost ticket tax revenue that this Congressional failure to act was causing. The reporter then noted that Republicans were holding up the bill by insisting that subsidies for little-used routes to small towns were wasteful and should be halted. They then reported that Democrats had offered to give up on the subsidy issue but that Senate Majority Leader Reid later reversed field and withdrew the offer. CBS essentially reported the same facts but added that when Reid made his offer, Republicans put forth their insistence that unionization by FAA employees be made more burdensome as a part of the reauthorization. Reid then withdrew his compromise because Democrats would not agree to make unionization more difficult. CBS gave us a much clearer picture of why Republicans were willing to put some seventy thousands workers out of work and sacrifice as much as a billion dollars in revenue at a time of high unemployment and deficit issues.

The media's preoccupation with simplicity was behind creation of the concept of red states (Republican) and blue states (Democrat) and the concept of the "Two Americas." Such an approach only perpetuates the division in America. This pop sociological nonsense portrays America as two-dimensional, by state, as if each state is a monolith of belief. Fancy computer-generated maps, colored in red and blue, give a false high-tech legitimacy to the simplistic casting of a host of people and events into either category. This portrayal of America provides supposed evidence that "real Americans" inhabit the red states while "elitist liberals" inhabit the blue states of the eastern seaboard and the blue confines of California and Hollywood. Conservative pundits have cashed in on the stereotype, alleging that blue-state liberals drink lattes, go to more museums and plays, and think they are more sophisticated and cosmopolitan than their counterparts in the red south and heartland; that they view the latter as simpleton farmers and good ol' boys. Could anything be more divisive or anger-inducing? Could anything be further from the truth? There are intellectuals and lunch-bucket workers, people of every political leaning and people out of touch in every state in this country. Some of the cable networks have even taken this foolishness right down to the county level within so-called swing states. This division has simply perpetuated the stereotype that Democrats are well-off, arrogant elitists living in blue states and blue, wealthy neighborhoods, while Republicans are the saviors of the hardworking common people of our nation's red breadbasket and oppressed post–Civil War South. Democratic leaders, in full shock and awe, have done nothing to dispel the stereotype, consumed as they are, running in fear from the liberal label. It is this kind of unchallenged stereotyping that can cast a mixed-race president as not a real American, as a socialist and a threat to real American values.

Vincent Van Gogh did not paint for an audience. Yet, as with broadcasting, in the publishing arena authors today are told by their editors to appeal to their demographic;

to write for a specific audience that will like and buy the material. That is what sells books: appealing to the beliefs and wants of the customers. And woe to the aspiring author who has no "platform"; a euphemism for notoriety. If you are famous in your field or have committed some notorious transgression, like bribery or adultery, then you are a saleable author. If you have brilliant new ideas or insight and no notoriety, the odds of a major publishing house picking up your work are somewhere between zero and none. Smart editors at major publishers know it is suicidal to take on an unknown, unproven author, no matter how brilliant. The risks are too great. As a result, traditional publishing is closed to much that is new and innovative, tending to recycle "proven" authors and editorial formulae. In addition, the public is exposed to books by highly unqualified pseudo-experts who have access to mainstream publishing only because they are TV personalities. Electronic publishing is creating an opening for the untested but worthwhile author here, but the ability to rise above the din and get noticed by the mass market is nearly impossible. Much that is valuable critique, innovative, thought-provoking, and even coalescing never rises above the noise that is our mass media in America. The end result of all of this appeal by various media to their respective demographics (audiences) is to further solidify and separate those demographic groups from one another and to intensify the divisions among us.

The Internet, despite its claimed savior status by Al Gore, is also proving very unhelpful in many regards. The available news on the Web is still dominated by news bureaus controlled by the conglomerates. There is also the tendency of people to go to websites that reinforce rather than challenge their beliefs. People generally prefer affirmation over a challenge to their preconceptions. Where challenging new information is made available, it is unlikely to circulate beyond the sphere of interest for that particular source; people generally tweet, email, and otherwise recommend to like-minded friends. There is also a plethora of misinformation on the Web that is passed off as if it were truth, with no independent validation or scrutiny. The anonymity of the Web also gives vent to angry, abusive comments and thinking that can exacerbate extreme and even violent leanings. What the Web has done, along with cable news, is to accelerate the news cycle, causing passions to gyrate even more precipitously and less thoughtfully.

The long-range threat all of this poses to our democracy should not be underestimated. In Russia Vladimir Putin consolidated his suppression of Russian democracy by taking over various media, directly by the State and through acquisition by his wealthy cronies, the Russian oligarchs. Many Russian journalists, who tried to report on corruption by wealthy businessmen or by the government they allied with, were fired or met deaths unsolved to this day. While it would be hard to envision politically motivated killings in the United States, the concept of a political leader aided by wealthy media magnates and corporations is not beyond the pale, to say the least. The knowing and unknowing complicity of the media in the vindictive outing of CIA operative Valerie Plame was a chilling example of executive branch intimidation through media manipulation at the highest levels.

As media concentration increases, so does the potential for other forms of abusive political alliance to occur. Money buys the shaping of public opinion at the hands of public relations and media professionals. Too much media concentration can mean the limiting, or outright elimination, of any effective rebuttal or scrutiny of the picture afforded by those with an agenda that may not be in the public's interest. The ability of powerful media interests to get their, or a key client's, chosen candidate elected through direct and indirect support creates a combination to be feared.

Even where objectivity is sought by print and visual media, there is still a tendency towards paternalism by some news producers. As Chris Mathews of MSNBC said, "We have to stop trying to be the parents of the American public." He was referencing the efforts of his producers to continuously sanitize reporting of President G. W. Bush so that Bush was always shown in a flattering light. MSNBC has been routinely criticized as antagonistic to Bush by Bush supporters, so his observation is all the more interesting. We need to know who our leaders really are, not be fed some selective representation that panders to preconceptions or achieves a balance for the sole purpose of *appearing* impartial.

The shocking lack of awareness, and misinformed views, held by many Americans about world events and world opinion is not aided by media more focused on gossip and entertainment than geopolitics. Reasoned analysis has been pushed aside in favor of sensationalism and sound bites. This has assumed ridiculous proportion in shows like *The O'Reilly Factor* on the Fox News Channel where in one episode "The Barbie Twins" were brought forward as commentators to discuss an offer by Hooters restaurants to fund the neutering of animals in Los Angeles. Apart from abject triviality in the face of significant issues in the world, the resort to individuals with no real expertise whatsoever is a complete disservice to viewers. For a channel that calls itself a "News Channel," this is especially inept and disingenuous. Fox is owned by Rupert Murdoch's News Corporation. Murdoch is well known for his political leanings and preference for voyeuristic muckraking. He has carried over those inclinations to Fox News which offers a clear example of selective presentation and ratings over reportage. That conclusion does not argue for censorship. Murdoch has the right to do what he does and his audiences have the right to watch his networks and read his publications. But it does argue for demanding better of ourselves in terms of separating the smoke and mirrors from the real substance. We must seek to be better informed and demand that of our sources of information. We must be more discriminating about what constitutes news and what constitutes mere opinion or thinly disguised entertainment masquerading as news. We should not hesitate to write to media outlets and hold them accountable; not for bias, but for completeness, being factual, and about presenting honest experts rather than simply talking heads or people of mere notoriety. It is also important to look at sources that offer differing perspectives. While we may not agree with all that is presented, it can provide us with information by which to better evaluate what is being presented by our preferred source.

As a democracy we are only as viable as we are informed. The Fourth Estate and media organizations seem to have lost sight of their critical role to separate fact from commentary and to be incessant in their search of the truth and knowledge. Unfortunately, that role is not what is being rewarded today. Attractive, likeable personalities and circus-quality commentary that boosts ratings are what are in demand. As with so much in our society, risk takers and intellect need not apply. Where are the Edward R. Murrows of this generation? Broadcast media have knuckled under to the entertainment competition from cable broadcasters who have no obligation to air public service material. Broadcast media are required to present a certain amount of material, such as news and public service content, that is in the public interest. This is part of the public trust they hold in exchange for their free use of the public airwaves. The resultant gray area between entertainment and news has been totally ignored by the Federal Communications Commission, which is charged with enforcing this obligation of non-cable broadcasters. We have gone from relevant reportage of news, driven by a professional desire to inform, to pandering for the sake of ratings. Just as it is incumbent upon our business schools to reinforce ethics in business, it is important for our journalism schools to stress that reporting is a profession, and what distinguishes professions is that they are supposed to exercise responsibility for their conduct. The cult of personality belongs, if at all, on stage and in theaters, not at the news desk. What is being passed off as present-day reportage by the major networks is an unprofessional abuse of the public trust.

Our professional and personal lives are inextricably tied to the politics and events of the day, whether we choose to be a part of them or not. The old adage has never been truer than here: knowledge is power. Our ability to have meaningful work and to feel a degree of relative security in which to live meaningful lives vitally depends upon being informed and knowledgeable. The current state of our media will change only when we support diversity of thought and demand accountability. It is folly to assume that people will turn away from entertainment-style reportage. But to the extent we demand better, we will get better. Rather than blaming the media for assumed bias, we should be demanding factual, complete, and honest presentation of issues, and access to real, informed experts. The result may not be as exciting, but it will be more informative. And who knows? Truth is often more interesting than fiction.

Chapter Thirteen

The Evolving Concept of Equality

We hold these truths to be self-evident, that all men are created equal, that they are endowed by their Creator with certain unalienable Rights, that among these are Life, Liberty and the pursuit of Happiness.
—Thomas Jefferson, Preamble to the Declaration of Independence

What so fundamentally distinguishes America from other societies throughout history is the concept of human equality of right. No other civilization has so uniquely established this form of egalitarianism. Recognizing that men and women have differing physical and mental characteristics, the Declaration of Independence and our Constitution proscribe that people must nevertheless be treated equally in terms of inherent rights that all people are assumed to possess. Ironically borne out of an aristocratic era, that concept, given greater expression in Constitutional amendments and court cases, forms the bedrock of our system of government. It is also the single greatest element of all that is meaningful about America. At once an elegantly simple concept, it is also one with immeasurably complex consequences. Because of its crucial role in both being the source of some of our disagreements, and a source for their resolution, a discussion and some background will be useful.

The "unalienable rights" referred to by Jefferson in the Declaration were not embodied in the original Constitution, as ratified in 1789. Without even the prospect of a "Bill of Rights," ratification of the Constitution as finally proposed would not have occurred at all. That is because leaders of several of the states were concerned that a purely administrative Constitution, focused upon giving power to the government, did not adequately address the rights of its citizens. The English philosopher John Locke originally detailed the concept of inalienable natural (as opposed to legal) rights that grew out of a broad interpretation of "property." His term was "life, liberty and property," an expression which Jefferson altered in the Declaration of Independence by substituting "pursuit of happiness" for "property," clearly relating the rights to more than what one acquired through one's labor. Locke saw the role of government as essentially protecting property. His "social contract" between government and its citizens formed the basis for much of the broader thinking that became the original Constitution. But this defining of the role of government, as contrasted with the rights of its citizens, formed the core of the debate concerning the Constitution. There was vigorous discussion between those arguing for a strong central government, so-called Federalists, and those whose focus was on safeguarding the rights of citizens from excessive government power, the anti-Federalists. James Madison, the principle drafter of the Constitution, initially did not see a need to set forth an enumeration of rights in the Constitution, as he and others felt the rights were self-evident as noted in the Declaration of Independence. Indeed, concern for too much power In the hands of the masses led to an initial Constitutional requirement of the election of senators by state legislatures and presidential election by electors, rather than directly by citizens. Jefferson and others were concerned that if not made explicit, the rights of the people would be usurped by the government through the implication of their absence and the exercise of expanding governmental authority. In the end Madison acquiesced and drafted a series of twelve Articles, ten of which were ratified into what we today refer to as the Bill of Rights, the first ten amendments to the United States Constitution. In addressing Congress in 1789, Madison referred to the amendments as a "provision for the security of rights." Although ratified by the requisite three-fourths of the States in 1791, it was not until 1939 that the last three of the original thirteen states (Connecticut, Georgia, and Massachusetts) adopted the amendments.

Today, more than two hundred and twenty years after the country's founding, we still struggle with the profound implications of equality of inalienable rights and the degree to which government should have power over our lives. Understanding the full meaning of our Constitution and the Declaration of Independence is a work in progress for America, much like a crustacean growing into its protective shell. Thomas Jefferson, the very author of those words in the Declaration of Independence referring to "all men," viewed blacks as inferior to whites in body and mind, while at the same time decrying their importation into the colonies as slaves. Others who participated in the drafting and ratification of the Constitution and the Bill of Rights were similarly varied in their views of equality with respect to women, people of color, and those whose religious views differed from their own. The debate whether the right existed to own other human beings in this country, many of whom were then citizens by birth, ultimately resulted in the only war to pit Americans against one another in combat, our Civil War. The subsequent Thirteenth Amendment, abolishing slavery, was in retrospect both a restatement and an evolution in understanding of what was already implicit in both the Declaration and the Constitution when taken together: the fact that "all men" should have equal rights to life, liberty, and the pursuit of happiness. Yet it was not until 1920 that the Nineteenth Amendment was enacted, extending the right of suffrage to women. There have also been instances throughout our history, such as the internment of Americans of Japanese ancestry during World War II, where we look back with regret that we let our emotions and fears do violence to the rights granted to all Americans, regardless of genealogy or national origin.

When we debate such health issues as abortion and the right to end suffering by knowingly choosing death over continued suffering, we are really talking about whether the right to make personal health decisions for ourselves and the right to end our lives in the manner we choose are inalienable rights. Our rights are of course not limitless. Attempting to define those limits is where the debate centers. Justice Oliver Wendell Holmes, in a case concerning the right of free speech, *Schenck v United States*, commented that the right of free speech "would not protect a man falsely shouting fire in a theater and causing a panic." Schenck had sought to distribute fliers opposing the draft during World War I, an action that was determined to be a "clear and present danger" to the war effort. The blocking of Schenck's right to protest the draft was upheld. The Schenk standard was later overturned by the Supreme Court in *Brandenburg v Ohio*, which adopted the present test that speech could be limited only when it was directed to, and likely to cause, imminent lawless action. Implicit in both rulings is the point that our rights reach their limits when they interfere with the rights of others. Our pursuit of happiness, our exercise of our freedoms, and the conduct of our lives as we see fit does not give us the right to do so when it threatens imminent harm to others. Nor do we have the right, within limitations that protect ourselves and others, to restrict our fellow citizens in ways that control their rights to live as they choose or to coerce them to live differently. It is at these intersections of right and limitation that the beliefs and values of some collide with the inalienable rights of others. The overturning of the Schenck case was part of our evolution, our growth into our protective shell, in a manner that expands our freedoms, not lessens them. It has not been a process of granting new rights by judges, but one of discovering and solidifying the implications that flow from the broad principle of equality of right.

American law finds expression and breadth through cases brought before our courts. There the facts of the case are deduced and applied to the requirements of the law. Even when enacting a particular law, ordinance, or administrative rule, the full implications are seldom appreciated, much less covered adequately in the language of the law itself. Borrowing from English common law, our legal system depends upon the precedents set by previous court cases on the matter (what lawyers call in Latin *stare decisis*) for guidance in applying the law to particular facts. American courts look for cases involving similar facts or issues and follow the holdings of those cases where applicable. The objective is predictability and a degree of uniformity. We can expect that under similar facts or issues the courts will decide the same way in the future. But the doctrine is not immutable, as with the Schenk case. When prior cases are found to have incorrectly applied the law courts have ignored precedent and reached different outcomes. Judges do make mistakes, and attitudes and beliefs evolve, even at the Supreme Court Level. Thus, as noted, our understanding of our Constitution is a work in progress. In 1896 our Supreme Court, in a case entitled *Plessy v Ferguson*, decided that discrimination against "negroes" was allowable as long as equal facilities were provided to those excluded: the so-called doctrine of "separate but equal." That doctrine was overturned by a later Supreme Court in the 1954 decision of *Brown v Board of Education*. The *Brown* case held that children of color could not be segregated into separate school facilities, whether those facilities were "equal" or not. That ruling overturned sixty-five years of prior decisions based on *Plessy*. Some look upon such cases, and the implementing segregation decisions that followed, and claim that so-called activist judges are infringing upon the legislative process by effectively creating new laws. Such critics do not fully comprehend our legal system in doing so. No law, whether in the form of a Constitutional pronouncement or a mere ordinance, can literally address all of the factual permutations that might arise out of its application. Indeed, in its Ninth Amendment, our Constitution itself recognizes that it does not expressly spell out all of our rights. It falls to our courts to apply the law to the facts at hand in order to give the law and our rights maximum viability wherever possible. Thus, in 1966 the Supreme Court ruled in a case entitled *Miranda v Arizona* that for a criminal conviction to comply with relevant Constitutional protections, police had to apprise suspects prior to interrogation of those protections (namely rights against self-incrimination, to have an attorney present to advise and observe them, and to have one appointed if they lacked the resources). There was no law or constitutional provision to this effect. It could be argued, and has been, that the Court was legislating: creating new requirements that did not exist previously. But without the decision, hapless (and presumed innocent) citizens could be taken into a room by overenthusiastic police (or racist police), away from any public scrutiny, and coerced into a confession to something they did not do. In establishing its holding, the Court could not make a law, but ruled that any conviction obtained without the warnings, or similar advice of constitutional protection, would not stand up on appeal. This was not the act of legislating. It was instead the act of giving life and viability to our right to be safe from torture, wrongful conviction, and harassment by the State through its police power. The ruling prescribed a course of conduct by police that would ensure our rights to liberty and due process were protected. The Constitution does not literally say such things. It does not define "due process" of law, nor does the Fifth Amendment call for police to tell you that you have a right against self-incrimination. Instead it is up to our courts to protect, implement, and give meaning to our rights. They do so by applying our constitutional and other legal rights to the real-world situations that present themselves in the form of cases brought before them. Without this court process, our laws would become hopelessly complex and in a process of constant amendment, while trying to plug every literal hole in the dike that sprang up. Without this vital safety valve of judicial interpretation, our rights would be subject to the whims of the powerful and our democracy a sham. It is why we must avoid at all costs the politicizing of the judicial process. Judges must be selected based on judicial ability, not litmus tests of belief. A free and independent judiciary is our only protection against abuses of power and injustice by the legislative and executive branches of our government. It is also the best guarantee that our constitution and other laws will be protected not only in their incarnation, but also in their application over time. Protecting our rights does not come at the cost that terrorists and other criminals go free. Rather it means that police and prosecutors must follow the law; that they cannot run roughshod over the rights of us all, who are presumed innocent until proven otherwise, in their desire to get a conviction. Miranda himself was retried and ultimately convicted by evidence beyond his mere confession. As a result of Miranda and related cases, the constitutional rights those cases address are not just words on paper, but have substance and effect in real life.

In this context the debates about the right to a medical abortion, gay marriage, the right to die, and religion in public life become easier to address. It ought to be clear to all that under our Constitution, liberty above all means freedom from oppression by others. That means we have the right to make our own determinations about our bodies, our beliefs, and our lives without the heavy, blind, and unfeeling hand of the state interfering. It is not for the unfeeling, indifferent voice of government to tell me when I have suffered enough from a terminal illness, or to force continuation of medical procedures when life support is in fact no such thing. Those ought to be decisions between myself, or my designee, and my medical expert caregiver. And it ought not to be for any of us to tell two loving people who have committed to each other that they cannot inherit or act for each other the way married individuals can merely because of their sexual orientation. The issue is not whether "marriage" is between a male and a female. That is a diversionary and fear-based argument. The issue is about the *right* of people in a committed relationship, to be equal to us all under our Constitution, to care and do for each other with *equal protection* of the state as those who have taken out a license of marriage and followed any state required formalities to solemnize it. Respecting that right will not do violence to the institution of marriage or the rights of heterosexual couples. Despite attempts by some to cloak marriage in religious garb, at its core marriage is a mere state-sanctioned contract in the United States.

Historically marriage has had many forms and purposes, from creating familial ties and rights of inheritance, to specification of sexual restriction and the creating of spheres of power and influence. There has been no universally accepted norm of marriage over time. Even monogamy is not a universally recognized characteristic of marriage throughout the world. While it is most often solemnized in a church or other religious setting, marriage is fully legal in every state without clerical intervention. A marriage, no matter how religious the partners, is only as strong as the commitment of those partners to one another. It is not religion that creates the bond between the people, nor even the contract of marriage itself. The religious implications are what lead us astray in the debate because we get into questions of morality and belief. Just as our Constitution grants us the right to our beliefs, it requires that we not deny the equal right of others to their beliefs, to their right to live as their makeup dictates: to inherit, to attend to health decisions for their partners, and to otherwise have the benefits that ought to flow from a committed relationship that has been formalized by the state. There is no good reason, beyond prejudice, to prevent the marriage contract or one similar, and the rights that would flow from it, to apply to people of the same sex who want to commit to each other in some formal manner. Even arguments about child rearing do not hold sway here. There are no credible studies to show that children of gay parents are any the less well cared for or less adjusted than children of heterosexual parents. Instead, studies have shown that the keys to well-adjusted children are the bond of the parents and their parenting skills, not their sexual orientation.

Those who, out of concern for unborn children, oppose a mother's right to make choices about her own body would do far greater good to devote equal concern to those children who are actually viable outside of the womb. Any rights of the unborn cannot take away the rights of the actually living. There are thousands of foster children in this country desperate for love and stability in their lives. They are also ones who seek and need help with the conduct of their lives. There are professionals to counsel the suffering, the pregnant, and the dying; but too few people to love and protect the lost children of our society.

If in the name of God we love our neighbor, that love should respect their right to freedom, to privacy, and to dignity. That is the hardest thing to do. When our beliefs collide with the rights of others, it is difficult to not want to prevent that which we revile. But that is the truest test of our freedoms: the ability to respect the freedom to others. When we hear the racist or blasphemer speak, we want to silence them. When we see people gather to protest what we might feel is a vital war to protect us, we want to take away their right to assemble and to criticize. And when we see public institutions that we might feel encourage immorality or lack of belief in God, we want to inject our religious views. But that is not our right in America. Instead we have the right to express our views and to be heard. But we do not have the unrestrained right to impose our standards and beliefs on those who do not share our standards and beliefs in America.

With rights come obligations. We have an obligation to understand our rights and to ensure their equal application to our fellow citizens in word and deed. And collectively we have an obligation to act toward the rest of the world in a way that is consistent with our principles. That means acknowledging the rights and beliefs of others outside the United States, even where we find those beliefs different than our own or even repugnant.

We do not have the right to impose our systems, culture, or desires on other peoples. If we truly believe in equality of right for all men and women, then we ought to be willing to respect the rights of others. How can we be true to our ideals and stand silent in the face of the deaths and atrocities wrought upon millions of men, women, and children, in Africa and elsewhere, from famine and oppression? How can we respect the rights of others by repeatedly interfering in the legitimate leadership of other countries? How do we honor our principles by denying rights to our fellow citizens because of their color, sexual orientation, or religious views? The answer is that we cannot.

As a nation we have been driven apart by those who fear, who resent, and who covet. For America to realize its most fundamental meaning we need to restore its generosity of spirit. Rather than focusing upon controlling others, it is time to return to a focus on helping those oppressed, discriminated against, and less fortunate. Our current priorities are fostering a horrific misallocation of human and financial resources. Instead of excessively rewarding economic achievement, we ought to also laud greatness in terms of the broader achievement of societal benefit. The billions of dollars in bonuses being paid to investment bankers for deals that richly benefit only a select few is nothing short of obscene. The hundreds of millions of dollars being paid to corporate executives in severance, even where they have failed their employees and shareholders miserably, is an abdication of responsibility by those directors who are grossly evading their fiduciary obligation to those shareholders. The billions of dollars being spent on spin doctors, consultants, and media by political candidates has severely warped our elections process and denied all of us the ability to be truly informed and wisely led. These are but a few examples of the diminishing of America through a distortion of the value proposition that we have been too willing to accept. But we diminish ourselves in other ways. When we tear down our fellow citizens, or deny them dignity and the pursuit of happiness, we diminish ourselves. When we limit constitutional rights in the fear-based hope that we will thereby be safer, we diminish ourselves. When we tolerate violence of any kind, and extol as a virtue power over reason, we debase ourselves. And when we do not make available to our children the resources needed to give them a world-competitive education, then we lessen ourselves and future generations.

We are justly proud of our democracy, and even seek to export it to other countries, yet our voting participation is among the lowest of democracies throughout the world. Our shining example to the world of equality of right cries out for participation. Not participation by those who seek to limit rights, but by those who want to protect the inalienable rights of everyone in America. It begs for support and nurturing, for creativity and leadership. There is wonderful personal meaning in participating in America, in being part of its greatness in every positive endeavor. From the act of voting with knowledge of the issues and candidates, to teaching our children and helping to feed and clothe the less fortunate, there is meaning. By speaking out against injustice in favor of help for the disadvantaged, there is meaning. By opening our minds to the great and wondrous possibilities afforded to us in America to do good in the world, there is great meaning. But the greatest meaning comes from respecting the equality of right of every citizen of the world to life, liberty, and the pursuit of happiness. Lifting up the hopes and aspirations of the many will be the greatest impediment to the dark and awful actions of the few. Meeting hate and violence with violence and hatred is a fool's errand. Providing knowledge, security, and sustenance creates an alloy through which hate cannot penetrate and violence has no fuel. This is no idealistic prattle, but a clear, productive, and meaningful direction for America. And it is a meaningful course for us all in our individual lives as well. Our collective force is immeasurable. The picture created by our national mosaic is colored by each individual tile. In word and deed we must aspire to integrity, respect for others, and a passion for excellence in all that we do. Find the meaning in your life. Make your tile shine. Help to create a national mosaic that respects the equality of all in the world to life, liberty, and their own pursuit of happiness.

Chapter Fourteen

The Terror Within

Violence in America

"Guns don't kill people, people do"........and most often with guns.
—Slogan by the National Rifle Association, with factual addition

To be clear at the outset, this chapter is not an argument against gun ownership. There are many Americans who use and enjoy their guns in a responsible way: some hunt, some collect, and for some guns are a business. At the same time, the fact is that America is a very violent place relative to other Western democracies. While we are shocked at the carnage we witness daily in Afghanistan and elsewhere in the world, measured by homicides, the United States is one of the most violent, if not the most violent, countries among the industrialized nations of the world. While the statistics from the World Health Organization and others are subject to issues of comparability, there is no question that the United States homicide rate is the highest of all the English-speaking countries. In 2007 (the most recent year for which domestic data was available as of this writing), according to the CDC there were 30,948 gun deaths in the United States, broken down as follows:

- 17,352 suicides (56 percent of all U.S. gun deaths),

- 12,63 homicides (41 percent of all U.S. gun deaths),

- 613 unintentional shootings (2percent of all U.S. gun deaths),

- 351 from legal intervention and 232 from undetermined intent (1percent of all U.S. gun deaths).

Numbers obtained from CDC National Center for Health Statistics mortality report online.

As early as 1992 according to its Attorney General, California became the first state to report that gunshot wounds had become the leading cause of death and injury in the state, surpassing even automobile accidents. Firearm deaths are second only to traffic deaths as a cause of injury-related death in the country as a whole. While street shootings make headlines, surprisingly much of the violence in the United States is perpetrated against family members or acquaintances of the perpetrator rather than against strangers. According to the 2010 FBI Uniform Crime Report, overall violent crime has been in decline over the past five years, but still remains shockingly high when compared to other western democracies. Firearms were used in 67.5 percent of the Nation's murders, 41.4 percent of robberies, and 20.6 percent of aggravated assaults. It is interesting to note that the FBI statistics come from 94 percent of law enforcement agencies participating and reporting, whereas the CDC numbers come from emergency and trauma center intake statistics. The reports serve to cross-check and reinforce one another.

These statistics, as contrasted with the rest of the industrialized and English-speaking world, ought to shock our collective conscience into concrete action. Instead we debate gun control, declining morals, money for more prisons, and attack judges as allegedly soft on crime. The tragic deaths of three thousand Americans on September 11, 2001, rightly stunned our complacency and caused us to spend hundreds of billions of dollars toward a "war on terror" (without commenting on the efficacy of those expenditures). But where are the billions to wage a "war on violence" stemming from the needless deaths of nearly one hundred fifty thousand Americans who were shot with guns in the ensuing five years? Without in any way diminishing the lives of those lost to 9/11, the sheer number of souls lost to gun deaths has been fifty times greater. Added to this is the staggering amount of non-lethal violence in the form of rapes, assaults and robberies. Violence has simply become an integral and tolerated part of the fabric of America, with the use of force being perceived by many as both a right and an acceptable strategy for solving conflict, exerting power and control, obtaining possessions, and satisfying emotional desires. We glamorize violence in all forms of entertainment, from movies and television to software games readily available to children. Games offer psychic reward for "kills," and there is even a game that involves using a car to kill pedestrians by running them down. Except for the witnesses, victims, and their families, the harsh realities of violence are shielded from us in sanitized news reporting designed to protect our sensibilities and occasionally the dignity of the victimized. Television and movie portrayals rarely display the agony of a violent death or the deep emotional scars remaining from non-lethal attacks.. But the reality of our violence is all a part of an America that constitutes background noise in our lives, surfacing on the evening news, and then obscured again in the stressful fog of our daily existence; at least until one of us, a relative or a friend, is directly affected, or a Columbine or Virginia Tech occurs.

As shocking as the statistics and our relative indifference are, they are compounded by the amount of violence we are witnessing perpetrated upon and between our children. Between 1979 and 2001, more than ninety thousand children and teenagers were killed by gunfire, according to the Children's Defense Fund and the National Center for Health Statistics. American children are far more likely to die from gun violence than in any other country. According to the Centers for Disease Prevention and Control, in one year guns killed no children in Japan, 19 in Great Britain, 57 in Germany, 109 in France, 153 in Canada and 5,285 in the United States! The Centers have also pointed out that statistically, American children are sixteen times more likely to be murdered with a gun, eleven times more likely to commit suicide with a gun, and nine times more likely to die from a firearm accident than in twenty-five other industrialized nations. While guns may not kill people, according to the NRA, even children are being killed at an alarming level by the use of guns in the United States. The year 2006 saw a sharp rise in the number of school gun deaths, with seventy-five shootings between the months of August and October alone, including incidents in Colorado and Pennsylvania, which were targeted specifically at female students by men from outside the schools. Then in April of 2007, the worst mass murder in U.S. history was perpetrated in Blacksburg, Virginia, on the campus of Virginia Tech by one of its students. These homicides represent only a portion of school violence which also encompasses beatings, rapes, and theft. The Columbine and Thurston massacres brought federal attention to the problem, but federal funding to prevent violence and substance abuse in our schools has actually been declining ever since, and was even recommended for outright elimination by the Bush Administration. Many now feel the program is too small to be effective.

When particularly shocking events such as Virginia Tech occur, the frustration of some is turned to cries for increased gun control. While characteristic of our need for quick answers, there has not been the political will in recent years to stiffen gun regulation in the United States. It is a political truism that strength in numbers is trumped by strength of action. Thus, a well-organized gun lobby has been able to thwart the beliefs of the majority of Americans who have not put sufficient actions behind their beliefs about the need for better gun control. There is a reflex on the part of some gun owners to the effect that any talk of gun regulation is the beginning of a government takeover and the loss of their ability to defend themselves. To be clear, the discussion here is not about taking away the legitimate rights of people to own and use their guns in a responsible manner. The issue here is violence in America, often committed with guns. The debate about gun control unfortunately diverts us from addressing the underlying causes of gun-related and other violence in the United States. The NRA is literally correct in their pronouncement that "Guns don't kill people, people do." The problem is that people in America are killing people primarily *with* guns. The real question is, why? Further, we don't seem to be doing a very good job of enforcing the gun laws that already exist. Under Federal law the Virginia Tech mass murderer should not have been able to qualify for a gun purchase. But because of a breakdown in the reporting schemes of various states such as Virginia, his disqualification under Federal requirements did not surface in Virginia, and was therefore not communicated to the Federal government for background-check purposes. Studies have shown that 1 percent of the gun stores sell the weapons traced to 57 percent of the gun crimes. Yet the enforcement of our gun laws is weak due to inadequate funding. It is one more of our misplaced priorities.

For a number of people, including some religious and community leaders, the problem of violence in America is related to a perceived moral decay in the country. For others it is traceable to a lack of religion in our public schools: what they feel is a permissive environment and the evils of teaching evolution rather than deity-based creationism. Whether religion's influence helps or hurts is fervently debated. The highest divorce rate in the United States exists in the so-called Bible Belt states. While there are many factors at work, including younger marriages in those states, at the very least it can be said that religion is not contributing noticeably to marital stability there. Increasing church attendance is also not correlating with lessened violence in the United States. Higher homicide rates as well are found in the Bible Belt states. The horrific slaughter of innocent children at the Amish school in

October of 2006 came at the hands of a devout, church-going Christian man. At the very time he was perpetrating the attack, his wife received a call from him while she was attending a prayer meeting. A relative described the husband and wife as a "devout Christian family." One of the highest homicide rates among industrialized countries is found in Italy, a predominately Catholic country, the home of the Papacy and one of the more religious of the industrialized nations. This does not mean that religion is a failure or cannot be a positive factor in the alleviation of violence. Religious precepts can certainly provide guidance and caring values. But values alone cannot always resolve deep-seated emotional issues, and can even be at the root of some of those issues. Religious differences can drive people apart and prevent them from supporting one another. Religious concepts of shame and guilt can create psychic harm as well as compulsion and obedience. As much as the deeply religious would like to believe that faith alone is the answer, there is more to contend with here than belief. Labeling killers such as Cho Seung Hue, the Virginia Tech gunman, as "pure evil" and "driven by the devil" does not direct us toward earthly answers and solutions. We can pray to heaven for the victims, but we should look to science for answers.

The root causes of violence in America have been examined for a long time by psychologists and other mental health professionals. While the kind of horrific violence experienced at Columbine, Nickel Mines, and Blacksburg is rare, these deeply aberrant events can help provide insight into lesser acts of violence. Although the circumstances of each violent act are extremely varied, certain common factors have been linked to these most severe attacks, as well as to many suicides. The first of these factors is a degree of self-absorption by the individual, whereby they focus inwardly on themselves and perceive they are victimized in some fashion. The victimization often takes the form of child abuse, bullying, or some other psychic injury that is initially reacted to with a sense of helplessness by the recipient of the injury. That in turn may create or feed a sense of paranoia in the individual. Paranoia itself is a common marker of individuals who commit the kind of sociopathic acts of violence such as occurred at Columbine and Blacksburg. Secondly, these are often people in great emotional pain who either do not seek, or who have been unable to obtain, constructive outlets for their suffering. Seeing themselves as powerless victims with no alternative, they act out their repressed rage in the form of violence against others. Rape and other sexual crimes, for example, are less about sex and more about power over the victim. But the sheer predominance of violence in the United States compels us to ask why it is so prevalent here. Are there aspects of our culture that now make us the most violent industrialized nation? Are there things we can do as individuals and as a country to remediate this deadly aspect of American life?

There is a strong sense of entitlement in our American society, an expectation of opportunity and largesse. We live in "the land of milk and honey," where everyone can supposedly be rich and famous. You simply need to apply yourself. There is an implication that if you are not wealthy and famous, it must be your fault. This belief can begin to address some of the frustration and rage felt by those who are forgotten or left out of the mainstream, whether through their own actions or otherwise. Cho, the Blacksburg killer, railed at "rich brats" and expressed repeated resentment of those with wealth. While that by no means explains the entirety of his complex and twisted motivations, it was an element that he expressed. One of his contemptuous plays alluded to a stepfather who had failed as a provider. The family had left impoverished conditions in Korea to improve their lot in the United States. The family was not wealthy and Cho, rightly or wrongly, felt outside the mainstream when it came to issues of economic well-being. The apparent relative wealth of fellow students gave his self-imposed isolation a further focus for his deranged anger.

There is also an inherent and perpetual dissatisfaction felt by many in our society. If we are not continually striving to better ourselves, then America's psychic message is that there is something wrong with us. In many other cultures, such as in Japan, the hotel doorman does not generally aspire to be prime minister or the CEO of the hotel chain. He simply wants to be the best doorman he can be and can find happiness in that. His limited expectations allow him to find satisfaction and accomplishment in his job without feeling pressure that he should be moving up in the hotel organization. There is less societal pressure there to be upwardly mobile and more focus on achieving personal best behavior. That focus on self, rather than blaming others or feeling victimized, along with cultural factors such as a degree of historic acceptability of suicide in the face of failure, has however resulted in Japan having a higher suicide rate than the United States. In the United

States we are bombarded by self-help programs and TV therapists, teachers, and counselors imploring us to be better than we are, to always be striving for more. Our social status and careers are an important part of who we are and how we value ourselves. Our self-esteem is strongly tied to our career successes and failures. Questions about what we do for a living are customary conversation openers in America. That would not be the case in Israel, for example, where other non-personal topics are customary with strangers. For most of us this pressure is tolerable. But for those who are not "moving up," or, worse, are falling behind, or who feel belittled by their station, the pressure can provide the salt applied to other wounds and weaknesses in their lives. Violent and abusive parents are often themselves the children of violent parentage. For those struggling with the burdens of past abuse, added societal pressures to strive and be successful, or peer pressure to conform, can create the camel-back-breaking straw. For those with any degree of paranoia, the depression that can come with a sense of failure can be turned to the rage of resentment of those who appear more successful. When these pressures are not alleviated and are allowed to build and turn to rage, the consequences can be deadly.

Our American culture also glamorizes appearance over substance. While the success of Bill Gates and others with more brains than looks has done much for the image of so-called nerds and geeks, the simple fact is that you are far less likely to be popular or successful if you are not handsome and athletic. Once again marketers flood our sensibilities with images of tan and buff males, youthful, svelte women with flawless smiles and full breasts, as the ideal to which we should aspire as respective males and females in America. The dramatic growth of fitness centers and weight-loss businesses in the United States has largely been driven by all of this "appearance" marketing. As noted shortly, it is not achieving overall fitness. Add to this barrage skin cream, deodorants, hair products, energizers, teeth whiteners, mouthwash, and other products, all of which play to our insecurities. The resultant stress is ironically having the opposite effect in one arena as obesity has been increasing in the U.S. to levels of 20 to 25 percent of the populace, up an incredible 75 percent over the past ten years, despite the growth of fitness centers and increased public awareness. The obesity rate is even greater in young children, an ominous sign for the future. The entire subject of food excess and abnormality, bingeing, overeating, and a need for so-called comfort food, are confirmatory more of the growing stresses in our society than of a general lack of will power. The pressure to be thin simply compounds the stress level. Nearly all weight-loss programs have shown an abysmal long-term success rate. If all of these appearance products and programs have not made one exceedingly anxious, there is a whole new cadre of health products assaulting our sensibilities from cures for restless leg syndrome to the pain and bloating of a recalcitrant digestive tract and the embarrassment of erectile dysfunction. For these with these actual ailments, such products may provide relief. But for others the persistent advertisements are merely another source of anxiety, if not annoyance.

From television to billboards to the Internet, we are inundated with directives about the physical ideals we should embody and the success we should achieve. If you are a child outside the norm, your life can be quite lonely and painful. Children can be terribly cruel to their fellow boys and girls if they perceive them as different. If your personal hygiene doesn't measure up, you have speech difficulty, your appearance is unattractive physically, or your clothes don't match the trend, your fellow students will likely let you know by their taunts or indifference. For a child who has been ostracized or bullied, the sadness and the sense of powerlessness in the face of implacable pressures can become simmering rage. Certainly not every such child commits heinous acts, but the ripples of that rage can find expression in anger acted out against themselves all too often in America. Dillon and Klebold, the killers of Columbine, were two such extreme outlyers, taunted and ridiculed by their peers. Cho referred to them as "martyrs" and saw himself as a martyr for the weak and the defenseless. In instances such as Blacksburg and Columbine, their communities were failed by the mental health and law-enforcement systems that might have reacted better to the warning signs. The signs of aberration were everywhere but the safety net was lacking. The ability to sense the isolation, suffering, and rage and provide a means for their functional dispersion was inadequate. The fact that Blacksburg and Columbine were extreme cases, albeit dramatic ones, does not lessen the point that we need to be vigilant to the pressures affecting people within our society. And we need to not be short-sided by cutting funds for mental health facilities, education, and treatment.

The expression that violence begets violence is not limited to physical force, but encompasses psychological abuse as well. A related expression might be that pressure begets pressure. Individuals under pressure can create pressure in others as they endeavor to release their own insecurities and rage or repeat response patterns they have suffered and learned at the hands of parents and friends. Pressure that is neglected can build until it works its way explosively out of rage contained. The end result can be violence against children, partners, or classes of people such as women or particular ethnic or religious groups.

Our American society is one of the most violent on earth, largely because we are one of the most pressured societies on earth and have not fostered sufficient means for the alleviation of that pressure. Not only does the pressure impact directly on those who act out, it impedes those who could help by desensitizing them to the warning signals going off around them. The outlets for that pressure as it affects those predisposed to violence can be highly dysfunctional, and can take the form of small vices or large. In the latter category are substance abuse and physical abuse. A huge component cause of crime in America is tied to substance abuse. People who turn to substance abuse do so most often for the same reasons some turn to violence directly: the alleviation of pressure. Ironically, the substance abuse can then spawn violence to support the drug needs.

Anger and depression are interchangeable responses as a reaction to perceived oppression. Depression grows out of resignation and withdrawal, a defensive reaction to implacable pressure. Anger is the offensive response to pressure that flows from a sense of entitlement and seeks a means to regain power. They are in many ways the modern-day incarnation of the primal "fight or flight" response to threat. The big bank that forecloses, the impersonal government that condemns property and imposes taxes, and the large out-of-state company that cuts benefits, wages, and downsizes can all contribute to a real or imagined sense of helplessness, with resultant depression and anger for those who do not see a conventional way out. The pressures to succeed, to conform, to go along, can all foster depression or anger. If there are not proper outlets and perceived recourse, the results can be tragic for the individual and others as well. Impersonal management practices and related work stress at the U.S. postal service led to a series of fatal mass shootings several years ago at post offices. The expression "going postal" then became a phrase to describe someone raging out of control in response to external pressures. Pressure needs release and redirection or eventually the containment bursts with dire results. A parent pressured by work can abuse their child, who then becomes an abuser and violent themselves, and the cycle continues.

The tendency of a mass culture to stress the normative means many are left out and isolated at what society deems to be the bottom or the top. It is no accident that many school shootings have occurred in smaller rural areas. There the opportunity for support from the comradeship of others with similar but unique styles and needs is reduced by the smaller population and lessened availability of sophisticated mental health resources for youth. These rural areas are also attractive to those who are inherently loners and antisocial, and whose family patterns are less social. Once thought idyllic, rural America is no longer a sanctuary of family and neighborly values, having been stained by the influence of big-city culture imported through the mass media. It is a culture that urges consumption, self absorption, and conformity, not self-acceptance. It is also a culture that glorifies violence as a means of problem solving, and weapons as an expression of manhood. It is a culture that implicitly sanctions taking what we want by lauding strength and cunning over effort. In the end it is a culture that has fostered increasing alienation from one another.

There are parallels in the United States to the violence we are witnessing in the Middle East and Asia. At its core the violence there often relates to the need for human dignity. The anger and hate that festers and is cultivated there grows out of the indignity that displacement, poverty, and illiteracy fertilize. The need for human dignity is so strong that it incredibly finds willing reception to its attainment through the killing of innocents and martyrdom. That need for dignity also finds expression in many of the murder-suicides we are witnessing in the United States. Here the object can be a form of martyrdom (thereby achieving a perceived dignity and value), retribution for perceived wrongs to one's dignity (expressed in the killing of others), and the perverse power that is found in controlling the end of one's life (expressed in the suicide, where there may also be a component of self-loathing). The point is simply that dignity is a tremendously powerful human emotion and need. As our society has grown increasingly isolating, the self-worth of many individuals in America is carelessly disregarded. And as we grow more insular in response to foreign threats, our resort to labeling minimizes the real issues underlying those threats. The failure to deal with human dignity has a great social cost both here and abroad.

None of this should be construed in any way whatsoever to excuse or justify violent acts. Our purpose is to learn from these circumstances of extreme behavior, so that we might be better prepared to prevent them in the future, and to lessen the overall level of violence in America. There are some in our society, however, who are simply beyond corrective action. Psychologists have discovered that there are individuals who do not have rational, normal response patterns as a result of trauma or birth defect, and irrespective of their upbringing and environment. Others have been irremediably damaged by their life experiences. Then there are the truly psychotic, who cannot discern reality from fantasy. But for all, the objective ought to be violence *prevention*.

We must find a better way to facilitate human dignity in the United States and provide more opportunities for the functional alleviation of perceived grievances where dignity has been impaired. That will go a long way toward relieving the dysfunction that ends in violence. It begins with learning and applying parenting skills that teach our children constructive approaches to conflict and the development of self-esteem. The American Psychological Association offers a number of helpful resources for parents and teens such as the ACT ("Adults and Children Together to prevent violence") publication "Raising Children to Resist Violence: What You Can Do**."** Other publications cover the identification of abusive relationships for teens, elder abuse, and guidance for teachers and counselors on violence prevention. In this arena the African American and Latino communities, where the highest incidence of gun-related death is occurring, have an opportunity, along with the full support of their larger communities, to address the root causes of that violence. Also in this arena we need to provide meaningful work for all who reside in this country, regardless of background. Talk of erecting barrier fences (which will pose no difficulty for someone determined to penetrate a single point in thousands of miles of border), deportation, or exclusion may be good political-speak, but it ignores the realities of the ten or more million undocumented immigrants already here. Driving them into hiding will not produce constructive outcomes. And the thinking that we can simply locate and round up millions of people and deport them- most of whom are integrated into our society- simply defies logic and common sense. We need to find more ways to reduce the stresses on individuals in this country and to provide support structures to help them through difficulty so they do not feel isolated and helpless and resort to drugs and violence. Creating *and publicizing* more "ombudsmen," pro bono attorneys, mental health resources, and telephone help lines can all provide constructive channels for frustration and resultant dysfunction. But these take resources that have to become higher up on our scale of priorities. We also need to consider the impact of the messages to succeed and be socially acceptable that we convey in our media and social discourse. We must become more inclusive of a broader range of personalities and types of people that we deem acceptable or at least tolerate. And we need to slow the pace of our lives long enough to look around at the faces passing by to see the ones in pain. So many times a person will commit horrific acts and end their lives by suicide, while those who knew them profess in shock that they thought all was well. But the signs were usually there all along, if we had been looking and open to listening. They are there if we look in the faces of our friends, co-workers, loved ones, and strangers. They are there if we truly listen rather than merely acknowledge the words people speak to us, and if we are observant of the changes in mood and action. This is also an area where law enforcement with proper training, physicians, and teachers can be especially alert to warning signs. Once we are observant, a kind word, an offer of help, or reassurance can make a difference, sometimes the difference between life and death. And we need to strike a better balance between individual liberty and the need to protect society from potentially danger-ous individuals before they commit heinous acts. We pay a price for our freedom, but we can still ensure individual liberty while finding a means to compel treatment of the mentally ill where warranted. Where mentally ill individu-als will not accept treatment, then the priority must shift to protection of others who are at risk. Institutions are under no legal obligation to teach or employ the aberrant who pose a threat to their fellow students and teachers or employers. There has been too great a tendency, with overcrowded facilities, to incarcerate only those who have committed an overt act of harm to others. We ought not to wait until serious injury has occurred before acting to remove the threat.

What could be more meaningful than to save a human life? How great the meaning in life to divert a child away from a life of abuse, to rescue a lost soul, or to show the way to help for a defeated spirit? Empathy for others can also alleviate our own suffering by turning us away from our own troubles and helping to find strength in a kindred spirit walking the same road. How meaningful is the courage to offer help for the aberrant, and then to take the action needed to protect others, when help is refused or otherwise impossible?

Finally, we need to examine our priorities. Vengeance may be viscerally satisfying, but rising prison construction expenditures and falling mental-health support, relative to total health expenditure, are a series of misdirected investments. According to the U.S. Department of Health and Human Services, an estimated 28 to 30 percent of our adult population will suffer from a mental or substance use disorder during the course of a year. In any given year, about 5 to 7 percent of adults have a serious mental illness. A similar percentage of children, about 5 to 9 percent, have a serious emotional disturbance. Yet as a percentage of total health-care expenditures, our mental health and substance abuse outlays are miniscule. Our failure to adequately address mental health issues is costing us greatly in dollars and lives. We can see the people in prison, but the silent suffering and violence of the walking wounded in our midst are harder to notice. Where we have chosen to provide help, in many cases we have moved away from active treatment facilities, due to budgetary constraints, and toward often unsupervised outpatient medication. The mentally ill are poorly equipped to monitor their medication. Drugs alone are also often not a satisfactory cure or palliative. Providing more mental-health professionals in our schools and communities will make it more likely that we will discern and treat the mentally ill and dysfunctional before they inflict harm upon themselves and others. It will also be more cost-effective. In California in the 1960s, then Governor Ronald Reagan began closing state mental-health hospitals, in favor of outpatient care and medication, because active treatment had cured and decreased the number of mentally ill in the state. As a consequence of the reduced number of treatment facilities, the number of mentally ill individuals needing treatment went back up significantly, along with total costs.

Before we leave this subject, it is worthwhile to reflect on the lives lost to violence and the resilience of the human spirit. Each life that is lost is not only someone's friend or relative, but a loss to all humanity in our efforts to grow. We are thus deprived of artists, scientists, and others, no matter how great or mundane, who would have made this world a little brighter and a little more humane. One of those occurrences was the loss of John Lennon to senseless violence. How many other potential John Lennons will we lose? Then there are the other entertainers and athletes who have died at the hands of others. It is unfortunate that times of tribulation, such as a Blacksburg, bring us together in our common shock and grief. But that resilience, that perseverance of the human spirit, should also inspire us to action in calmer times.

So much of what has been discussed in this book relates to things that push us apart in America. Whether it is the politics of fear, work and social stresses, religious differences, or the labels we place on one another, we are becoming increasingly alienated from each other. We need to reverse this negative trend with all deliberate speed. That reversal starts with each of us in our daily interactions with one another, continues with the integrity with which we manage and the choices we make for leadership and public expenditure. Great meaning comes from those actions which draw us together: those efforts to find common ground where we can share hopes, aspirations, and needs. That should again become part of the character of America.

Chapter Fifteen

Beyond Belief

The Ungodly Misuse of Religion

I do not consider it an insult, but rather a compliment to be called an agnostic. I do not pretend to know where many ignorant men are sure— that is all that agnosticism means.
—Clarence Darrow, Scopes trial, Dayton, Tennessee, July 13, 1925

Men never do evil so completely and cheerfully as when they do it from religious conviction.
—Blaise Pascal

Religion has already been discussed in a limited way and in a variety of contexts in this book, but the central role it plays in human existence calls for separate consideration. Religion is at once the most uniting and most dividing of human belief systems. For many it provides the structure and purpose to an otherwise inexplicable and amoral world. For others it is an instrument of coercion and repression, a powerful tool to enlist and mold soldiers in the army of those with agendas beyond the mere service of their God. Because it addresses man's deepest fears and insecurities, religion has a compelling attraction. Man has engaged in various forms of religion, most likely even before recorded history. The statistics vary depending upon the source, but in relative magnitude today there are roughly 2.1 billion adherents to some form of Christianity, 1.2 billion Muslims, and 1.1 billion secularists in the world. Hundreds of millions of people are Hindus, Buddhists, and Chinese traditionalists, along with followers of scores of smaller religions. The number of estimated Muslims in the United States varies dramatically, from 1.1 million to as many as seven million. The variance stems from both the source of the information and the degree of actual practice, but the number of practicing Muslims in the United States appears closer to two million. Islam has been growing at a rate of 2.9 percent per year throughout the world, while Christianity has remained relatively stable in terms of adherents worldwide. In fact, Islam is projected to surpass Christianity by the middle of the twenty-first century as the most ubiquitous religion, if present trends continue.

To better understand the influence of religion, it is useful to look at some of its more extreme manifestations, where religious belief leads to action at odds with the basic tenets of the religion. Virtually every religion has found extreme expression in one form or another. When belief is stretched to the extreme, aberrant actions are sure to follow. That is a lesson that applies to more than merely religious belief.

A good place to start, especially for Americans, is with Islam. Despite Islam's growth and pervasive influence throughout the world, until September 11, 2001, Islam was little noticed by most Americans. It is but another example of how our relative insularity has diverted us from even the most apparent of conditions beyond our borders. Until then we had been largely blind to the gathering storm outside our country, and subsequently to the insidious erosion of our secular values within. The events of 9/11 did not occur in a vacuum. They were part of a continuum of religious manipulation and hegemony that had its roots many years before. Bin Laden's ostensible justification for the 9/11 attack was the sullying of ground sacred to Islam by the maintenance of American troops in Saudi Arabia. That was a convenient pretext perhaps. But incitement had surfaced far earlier in the attack on our humanitarian efforts in Mogadishu in 1993 (the infamous "Blackhawk Down" incident where our elite forces were surprised in a brutal ambush), and had its genesis as early as 1989 according to the November 4, 1998, Justice Department indictment of Osama Bin Laden and his military director, Mohammed Atef. As in Iraq, our presence in Somalia was motivated by outwardly honorable intentions. The venality with which we were greeted in Somalia, and the Mogadishu attack in particular, should have been another omen of history to temper our expectations for Iraq. But those who shaped the Iraq strategy out of ideology rather than knowledge ignored the lessons of history, including Somalia as well as Lebanon and Vietnam some forty years prior. They also ignored the political realities of the region and the growing and sinister manipulation of Islam by those with dark political agendas. Various statements by Bin Laden suggest that he made several attempts to bait America into violence against Muslims, including the attack on the USNS *Cole*, with the object of creating a rallying cause for his own aggrandizement. He could not have asked for a better response than the invasion of Iraq, which by all accounts radicalized tens of thousands more Muslims throughout the world against the West and enshrined Bin Laden as a hero to many Muslims. Among those who decry his and other terrorist atrocities against innocent men, women, and children, there has been at least a degree of grudging admiration by some for his ability to tweak the nose of his adversaries with relative impunity. In their eyes the weak and the disrespected have been empowered. This sense of empowerment has strong appeal for those who have been marginalized and ignored. It is a key element that draws support to extremism.

All of the horror we witnessed on 9/11, all of the carnage in Iraq and Lebanon, Gaza, Israel and elsewhere, had their origins in religion. The use and misuse of religion continues to have a very significant impact upon our world. Religion has been used throughout history to appease the downtrodden, to ennoble the most heinous of actions, and ultimately to further the political and personal aims of those who would twist it to their purposes, all in the name of a supreme deity. Because of its emotional power, where religion is involved reason is often a casualty. It is thus easily perverted to accomplish the ends of its supposed champions, because people are willing to disregard reason in favor of emotional assuagement of their deepest fears and anxieties. It is a dangerous bargain, but one often readily made, and with sometimes horrific consequences for the bargainer and others.

It is not religion that is bad, but rather its distortion and proselytizing by extremists and fundamentalists who seek to manipulate it for their own ends and prejudices. Whether it is an evangelist enriching himself at the expense of his congregants, a self righteous bigot seeking to justify their hatred, or an extremist of any sort with an agenda, religious teachings can be easily distorted to achieve a desired end. Because of the great harm that religious extremism is capable of engendering, it is crucial that we understand both the methods used by the extremist to build support and the receptivity to extremism exhibited by those drawn to it. Although the extremist rarely if ever characterizes his views as extreme, by definition the extremist advocates positions that are far from center and even radical. This is necessary in order to justify the aberrant behaviors sought by the extremist, because at their core most religions advocate tolerance and peace. The appeal of the extremist is thus to emotion rather than reason, because reason would question the deviance and undermine support for the extremist's goals. Reason and debate are the enemies of the extremist and why extremists abhor democratic processes in favor of unquestioned and fanatical allegiance based in ideology and emotion. The avoidance of reason and the elimination of debate are accomplished through a variety of means. Extremists deal with their critics and opponents by attacking the questioning person or group rather than addressing the facts and issues raised by the questioner. They will do this by questioning the motives, qualifications, character, and values of the opponent as a means of diverting attention away from debate and discussion and toward marginalizing the opponent. Emotionally charged speech is useful in this regard through resort to labeling and name-calling such as describing the opponent as immoral, an infidel, fascist, and racist, un-American, a crackpot, too liberal, or too conservative.

As we have noted, labeling is an effective way of dispensing with thoughtful examination in favor of simplistic emotional packaging. Often the opponents of the extremist adopt the rhetorical ploys of the extremist. In that regard it is noteworthy and a bit ironic that both George W. Bush and Osama Bin Laden each labeled the other as a "terrorist." The banners and slogans seen at rallies of extremist groups are emotional incitement to others to join the cause without regard to argument. The rallies themselves are attempts to demonstrate mass support, and thereby attract the recalcitrant who do not want to be isolated. Symbols become important here, for both advocate and opponent, such as the swastika, the clenched fist, and the burned flag. They are but emotional labeling in symbolic form.

Extremists' most powerful weapon is to play upon and incubate the fears of those they seek to win over. They do so by casting their antagonists as essentially evil or threatening to those the extremist seeks to influence. In a religious context the opponents are defilers, infidels, or the Antichrist, to name a few epithets. One of the most egregious examples of such techniques is the infamous "Protocols of the Learned Elders of Zion." This blatant anti-Semitic fraud was conjured up by Okhranka, the Tsarist Secret Police, in the late nineteenth century to support the suppression of Russian Jews, many of whom were advocating reforms. It alleges a Jewish plot to enslave the world and drink the blood of non-Jews by gaining control of the media, banking, and politics through a set of strategies called protocols. The argument that a religion comprising .2 percent of the world's population could enslave the other 99.8percent is ludicrous on its face, but it demonstrates why reason and logic play no part in extremism and are to be avoided at all costs by the extremist. This hateful scourge was employed in Europe to justify the mass extermination of millions of Jews, and was required reading for German children during Hitler's era. It has been translated into Arabic and Farsi by Sunni Islamist groups, the Muslim Brotherhood, and governments such as the Shiite Islamic Republic of Iran. The calls for the destruction of Israel and the denial of the Holocaust by Iran's President Mahmouhd Ahdminejad can be better understood with that frame of reference. It is also no accident that the Protocols are one of the most widely available books for sale in Islamic marketplaces besides the Koran, and is a best-seller in Syria.

There is great debate about whether Islam is a religion of peace or one that seeks worldwide hegemony, necessitating the hatred of all nonbelievers such as Christians and Jews. A former Muslim professor himself, Mark Gabriel argues forcefully, through references to the Qur'an in his book *Islam and Terrorism,* that Islam does ultimately have as its objective the conversion or death of all nonbelievers. Whether that is true, and whether we have been lulled into a false sense of belief about so-called moderate Islam, as he also argues, remains to be seen. No religion, including Islam, is monolithic. There are believers of differing views within every religion. Judaism has Orthodox, Conservative, and Reform branches, as well as subgroups within those. Within Islam there is great division, which is evident in the violence between Sunni and Shia in Iraq and elsewhere. Again, the religion is not the problem, but its perversion by fundamentalists and radical ideologues, that creates the problems for all, inside and outside the religion. The credo of the Islamic Brotherhood, as stated on their internet homepage states:

Allah is our objective.

The messenger is our leader.

Quran is our law.

Jihad is our way.

Dying in the way of Allah is our highest hope

Officially the Brotherhood disavows terrorism and has condemned the 9/11 attacks. Its members have themselves been the victims of harsh repression in Egypt and Syria. However, leaders in those countries and others assert that factions of the Brotherhood encourage and finance terrorism. It is easy to comprehend why the language of their credo could be seen to endorse the very actions they claim to disavow. These inconsistencies and claims to peaceful advocacy are part of a process of planned subterfuge, according to Dr. Gabriel. What is clear is that there are those Muslims who openly advocate and commit violence against others in the name of their view of Islam. No group, however, in recent times has suffered more greatly in sheer numbers from Muslim violence than Muslims themselves. It falls to the leaders of Islam throughout the world to question whether tolerance, or outright endorsement, of violent means within the religion is ultimately in their best long-term interests. While there are those Muslims who have argued that the deaths of thousands of innocent Muslims, not to mention non-Muslims, is justified by the goals (the end justifies the means), rational Muslims should ask, is there not a better way? And they should have the courage to challenge and debate those whose actions bring discredit and death.

The nation of Israel's attempts to defend itself and its actions in the occupied territories have provided modern-day flash points for Islamic hatred that was initially cultivated far earlier. That hatred has become an ideology, an ideology that Israel's own pre-conditioning has only reinforced through occupation. Ideology takes the form of dogma such that you don't have to know anything more or search for anything further. You already know the answer to everything, and facts inconsistent with the dogma are explained away or ignored altogether. It is why negotiation with the ideologue is difficult if not impossible. Ideology is at the core of all religious extremism, with its intolerance for any divergent thinking. Peace will come between Palestinians and Israelis when moderates on both sides see more to be gained by peace than bloodshed; when dignity is recognized as crucial to Jew and Muslim, alike; and when the profit is taken out of the conflict for leaders who pocket funds meant for their people.

Building upon the fear turned to hatred, borne of ideology, the extremist appeals to the piety and conviction of their followers. That in turn becomes the litmus of loyalty in the face of extreme demands. The appeal to martyrdom, whether through suicide by bomb in the Middle East or poison in Jonestown, Guyana, is an extension of this approach. In the end there is nothing too extreme for the truly devout when done in the service of their God. Indeed, the more extreme the act, the more the adherent proves his devotion. In their quest to keep reason at bay, extremists also often couch their positions in broad emotional terms that are vague enough to defy analysis but specific enough to resonate with the fears, needs, and anxieties of their followers. They accordingly make sweeping claims and assessments on little or no factual basis. The Protocols of the Elders of Zion again come to mind here. While the appeal is to emotion, often the extremist will try to give the impression of employing logic even though none exists. Thus, they will analogize that because something is true in one context, it is true in all contexts. If, for example, a country has taken military action against a predominantly Muslim country, it must be a threat to all Muslims. Or the extremist will simply make a sweeping statement vaguely connecting two things that followers are asked to accept. If Jews are involved in the media, politics, and banking, it must be because they seek world domination. Or if someone is a homosexual, they must want to convert others to their sexual orientation. Such sweeping generalizations ignore the detailed facts of the matter and are faulty, unsupported logic as well. But they can be effective to the predisposed. By appealing to the prejudices and beliefs of the followers, the leader can gain support and avoid true logical argument. Hearing what they want to hear, the followers do not see the need to question.

The use of apparent logic is not limited to analogy alone. Another device is to suggest that because something followed something else, it was the cause of what followed. Some have argued, for instance, that because

AIDS has afflicted homosexuals that it is God's punishment for their supposed transgressions. That fallacious argument of course ignores, among other things, the factual tragedy of the AIDS epidemic in Africa that has spread largely from unprotected heterosexual sex. In many instances that sex took has taken the form of rape, creating a double victimization. Extremists hold their opponents to a high standard of truth, but that is not the standard to which they hold themselves. Often they excuse this double standard by resort to sympathy for their cause arising from special circumstances such as persecution, economic disadvantage, or piety. For the extremist the world is black and white, right or wrong, good or evil. For the extremist you are either with him or against him. There is no middle ground. To allow diversity of view would weaken the extremist's power and open the door to debate and factionalism. That is why it is critical for the extremist to limit dissent altogether in the interest of strengthening the cause. Debate thus becomes disloyalty and even treasonous, justifying intimidation and threats against those who would question. This has been an effective tool to maintain acquiescence from the masses that are taught through example to fear retaliation from any resistance. The brutality encouraged and directed by extremists feeds not only the sense of power in the followers, but also engenders compliance from those who would otherwise challenge the extremist.

It is again noteworthy in this context that those who oppose extremism can be drawn into some of the very same tactics employed by the extremists. Thus we find ourselves in the United States using labels to describe complex groups and situations, and the use of intimidation and limitation of dissent, in the face of terrorist threats. Using terms like "Islamo-Fascist" and "axis of evil" does nothing to shed light on solutions or even lead to productive discourse. Claiming that those who oppose the leadership are "unpatriotic," apologists, or even "treasonous" is intended to intimidate and stifle opposition, even if the labeler is well-intentioned. Such tactics ought to be anathema in a free and democratic society. These are emotion-charged words, not factual exposition or even reasoned argument. Abridgment of the protections against unreasonable search and seizure and the guarantees of due process threaten the very freedoms we cherish and seek to protect. Terrorism is not an excuse to sacrifice our rights and protections as Americans. Such misguided efforts to limit our rights protect neither America nor its values.

A fundamental antidote to extremism, religious or otherwise, is information, not repression or counter-violence against those susceptible to extremist appeals. The free exchange of ideas and reasoned debate provide a means to find solutions to inequity and injustice, as well as a relief valve for discontent. Information, as opposed to emotional appeals or threats, helps to alleviate the underlying anxieties that support prejudice and the resultant hatreds. Free discussion and debate also generate productive strategies for combating extremism and a means of critiquing and checking approaches to extremism that are ineffective. That is why extremists do not brook competing ideas and instead demand unquestioned loyalty. That is why they use every means to incite rather than inform or engage in dialogue. It is also why attempts to reason with the extremist fail. The answer to extremism is to remove support from the extremist. To understand how that can be done we need to understand what compels some to willingly become the followers of religious extremism and participate in all of its egregious excess.

It took a self-taught longshoreman, not a PhD in psychology or sociology, to write a definitive work on the underpinnings of mass movements. Intrigued by the rise of Nazism, Communism, and other mass movements, longshoreman Eric Hoffer sought to understand their genesis and attraction. Referring to the incredible rise of totalitarian Nazi Germany he noted, "I can never forget that one of the most gifted, best educated nations in the world, of its own free will, surrendered its fate into the hands of a maniac." His conclusions were expressed in a book entitled *The True Believer: Thoughts on the Origins of Mass Movements.* Hoffer observed that while mass movements differed in their beliefs, there was a commonality in their attraction. That linkage was an appeal to the frustrations of the converts. Frustration could take the form of economic or political oppression, isolation, or all three. That frustration led individuals to surrender themselves to a movement as a means of escaping their plight. He noted that, "A rising mass movement attracts and holds a following not by its doctrines and promises but by the refuge it offers from the anxieties, barrenness and meaninglessness of an individual existence." The less control people feel they have over their lives, the more attractive the message of mass movements will be (a sobering point for an increasingly alienated populace in the United States). Thus a defeated post-WWI Germany, with its economic subjugation, and Tsarist Russia, mired under political and economic oppression, were fertile spawning grounds for the mass movements that sprang up in those countries. The French Revolution grew out of the dire circumstances and sense of helplessness felt by the French underclass. Even the United States had its origins in a disaffected group that broke away in search of control over their lives and freedom from what they saw as an oppressive monarchy in England. Not all mass movements are bad, but the conditions that compel adherents share a common genesis: frustration and futility. When the frustration and futility are removed, the extremist loses his attraction.

Extremist religious movements have similar appeal to the disaffected. Those enduring crushing poverty and a sense of powerlessness in a world that seems to have passed them by surrender themselves to an ideology that blames others for their plight and that appeals to their dignity and sense of purpose. Religious fundamentalism that sees modernity as anathema comforts those who lack the barest of necessities. Thus in the Islamic world, extremism finds its greatest following among the poorest and most oppressed. The tenets of Islam are activist. They involve a sense of destiny and control by articulating a detailed code of conduct and rules for the meting out of justice. While there are various forms of Islam and many interpretations, the point here is not to denigrate Islam, but to recognize how its extreme forms can find special receptivity among those who feel their dignity has been denied and that their sense of self-worth has been diminished. Placing blame for their ills on Christians and Jews, as well as the alleged excesses of the West in general, resonates with many of Islam's oppressed. Circumscribing women's roles and condemnation of sexuality, modern inventions, and modern comforts appeals to those who see no path to such things or have been taught to see them as evils and that asceticism is more in keeping with God's requirements.

Having an army and being unwilling to deploy it is as unwise as deploying it without full appreciation of the consequences. When we attack a nation because of the acts of some within its borders, we inflame all. It is a natural consequence of war. The terrorism the world faces today is insidious and cross-national. The most productive way to reduce extremism, and the terrorist actions it fosters, is to remove the support for extremism, not to sweep all up into a large-scale military attempt at conquest. We diminish support for extremism when there is a focus on the underlying receptivity to extremism: injustice, poverty, isolation, limited education, and diminished self-worth. The billions we spend on warfare have become a blunt instrument that encourages more terrorism than it alleviates. That does not mean all military actions are all without merit. It simply means that wholesale invasion is counterproductive when confronting terrorist elements that move about in multiple nations. Our resources could be better applied to supporting broad-based education (not hate mongering madrasas), jobs, justice, and economic growth in areas where these are lacking. This does not mean direct expenditure, necessarily. It means providing support to moderate leadership and groups that seek to improve the quality of life of their people rather than self-aggrandizement and hegemony. This quality-of-life vacuum is itself being exploited by the extremists, such as Hamas, Hezbollah, and the Brotherhood of Islam, who regularly provide education, health care, and food to those they seek to win over as converts. They are filling the vacuum left by ineffective, corrupt governments.

Addressing the needs of the misbegotten is not the quick fix we would all like, because there is no quick fix. We are where we are because of decades of foreign policies that have largely ignored the needs and beliefs of people following the world's second-largest religion, among others. We have been more interested in their resources, such as oil and timber, and the related political strategies to secure those resources for Western interests, than in the welfare of the inhabitants of resource-rich countries and their neighbors. We have alternatively supported despots, such as Saddam Hussein in Iraq and Suharto in Indonesia, and then opposed them. Our shifting allegiances and priorities have angered leaders and followers alike. Our attempts, if they can be called that, to promote peace between Palestinians and Israelis reached a new low during the George W. Bush years. And our lack of knowledge of the Islamic world is endemic. Indonesia, the most populous Muslim majority country in the world, is a mystery to most Americans. One would at least expect that those charged with antiterrorism would be enlightened, but even after 9/11 only thirty-three of our of twelve thousand FBI agents spoke Arabic, until recently. Their cultural training has been similarly abysmal. And, as we have observed, the cultural education of our children is severely limited and ethnocentric.

Dealing with the poverty, prejudices, and limited education that afflict many of the followers of religious extremism outside the United States, and those potentially receptive to it, is of course not the sole answer. But it comprises a critical foundation for the political actions that need to accompany these efforts. The prospect of a nuclear Iran and the other political realities of the Middle East and elsewhere need to be taken into account. In dealing with Iran, for example, we must employ every economic and political means of persuasion to encourage China and Russia, indispensable to meaningful U.N. Security Council action, to move beyond platitudes and into coordinated, effective efforts to prevent Iran from developing nuclear weapons capability. The radical ideology of Iran's leadership, coupled with nuclear weapons power, is a frightening prospect. The willing participation of China and Russia can alter the present course of worsening instability in the region and a growing risk of nuclear terrorism. But China and Russia must see it in their interests to do so, interests that must outweigh the current economic and political benefits they derive from the status quo. We also cannot afford to continue our isolation from problematic countries and issues. The essence of diplomacy is the recognition of mutuality; that nations are interconnected by their needs. Without dialogue those interconnections cannot be negotiated. It took forty years of tense and often seemingly inconclusive discussion to end the Cold War, but it ended in mutual benefit.

Religious extremism in all its forms and denominations is a threat to the stability and freedoms of all people everywhere. The efforts by some Christian fundamentalists in the United States to create a Christian theocracy here have already been mentioned. For a more detailed exposition please see Kevin Philips' excellently researched book *American Theocracy*. These efforts to create a Christian-directed government stem from an ideology: a belief by its proponents that they know the true word of God and that it should be embodied in our laws and actions as they see it. Former senator and U.S. ambassador to the United Nations, John C. Danforth, himself an ordained Episcopal minister, said in an article in the *New York Times*, June 17, 2005, entitled "Onward, Moderate Christian Soldiers":

> Many conservative Christians approach politics with a certainty that they know God's truth, and that they can advance the kingdom of God through governmental action. So they have developed a political agenda that they believe advances God's kingdom, one that includes efforts to "put God back" into the public square and to pass a constitutional amendment intended to protect marriage from the perceived threat of homosexuality.

Danforth went on to point out that moderate Christians go to church, read the Bible, and are just as pious as their more fundamentalist friends. However, Danforth stressed,

> for us the only absolute standard of behavior is the commandment to love our neighbors as ourselves. Repeatedly in the Gospels, we find that the Love Commandment takes precedence when it conflicts with laws. We struggle to follow that commandment as we face the realities of everyday living, and

we do not agree that our responsibility to live as Christians can be codified by legislators.

Danforth is not alone in trying to strike the proper balance between piety and politics.

Others in the clergy have argued that Judeo-Christian principles include caring for the less fortunate, protection of all that God has created in the environment, and tolerance for divergent beliefs. Their view is not one of exclusion and fearmongering, but of inclusion and actions that express care for their fellow men and women of all persuasions. At their core Judaism and Christianity, and nearly every other religion, have in common a belief in charity and a desire for peace and tolerance. The tenets of moderate Islam also recognize the need for peace with nonbelievers.

What is fundamental to our Constitution is one's right to believe as he or she chooses. The Constitution protects "the free exercise" of religion. What is not protected is one's right to impose their beliefs on others, whether Christian, Islamic, or agnostic, and one surely does not have the right to embody their spiritual beliefs in the laws that apply to us all. One of the first things an American law student learns is that laws are not moral. There is nothing moral about a stop sign or a law prohibiting arson. Laws are meant to be pragmatic: to provide rules that benefit and protect. In all cases we seek to apply laws in a manner that achieves justice, but that is not always possible. All of us have a sense of fairness or justice. Not all of us can agree on what is moral. And that is the dilemma. That is why our system (of common law) is based on precedent rather than morality. Courts interpret and apply our laws in a manner consistent with prior decisions so as to maintain consistency and a degree of certainty. Any attempt to use a standard as vague as morality would create great uncertainty. Those religious fundamentalists who criticize our judges and lawmakers on moral grounds misunderstand our legal system and our Constitution. Those who criticize our Federal Court justices as "activist" ignore the reality of time. We live in conditions that never existed when our Constitution was written and that were never contemplated by its framers and amenders. It falls to the courts to fill in the voids in a manner that preserves the intention of the document. To do otherwise would make the document of severely diminished use in modern times. The cumbersome process of amendment is reserved for new directions, not clarification or fleshing out of already established precepts.

Religion was felt by the Founders to be of such great import that it is discussed in the very first amendment of the Constitution. The First Amendment requirement that "Congress shall make no law respecting an establishment of religion," is given life by requiring that the prohibition against "establishment" is not merely against a state-determined religion, but also prohibits any state support or sanction of a particular religion or religious practice. While the First Amendment refers to prohibition of religious "establishment" by Congress, its provisions have been extended to the states, under the Due Process Clause of the Fourteenth Amendment, through Supreme Court rulings in 1940 (free exercise) and 1947 (establishment). Together these do not prohibit anyone from religious practice, so long as it is not through the use of facilities or funds that are owned by the public. Instead of allowing all religions access to state support, and thus inviting arguments over degree and fairness, the Constitution treats all equally by precluding state support of any religion. This principle protects all religious and nonreligious expression by prohibiting the state from favoring any such expression. The religious faction that seeks to weaken this principle does not seem to understand that they do so at their own peril. Shifting majorities would mean shifting support for their own religious views.

Most of America's earliest settlers came here out of religious motivation. Indeed, some of the original colonization, such as the Massachusetts Bay colony and the Plymouth colony, was directed at specific religious views. But over time those with the great wisdom to fashion our democracy came to realize the innumerable benefits that flowed to all, religious and agnostic alike, from a separation between government and religion. Thomas Jefferson noted that

> No provision in our Constitution ought to be dearer to man than that which protects the rights of conscience against the power of its public functionaries, were it possible that any of these should consider a conquest over the conscience of men either attainable or applicable to any desirable purpose. (Letter to the Methodist Episcopal Church at New London, Connecticut, Feb. 4, 1809)

The debate as to where the line should be drawn continues to this day. Our currency refers to trust in God, our Pledge of Allegiance expresses that we are a "nation under God," and our Congress begins its sessions with an invocation, to name just a few incidences of where we have intermixed government and generic religion. For some, political correctness would eliminate all references to a deity and all symbols of religious expression in public places and actions. That in turn has angered those who see such limitation as an attack on their particular religious beliefs. For them it is an expression of the decline of morality and values in the United States. But morality, as we have observed, is a matter of interpretation. Moreover, morality is not the province of religion alone. We engage in this debate over religion and government because we do not fully appreciate the need to keep them separate, even for the sake of religion itself. In 1773, Isaac Backus, a prominent Baptist minister in New England, observed that when

> Church and state are separate, the effects are happy, and they do not at all interfere with each other: but where they have been confounded together, no tongue nor pen can fully describe the mischiefs that have ensued.

We need only to observe those nations, such as Iran, where theocracies exist to understand how religion can corrupt the otherwise legitimate ends of government. And any reference to history will disgorge the plethora of nations that fell from their zenith when religion began to direct their progress rather than pragmatism, such as the Roman, Spanish, and British empires. Just as religion can corrupt government, government can corrupt religion.

When religion becomes entwined in government, it becomes dogmatic and perverse for all but its ideologues. The horrific violence we are witnessing in Iraq and elsewhere has its origins in a struggle to control government by those with differing religious beliefs.

The meaning of America is freedom: specifically, freedom to believe as one chooses, freedom to act in response to one's true self, and the freedom to pursue personal happiness. The only limitation upon our freedom is where it intersects with the freedom of others. That is where religious freedom finds its limitation, when it conflicts with the religious freedom of others. Helping to ensure our freedoms is where we can find great meaning in America. Respecting and learning from the views and lifestyles of our fellow Americans can only enrich our lives, not diminish or threaten them. And in the diversity of our American culture lies great meaning for us all. Finally, understanding the origins and effects of religion in the extreme can help us prevent the consequences that would otherwise occur. The character of America should be to respect all religions, and to guard against extreme usurpation by any religion.

Chapter Sixteen

Why It's Not Working

Our Jobs, Our Lives,

Our Badly Flawed Economy

Capitalism is the legitimate racket of the ruling class.
—Al Capone

Capitalism works better from every perspective when the economic decision makers are forced to share power with those who will be affected by those decisions.
—Barney Frank

The face of corporate America has changed dramatically over the years. What used to be the economic equivalent of democracy, individual stock ownership, has succumbed to primary ownership of major corporations by yet other organizations: hedge and mutual funds, and program, or "black box," traders who transfer ownership of companies and commodities in microseconds. Investments are being made and capital is being allocated in accordance with stratagems never before envisioned. Professional investors have moved from an emphasis on the long term to the short term and now to trading on instantaneous anomalies and relationships. Those relationships involve commodities, bonds, derivatives and stocks that trade worldwide and are affected by factors far beyond our borders. Automated, high-frequency trading is now believed to account for more than 70 percent of the volume of major exchanges. The effects on the management of companies, their employees, individual investors, and American citizens who don't own stocks or bonds have been profound, as we shall see.

As with so many other aspects of American life, the workplace is becoming a more stressful, less meaningful part of our lives. For many millions of Americans today there is no workplace at all, despite an urgent need to be employed. Others are working reduced hours or have accepted wages at greatly reduced levels from what they experienced in previous years. A great many have met with such immense frustration seeking work that they have just given up. True unemployment is reaching Great Depression levels in states like California. Some job listings have even openly stated their disinterest in hiring anyone not presently employed, and the prospects for older job seekers have perhaps never been grimmer. Currently, nearly forty-six million Americans are receiving food stamps. At the same time, corporate profits are at an all-time high. Instead of hiring, a number of companies have been using the cover of recession to lay off employees, reduce hours, and outsource work in order to reduce costs and enhance the bottom line. Justifying large executive bonuses and mega salaries requires such tactics when demand is softer. Workers who remain employed can be compelled to work harder, and processes are revamped to cover for those laid off, so that even as demand improves, companies are reluctant to rehire. Companies that are unsure of the future are also reluctant to make other longer-term commitments and are thus sitting on major hordes of cash.

Foreign competition and foreign wage levels continue to create major structural changes to the American economy. Higher-wage manufacturing jobs are being sent abroad, and demand for products at home is being increasingly met by foreign producers like China. Our trade imbalance is like a wound from which our economy bleeds. Our failure to invest adequately in our future through expenditures for research and education is eroding the very source of vitality in our economy and the ability to staunch the bleeding. The current state of extraordinarily high unemployment has forced some to remain in jobs they would have previously left and encouraged others to take jobs they would have otherwise rejected. To all of this must be added the efforts from some quarters, notably Republican, to further weaken union organizing efforts and to deprive workers of collective bargaining tools. At the same time, union-bargained gains in wages, benefits, and retirement have placed nearly insurmountable burdens on state and local governments and saddled businesses with uncompetitive cost structures. The current difficult state of work life and our economy in America compels us to look at how we got here, where we are headed if current trends continue, and what we can do to alter the paradigm.

Previous generations have had different expectations with respect to their work. Some took satisfaction in their craft or in their contribution to a significant project such as a dam or building. But for most work was a means to survival, a way of putting food on the table. The expectation that a job should be emotionally rewarding was not a major part of the equation. The Great Depression scarred many who were only too happy to have work at all. One of those so affected was my father who became a pharmacist, not because he wanted to—he did so because his father got him admitted to a medical school. To support his new wife, he dropped out with a degree in pharmacy, rather than continue to get his MD. Although dropping out prematurely was a decision he regretted the rest of his life, he nevertheless encouraged me to become a pharmacist as well, because it was steady work. But I and others of the post–World War II generation had broader horizons and greater expectations.

My generation, the so-called Baby Boomers, found itself in the middle of the Sputnik era where the Russians had internationally embarrassed America's sense of complacency about our technological superiority. On October 4, 1957, the then Soviet Union launched a rocket from Kazakhstan that placed a satellite into orbit around the earth, emitting radio beeps back to earth. This was followed by the Russians putting Yuri Gagarin into a space capsule, where he became the first human in space. Coming as it did toward the end of the McCarthy communist witch hunts and a general period of hysteria about nuclear war with Russia (children used to practice "duck and cover" drills in school during practice "air raids"), the event caused great concern rather than admiration for the Soviets. Once again fear became a motivator of national policy. Suddenly there was great national emphasis on a college education and support for technological research.

An increasing standard of living following World War II began to place college in reach for more and more high school graduates, especially with the GI Bill (officially the Servicemen's Readjustment Act of 1944), which provided college and vocational assistance to returning servicemen. This was a time when Congress willingly had the foresight to look longer-term and to make crucial investments, like in infrastructure and education, in America's future. The result was a dramatic expansion of schools and enrollment across the country. The concern became less and less about getting work and more about choosing a "career." College graduates had a broad range of opportunities in a growing post–World War II economy. There were roads and bridges to build and new products and services to be provided. During this period business became more paternalistic in an effort to attract and retain workers. Some companies even offered work/study programs that made college accessible and affordable, and began to provide increasing noncash benefits such as prepaid health insurance and pensions. Union organizing efforts were flourishing as well. Financial institutions and public utilities were places where job security was largely guaranteed, despite the vagaries of the economy or even a degree of poor work performance. It was a gentler, less competitive time. In most households only one partner worked and a workweek significantly beyond forty hours per week (apart from overtime situations) was somewhat of a rarity. Union bargaining and growth provided an ever-increasing wage level that helped build a growing middle class. And people with a modicum of wealth invested directly in stocks of American companies.

As time passed more and more American companies began to develop international markets, and foreign companies gained more entry in our marketplace. Nowhere was the latter factor more noticeable than in the automobile and consumer electronics businesses. The Japanese automakers, in particular, rapidly adapted to the U.S. market, which they saw as a rich opportunity. They quickly came to understand that they had to compete not only on price to break into the American market, but also on quality. Suddenly, the relatively higher-paid and independent American worker was pitted against a low-cost labor force in Japan, where obedience and conformity were cultural virtues. This pattern repeated itself in other industries such as toys, machinery, clothing, and consumer electronics. Soon, manufacturing company after company began to disappear from the American business landscape. Union gains in wages and benefits had become costly, uncompetitive burdens for many companies. Even where unions were not involved, the general cost structure of many U.S.-based companies had become uncompetitive. The American auto industry did little to help itself, continuing to produce bland, relatively expensive, and poorly made cars as it continued to lose market share. In its clumsy effort to control costs and win back market share, General Motors abandoned its differentiation between product lines. Buyers of Pontiacs, Chevrolets, and even Cadillacs discovered their cars had generic motors and frames and differed little but for trim. The exclusivity of Cadillac was watered down, and the previously successful step-up marketing of models from the entry-level Chevrolet through the Oldsmobile, to the

Buick and ultimately Cadillac, was lost to the directives of the finance department.

The increasing competitive pressure to cut costs found expression in the outsourcing of jobs to independent domestic contractors, a process that then began to result in outsourcing to foreign subcontractors as the global economy assumed an ever-greater impact on the American economy. Cost pressures also inspired efforts to increase productivity through increased mechanization and other forms of technology. Routine record keeping and processing increasingly began to be performed by machine, as did complex calculation and analysis. In one sense this removed some of the mundane from the workplace, but the tireless computers did not reduce employee workloads; they instead increased them. And work became more impersonal. Human interaction with the computer increased, while enriching direct interaction with coworkers often decreased. With the advent of e-mail, this alienation has become even more severe, with an increasing number of individuals working in complete isolation at home. This latter development has manifest advantages for business, which does not have to provide office space or as much support for these off-site personnel. The supposed trade-off for the employee is the ability to stay at home with one's family, and reduced transportation costs. In contrast, the isolation from coworkers and from the corporate culture is a distinct negative.

Today's office workers are frequently deluged with e-mails, meetings, difficult co-workers and deadlines, each providing its own form of stress. All the while production employees must relate more and more to machines in their work, engaged in repetitive tasks that separate them from the satisfaction that flows from any connection with the finished product. As companies merge in an effort to remain competitive and grow, the turmoil and uncertainty of these changes provide added insecurity, regardless of competence. Many have watched as valued employees are let go in the wake of a merger; no matter that they gave years of dedicated service and positive results. In addition, the larger the company becomes, the more likely workers are to become disconnected from management and corporate purpose.

All of these trends collided head-on with growing affluence and an increasing expectation that work should be "meaningful." The paternalism of the early postwar era began to vanish from most companies, with a corresponding effect upon employee loyalty. A "what have you done for me today" mentality exists in many companies now, both for the employee and the employer. Benchmarks and quotas have substituted for a more interpersonal form of management. This state of affairs only increased the sense of alienation and willingness to change jobs and to cut staff without regard to the investment in training and experience. The business lexicon now includes the term "human capital" to refer to employees, as if human beings were the equivalent of dollar bills. In such an environment, it is little wonder that many Americans became increasingly dissatisfied with their jobs and also fearful of the future.

There are a number of things that can be done to alter the landscape. With respect to union employees, their leadership must abandon the "us versus them" mentality. While demands for uncompetitive wages and seniority over competence may please the rank-and-file, what good are such things if the jobs are ultimately shipped overseas or the plant closes? Unions are also fighting a battle for their very existence, viewed by some as unsupportable by state and local governments. Workers and employers have an area of common ground when it comes to health care and benefits such as pensions. As long as we fail to address fully the issues of universal health care and provision for retirement in the United States, employees will continue to absorb a greater share of health-care costs as well as providing for a greater part of their own retirement. And employers will continue to be saddled with burdens that are not sustainable. Yet this continues to be a battleground for employees and employers. It is a losing battle between them that they ought to join forces on. The recent convoluted attempt to overhaul government's role in health care did little to alleviate the responsibility for coverage that is overburdening American businesses and depriving millions of American citizens of decent and affordable medical care. Instead of addressing health-care costs, we have focused on broader coverage of people within the framework of the existing costly health-care insurance structure. Attempts to cut Medicare and Medicaid reimbursement rates are resulting in fewer and fewer choices and more and more providers opting out. Employers and employees have a mutual interest in seeing cost-effective, single-payer universal health care adopted in the United States, rather than wasting their energies arguing over vanishing benefit dollars. Many employers have bought the argument that increased taxes from universal health care would cost them more than the current system. That is not borne out in countries that have universal health care. Businesses in those countries are able to be more competitive without skyrocketing health insurance overhead. And the productivity of their workers is enhanced by better preventative care on average. Finally, the purchasing power of government, *applied wisely*, can help drive down health-care costs.

Instead of fighting over expensive health-care and other benefit dollars, employers should provide, and employees should seek, a greater participation by employees in the nature and details of their work. To the surprise of many senior managers and corporate boards, compensation surveys consistently show that employees value job satisfaction ahead of compensation. And in my business experience that has repeatedly been the case. If people enjoy their work, they are more likely to remain with the company and to work for relatively less money. Job satisfaction is derived largely from the satisfaction one gets from the product produced, whether tangible or intangible, and secondarily from a positive work environment that rewards achievement and respects the individual. If the employee feels the product is worthwhile, and they have a discernable part in it from which they can take some degree of pride, there is satisfaction from having helped to produce it. But if the employee has no input, and cannot tie their effort to a positive outcome, then he or she feels devalued and disconnected from their work. The Japanese auto industry recognized this many years ago when they began to involve assembly-line workers in manufacturing and design discussions. These "quality circles," or *kaizen,* resulted in fewer defects, lower costs, and better-built cars.

Workers on the assembly line, who intimately knew the work involved, came up with ideas that their chair-bound executives could not. But most importantly this process connected the workers with their jobs and provided an element of greater satisfaction through a sense of control over their work. This concept is certainly not a new one, and is employed to varying degrees in many manufacturing companies today. But few companies have applied the concept to the rest of their operations beyond manufacturing. The impersonal "suggestion box" needs to come off the wall and take the form of regular interaction between coworkers at all levels, right up to the CEO and board of directors. Imagine the impact if board members regularly heard from line people about issues in the company. Instead, most American boards exist in an ivory tower environment, spoon-fed and isolated by senior management. This abrogation of the board's fiduciary obligation to shareholders by many boards of directors in the United States has led not only to significant management abuse in compensation and financial reporting, but also has aggravated workers' sense of alienation. Watching senior management walk away with millions of dollars in salary, bonuses, and severance, even when the company has performed poorly, does not build employee morale or create job satisfaction.

There are other factors existing in many corporate boardrooms today that inhibit our competitiveness and the underpinnings of a better economy. Too many corporate boards have lost all sense of value by awarding hundreds of millions of dollars to senior executives, sometimes regardless of ultimate performance and far beyond what should be necessary to attract and retain good management. CEOs who have committed illegal acts, driven their companies into bankruptcy, and otherwise destroyed shareholder value have been rewarded with huge severance payments and lavish retirement benefits. These same individuals then often reappear as the CEO of another company. In a recent example, Hewlett-Packard fired their CEO, Leo Apotheker, who had previously been let go from software maker SAP. During Apotheker's brief tenure at HP, which lasted only eleven months, HP's shares fell 46 percent- a loss of market value to shareholders of nearly $40 billion. Despite that, Apotheker was still awarded $2.4 million under HP's "pay-for-results" plan and walked away with a total of more than $13 million in cash and stock. This not only raises questions about the HP board's judgment in agreeing to such terms, it raises questions about the initial hiring decision, itself.

Even where boards have been well-intentioned, they have been hamstrung by poorly crafted employment agreements prepared by law firms seeking to curry favor with the CEO. Boards need to utilize independent counsel for the drafting and overview of these arrangements to ensure full authority to fire and cancel compensation. It has been a common joke among many CEOs that you are better off to perform poorly and get booted with a huge severance than to have to stay and work to earn the same amount or less. For some companies even the "outside" board members are insiders. They have a too-cozy relationship with senior management, such as existed at United Health, mentioned below. A smart CEO makes sure his board is populated by sympathetic directors who are well compensated through stock options and other perks, like use of the corporate jet, that tie them to the CEO.

In 1980 CEO pay was ten times the pay of the average worker. Today the average CEO's pay is a staggering 430 times that of the average worker. Clearly the importance of the CEO has not increased by this magnitude relative to the worker in this time frame. From 1995 to 2005, average CEO pay rose nearly 300 percent, while average wages for workers rose only 4.3 percent and corporate profits rose 103 percent. These are dollars that could have been better spent distributed throughout these companies to attract and retain talent at all levels, enhance innovation, and increase competitiveness. But until shareholders (often large institutions themselves, such as pension and mutual funds) demand more from boards, those boards will not demand more from management. There has also been only grudging acceptance by boards of the need to tie compensation of senior management not only to short-term results, but also to longer-term performance. A CEO should not make a windfall compensation level one year only to stay at the same level despite the company doing poorly the next year.

The Sarbanes-Oxley legislation that grew out of the Enron era has been a costly boon for accountants and lawyers, but ultimately does nothing to address fairness and management effectiveness. These cannot be legis-lated. They must be voted upon by shareholders who take a longer-term interest in the companies they own by ques-tioning board and management actions and recommen-dations. Until such time as those who exercise corporate voting power find it meaningful, as well as in their best interest, to become more involved and demand accountability, the excesses will persist. Too many merely accept the proxy submitted by management or do not participate at all. Regrettably, one of the other trends in our economy is the increasing separation of stock ownership from those with any long-term interest in the company. In some cases stock changes hands in a microsecond as the result of programmed trades generated by computers. Such trades may have no relationship to the expected performance of the company, relating instead to such things as momentary market anomalies and efforts to hedge other trades. Today the major holders of stock for any length of time are largely pension and mutual funds that again lack a long-term commitment to the companies they own. Rather than pressure management for change, they simply move on to more desirable companies. The implications of this include more running of the company for the benefit of management than for shareholders. The implications for those individuals who invest in the stock market directly are that they are very much on the outside without even a view in. Traditional investing analysis no longer applies in cyber-traded markets manipulated by hedge funds and high-frequency trading. The traditional democratic ownership of stock directly by individuals has become a relic.

The disengagement between shareholders and management is paralleled within the companies themselves. There is a huge disconnection between management and staff at most companies today. It is rare for senior management to "manage by walking around;" to find out what is truly going on in their companies and what their employees think outside the executive suite. This entails random and unscheduled one-on-one visits, not orchestrated "appearances" by the boss. Instead, policies and procedures get promulgated by little fiefdoms within the organization that build power at various levels, from human resources to legal, all the while destroying initiative. Creativity is too often squelched in larger companies, either because the ideas cannot find a path to decision makers or because ingenuity and change are perceived to threaten coworkers' job security. There is frequently a dumbing down and don't-rock-the-boat mentality that exists in bureaucracies where the creative individual is the outlier, viewed as the nonconformist or the problem worker and resented. And yet it is these very individuals who can help reinvigorate the workplace. Once creative and agile, Microsoft has become the poster child of corporate sloth. Years behind schedule with a new version of its Windows operating system, Vista, that had to be rapidly replaced by Windows 7, it has allowed itself to wallow in unproductive litigation, add layers of management bureaucracy, and stifle creativity in the process. Despite allocating $7.5 billion for research in 2006, it produced few new ideas and had to play catch-up with the likes of open source freeware such the Mozilla Firefox browser, the Google juggernaut, and Apple's creativity. Instead of streamlining its flagship products, Microsoft kept enlarging them into "bloatware" that slowed their operation and made comprehension more difficult. Apple Computer has managed to produce breakthrough products during this same period, such as the iPod, iPad, and iPhone, largely because of the continued involvement and vision of its founder, Steve Jobs. Execution has been the key. Apple didn't invent the tablet computer; they produced one that sold in large numbers by identifying key needs. Microsoft's lame offering in preceding years was to foster "tablet computing" that was simply a flat, cumbersome PC rather than an innovative new tool. The Xbox lost money for years and did little to set itself apart from competing gaming machines like the creative Sony Wii that employed a motion-sensitive controller. Late to the party, Microsoft finally produced its own motion-sensitive system. Then there was the failed Zoom. We have to ask ourselves why companies like Microsoft and Xerox, the latter whose very name became synonymous with photocopying, fall from leadership. Are there parallels between our companies and our governments in terms of people management? The answer is a resounding yes.

The challenge for management in America today is to cast off their hubris, with its top-down arrogance, and give expression to creativity in their organizations. Empowering employees enhances their individual job satisfaction and benefits the organization as well in the form of better products and better customer service. Angry, dissatisfied employees make angry, dissatisfied customers and coworkers when those employees vent their frustrations on the only outlets accessible to them: the people they come in contact with. The current pop psychology of management says that workers are being involved, but the statistics say otherwise. So many useful tools, such as Six Sigma, are mindlessly put in place by supposedly progressive managements with little understanding of either the underpinnings or the application to their specific company and its employees. The institutional barriers built up through layer upon layer of departments need to come down. Like teaching, effective management is an intensely personal avocation, where success cannot be achieved by resorting to highly automated or formulaic approaches, nor cumbersome management structures. Grades, performance levels, buzz words, statistical analysis, and the like diminish outcomes when misapplied by unthinking managers in bureaucracies, and contribute to even greater worker alienation. Formulaic approaches and layers of rules and structure get implemented as the organization grows in order to retain control from the top. It is not only an illusion, these control mechanisms become the sticky tar that slows the organization down and inhibits creativity. Innovation and creativity flourish in unstructured environments, not rigid bureaucracies where turf and silos prevail.

The issue is not just about providing meaningful work for staff and outlets for creativity. The approach discussed here has equal value for managers. It is truly lonely at the top for those managers who cannot, or will not, connect with the needs, aspirations, and ideas of their subordinates. There is great satisfaction to be obtained by seeing your employees thrive and succeed, unless you are insecure in your own position. We have created false direction for managers by placing too much emphasis upon compensation as the yardstick of success within business and within our culture. Rather than finding meaning in their jobs, many managers seek to "buy" meaning in their lives by making more and more money in order to buy more and more things. The money and the things are the scorecards of their success. This has reached absurd proportion with some CEO compensation schemes, as we have noted.

In my business career, which has included being a CEO, I have often been struck by the number of CEOs who have resorted to illegal or unethical means to put even more money in their pockets, despite already earning millions in salary and benefits. It is as if they cannot earn enough, no matter how much they make. The money has become a narcotic that requires more and more to stay high, even to the extent of illegality and immorality to achieve it. For some of us there is no satisfaction in winning by cheating, but for those individuals with unquenchable thirst it is about power, and the money is merely an expression of their power. Take for example the epidemic of stock back-dating that occurred only a few years ago. Stock options granted to senior executives are supposed to provide incentive for them to enhance stock value going forward. Instead, for several companies the option grant dates were retroactively set back to dates when the stock value was lower than at the true grant date, thereby producing an immediate gain to the executive, even though there was no assurance of future performance. The net effect was to grant compensation without declaring it as an expense (as required by accounting and tax rules), thus overstating earnings and effectively taking money from shareholders without their knowledge. Another consequence was to disqualify the options for capital gains treatment but act as if the requirements were in fact met. Not only were share-holders cheated, so was the public, through reduced tax revenue. One of the most egregious of these schemes was sanctioned by United Health Group's Chairman and CEO,

William McGuire. His millions of dollars in compensation, and nearly two billion dollars in stock options, were apparently inadequate, in his judgment. Not only were his most recent years' options backdated (the *Wall Street Journal* computed the odds of his options having been correctly dated at each of the low points for the year at roughly two hundred million to one), but he even managed to finesse getting an award doubled. He requested that one award be suspended (because the stock price had fallen below the option's exercise price) and replaced by a substitute award set at an even lower execution price. Later, when the stock recovered, he reinstated the original award, thereby doubling the award. For some CEOs the money is a measure of their brilliance, and they simply cannot get enough of that. Compliant boards, in too-cozy relationships with the CEO, are often their too-willing accomplices. In United Health's case, the head of the compensation committee of the board was being paid by the chairman and CEO, McGuire, to manage a trust for McGuire's children. McGuire had also invested substantial sums in the board member's management firm. The board did not ascertain or admit knowledge of these schemes until embarrassed by a *Wall Street Journal* article, and then took over six months to ferret out the details.

Americans are working longer hours than most other nationalities (the trend of decreasing hours reversed during the 1980s), even more than the Japanese and Europeans, yet our productivity per hour has been less. Total productivity of American workers (GDP per worker) is greater, though, because we have chosen to work more hours. Despite great strides toward increasing technology in the workplace, our answer to world competition has been largely to work harder, not smarter. We spend too much unproductive time e-mailing and meeting, as if communication was an achievement of itself. We spend too little time collaborating. We spend too much time seeking more money and not enough time seeking satisfying work. The end result is more stress, less meaningful work, and lessened competitiveness. European economies have their own issues to deal with, such as persistent and high unemployment, especially at the entry level and for youth. Several European economies are also experiencing financial woes from mismanagement and corruption within their economies. Yet Europeans seem to have struck a better balance between work and leisure.

It is time to rethink our corporate paradigm in America. Larger corporations are no longer an extension of democracy through direct voting by human shareholders; they have become the corrupters of democracy, acting disproportionately for their narrow economic interests. Where these corporations are multinational, their interests become even more disconnected from those of the American public. Barely accountable senior management and conflicted governance by corporate boards have resulted in companies run more for the aggrandizement of senior management than for enhancing shareholder value, in too many cases. It is time to reexamine our assumptions about the relationship between line, management, and boards, so that management becomes more informed and workers at every level become more empowered. The satisfaction of craft needs to reemerge in the American workplace, where achievement becomes valued over monetary status. This involves elevating integrity to its rightful place in all aspects of work, from the most senior managers and board to the line workers. Integrity is not just about honesty. When a product is well made we say it has integrity. Integrity involves dedication to a job well done. And like a smile, integrity is infectious. Integrity also involves organizing for achievement as opposed to control as the primary objective. Organizing so everything can be controlled from the top, with supposed efficiency as the primary driver, is what drives out creativity at the intermediate and subsidiary levels of an organization. Creative people do not want to work where they have minimal control over their areas but all the responsibility for the outcome. This means institutionalizing creativity and accomplishment with far more than "employee of the month." It involves delegating management authority for critical personnel, sales, and operational functions along with accountability for clearly specified and agreed-upon outcomes that are desired by the larger organization. That can be a win/win proposition.

While investment bankers and overpaid CEOs invest their considerable compensation in yachts, hedge funds, and multiple homes, many hardworking Americans are finding it more difficult to put children through college, buy a single home, and grow their standard of living. A less affluent middle and lower income America is a grave threat to the primary driver of the U.S. economy, consumer spending. Luxuries and so-called hedge fund investments will not sustain growth in the United States nor ensure long-term stability. In fact, the diversion of billions of dollars to financial trading, as opposed to capital investment, is another misallocation of resources working against us. The growing fissures in the American economy require an effort to more broadly distribute income in the United States, not by fiat but by how we structure and prioritize things in our economy. The rumble of calls for less regulation and reduced government, to the extent they are heeded, will continue to worsen the standard of living for the majority while favoring the wealthiest few of our populace. It was the broad distribution of wealth that built this country, and the concentration of wealth that helped damage our economy in the 1930's. Without consumers there is no need for suppliers. This isn't about class warfare or destroying incentives for the "job creators." Those are just labels. The American economy and our standard of living will improve only when we make its benefits available to more people, not fewer. Attempts to cripple or even eliminate social programs like Medicare and Social Security take money and demand out of the economy, and weakened demand means a weaker economy. The destructive drive for an undefined "less government" also takes a source of demand from the economy in mindless fashion. More favorable tax treatment for individuals outside the top brackets and small business (including consideration of moving toward a simplified tax that would be far more efficient in terms of the massive sums spent today to cope with our ridiculously complex tax code), a reevaluation of compensation schemes and relative levels, a greater emphasis on preparing Americans for competing in a global economy through education and social and tax programs that alleviate middle and lower class burdens, such as college costs, are all areas that can help restore vibrancy to our economy. So far, however, this subject of inequality has been merely a political football tossed between the two major parties without substance.

Universal health care, an issue that inspires intense opposition, does not exist in a vacuum. Health-care costs are a significant factor in the reduced competitiveness of American companies under the current private-insurance-based system and the consequent strains on middle class American individuals. The education crisis in America does not exist in a vacuum. It exacerbates the income disparities, the lack of international competitiveness, and any hopes for upward mobility for millions of Americans; not to mention the threat it poses to our democracy from an electorate that lacks the best broad-based education we can offer. The failure to prioritize and invest in education and research deprives us of the drivers of innovation and skills that will spur broad-based growth for the whole of the economy. At the same time, we have roads and bridges that are crumbling, buildings that need modernization and energy efficiency, and a host of other investments in our future that would also put people back to work. Instead we are losing valuable time to ideological intransigence, political gamesmanship, and to policies that con patriotic Americans into self-defeating actions that benefit only a wealthy few. Our misdirected priorities and lack of leadership are slowly sapping the vitality, the health, and ultimately the well-being of America. More importantly, there are no quick fixes. These are issues that will take time and resources to reverse, even if we began today. But in our current state, we are not even aware of the magnitude of our difficulties, the degree of impending harm, or the institutional impediments to change that we have built in because of our inability to come together in solution. Until we cease looking to "others" to move us in new directions, until we open our minds and information sources to different approaches that build bridges between us rather than lend credibility to people who tear them down, we will continue to drift with all the frustration and ultimate damage that will incur.

Chapter Seventeen

Pebbles of Change

We would rather be ruined than changed;
We would rather die in our dread
Than climb the cross of the moment
And let our illusions die.
W. H. Auden

Never believe that a few caring people can't change the world. For, indeed,
that's all who ever have.
—Margaret Mead

In times of difficulty we yearn for change. Then change becomes the difficulty. When change moves from the abstract to the specific, it raises questions and alarms, especially from those who feel they may be negatively impacted. Those apprehensive of the change then become easy prey for those who seek to preserve the status quo. It is always easier to oppose progress than it is to justify new directions and calm the resultant concerns. The situation is made far more difficult when opposition comes from powerful interests with a stake in maintaining their gains and advantages. The American people have resisted their fears and come together to address great challenges so many times in our history. This time, however, too many see our future as a return to an illusory past; too many want to tear down, clashing with those who turn to government for solutions. And that is where we find ourselves in America today: afraid to climb the cross of the moment. We have allowed deceptively attractive propaganda and ideology to manipulate the fears and hopes of good people, causing many to act against their own best interests, and against our interests as a nation, for the exclusive benefit of the wealthiest and most powerful. We have been reduced to quibbling about the mortgage while our home is being robbed of its treasures. All the while too many of us have been largely indifferent to the silent corruption of our political processes, making only token protests while our democracy has withered and plutocracy flourished at all levels.

Change occurs whether we want it to or not. The vast majority of the changes over the last few decades in America have not been favorable. The only issue now is whether we will change for the better or continue to change for the worse, whether we will seize a brighter future for ourselves and our country or continue to cede control to the few at the expense of us all. We will not progress as a nation as long as apprehension guides us and ideology divides us. There are approaches to our problems that can unite us if we address our collective needs rather than argue about the superiority of individual beliefs. Some of those approaches have been set forth in this book. There are many more available to us if we are willing to consider our alternatives with an open mind and a desire to be respectful of one another rather than antagonistic. That is why so much time was spent in this book challenging belief and stressing the need to be cognizant of the impact on our thinking of fear mongering and stereotyped labeling. We cannot build our country by tearing it down. We cannot pursue new directions by disregarding the lessons of history or personally attacking the proponents of new ideas while offering none in return.

We have become like the rancorous crew mentioned in the Preface: arguing among ourselves while our ship, our country, gets ever closer to being dashed upon the rocks. The single most important thing we can do is to begin to talk *with* one another rather than *about* one another. The disparagement, the finger-pointing, the emotional responses need to stop. They get us nowhere. While we may have divergent beliefs, we have many shared needs as citizens of the same country, exposed to the same challenges. The Iowa corn farmer who is a religious, fiscal conservative may find he has much in common with advocates of a healthier lifestyle who support social change. The guy who can overhaul a Chevy 283 may find camaraderie with a college professor who shares with him a love for cars. The point is that we all, as Americans, have much in common with one another when we set aside our beliefs, look beyond the simplistic labels, and take the time to see the complex individuals that we all are and the needs we share. What we share in common can begin a dialogue that may lead to the discovery of even more that is shared, and from there the ability to bridge differences. A guiding principle of any such dialogue is that the discussion must center on needs rather than beliefs. That is why discussions of religion and politics so often end badly, when irreconcilable beliefs collide. But people's needs can usually be accommodated through discussion, where the effort is made to achieve the needs of both rather than one at the expense of the other. That is the proverbial "win, win." We also need to be willing to maintain dialogue on other issues, even where we cannot come to agreement on a particular issue. Regardless of how strongly we might feel about a particular issue, it should not become the *only* issue at the sacrifice of all else. We all lose when that happens. The debt-ceiling debate of July, 2011, was a good example. There were no winners in that fiasco.

Dialogue between us as citizens is a start. That can then enable us to address our badly flawed political system. New politicians and new ideas will never make it through the gauntlet of temptation, manipulation, and entrenched power as it exists today. Even well-meaning politicians and bureaucrats cannot escape the impact of the current system. Until we change that system, and its captivity by special interests, the kind of change for the better that we all desire, the kind of change that fulfills America's promise for all of its citizens, will never come to fruition. It is absolutely vital to our future as a nation that we remove the disproportionate influence of money from our elections and our government. First, and foremost, we need to move to the public financing of elections whereby candidates who meet eligibility requirements have equal funds by which to present their case for why they should be elected to the office they seek. That will require state and federal legislation and a grassroots effort to obtain it. Entrenched politicians will resist such a change mightily, along with all of the others with a vested interest in the current corrupted system. The enormity of the task, however, is not a reason to shrink from it. The means to organize a national campaign are easily within our grasp, using social media and other Internet tools and grassroots local efforts. This is a nonpartisan issue that we all ought to be able to come together to resolve. With a concerted effort, pressure can be brought to bear on our state legislatures and Congress to enact such legislation in simple fashion and without loopholes.

The next obstacle to restoring our democracy is the idea that corporate and other organizations are somehow "super citizens," who can affect citizen and legislative votes through the disproportionate power of their wealth. The Supreme Court decision in *Citizens United v FEC* currently stands as a bar to effective reform by treating money as freedom of speech for these organizations. If we are to remove the disproportionate influence of PAC and other corporate, union, or other organization money upon our government, it will require a constitutional amendment that states the following:

> The freedom of expression of corporations and other legal organizations under this Constitution, who are not natural persons, shall not extend to the right to contribute money or other value (excluding factual information) directly, or indirectly through individuals or other organizations, to any candidate for federal office or to any federal employee or federal office holder, for the

purpose of influencing the decisions of the candidate, office holder or federal employee or for the purpose of influencing the outcome of any federal election.

Our forefathers, who were justly suspicious of corporate power, never envisioned that corporations would become "super citizens" in our democracy with the power to buy votes. This amendment would not only eliminate the disastrous inequality of the Supreme Court's decision in *Citizens United v FEC*, it would remove the ability of corporations, unions, and other special-interest groups to buy candidates, legislation, and elections. This would be a giant killer. It would put the true power of the vote back into the hands of citizen voters responding to candidates' positions and the factual merits of legislation rather than to special-interest influence. Imagine federal elections without slick attack or issue ads. Imagine legislation that was based solely on factual information, relevant expertise and independent legislative judgment rather than assurances of campaign contributions or future employment, or deceptive attempts to influence public opinion.

The above amendment does not provide sanctions. Instead, it enables Congress to enact true campaign and influence reform and to provide for appropriate sanctions for violations. But make no mistake. The attempt to pass such an amendment, and its implementing legislation, will meet with huge opposition from those who extract billions of dollars from our economy through the manipulation of public opinion for the benefit of special interests.

These are the same powerful people and organizations who want to divert people's attention away from the entrenched plutocracy they maintain and toward divisive social issues like abortion and seemingly sound economic foolishness like a balanced budget amendment. Many proud Americans understandably respond to appeals to liberty and freedom. But such generic appeals, coming from well-funded entities masquerading as grassroots organizations, are smokescreens for devious ends that erode liberty and weaken freedom. The concepts become divisive once they are attached to different beliefs held by different Americans. There are no "true Americans;" no exclusive club of people with the only correct American perspective and thinking or who have a lock on patriotism. There are just Americans who hold a variety of political and economic views and span the gamut of races and religions. That diversity is at the heart of what America is all about. It is that diversity of people and thought that have made us a great nation. We should embrace our diversity, not be antagonistic towards one another, at the behest of an organization, or suggest that one group or individual is more American than the other. The intellectual should not look down on the less-schooled, nor should the worker resent the professor, merely because of their respective occupations or outlooks. All of us are Americans with a common interest in the betterment of our nation. Corporations and other organizations, on the other hand, are not "Americans" in this sense. Many of these organizations have interests and allegiances throughout the globe, with many not even headquartered, or without major operations, in the United States. That is why this proposed amendment is so important; to ensure that our democracy is not diminished, directly or indirectly, through the undue influence of money as "free speech."

Not only would this proposed amendment to our Constitution prevent the extraction of billions of dollars from our economy from favoritism, it will eliminate billions of dollars of wasted, unproductive expenditure that could be better used by corporations to do research, hire people, and improve their products and services so they can be sold without subsidy or special protection. Instead of money wasted on lobbying, those funds could be applied to the benefit of the organizations' memberships and to their stated purposes.

If we want our political parties to be more effective, then we need to stop ceding them to cliques and groups with single-minded agendas. That means getting involved at the grassroots level to ensure that there is a breadth of input. And it means abandoning the sloganeering and supposed "contracts" with "the people" in favor of platforms that detail specific objectives rather than lofty-sounding platitudes that are soon forgotten. Angry denunciations on blogs and waving signs may feel like participation, but it isn't. Helping to register voters, going door to door, contributing time and money are things that help create outcomes. But before action comes preparation. Learn about the issues from facts, not from hyperbole or propaganda. Be an informed participant; not from talk shows or politicians or special interest groups, but from *independent* sources that are credible. That doesn't mean you shouldn't belong to the NRA or NARAL, but get information from more than your favorite organization. Seek statistics and other facts from reputable sources, like census data and the National Institutes of Health or other sources that keep accurate data on subjects of interest to you. Don't rely on sweeping generalizations or repetition to make things true. And within your organization, hold it accountable for the accuracy and merit of its objectives.

Finally, we need to have legislators who know how to create simple legislation. That is a better goal than simply "less government." Laws that take several thousand pages to create become almost impossible to administer and are more likely to be chock-full of special interest exemptions and benefits. A truly smart lawyer doesn't try to craft a document with verbiage to cover every conceivable contingency. Instead, he uses the careful choice of words to succinctly cover what is needed, no more, no less. The original Glass-Steagall Act, that prevented "too big to fail" until its repeal in 1999, was thirty-four pages. Our tax code and the related regulations have become millions of Band-Aids to cover millions of circumstances. We simply ought to start over. Trying to repeatedly amend the existing Tax Code has produced a prodigious mess of special interest provisions that become impossible to remove one at a time.

Lessening the influence of special interests will go a long way in terms of creating better legislation. In fact, it is ironic that these same special interests, who demand less regulation, are the very people who contribute to its proliferation through lobbying. They are the ones who submit all the ins and outs and obfuscation into practically every bill before Congress. This is but another reason to eliminate special-interest influence: the simplification of our lives and simpler government.

Single pebbles strewn about a streambed have little effect on the flow of the water: a riffle here, a swirling eddy there. But the water still washes over them and wears them down. Pebbles drawn together become an instrument of change that can stand up to the force of the water and divert even a mighty stream into more productive paths. We became a great nation because individuals have come together at critical times to achieve the common good. This is just such a critical time. Our divided house is falling. We must come together as a people to restore the foundation of our democracy so that our house, our nation, may stand as a shelter of opportunity for all of our citizens, not merely the wealthiest among us. The suggestions and changes presented in this book, as well as others, are just words if we cannot put aside our egos and our preconceptions and work with one another for the benefit of us all. Everyone has something to offer at the table. The CEO can learn from the employee. The laborer can learn from the professor, and vice-versa. The retiree and the student can learn from each other. That is what truly made this country great: the melding of cultures and viewpoints to produce a sum greater than the parts. For too many in America, it has become about getting all you can. For others the power that comes from wealth or political triumph has blinded them to the consequences of insensitivity to the needs of those who are trying to succeed when all is stacked against them. As a nation whose revolution grew out of just such a circumstance, we should know better what happens when power is not widely shared.

The character of America will change only when we individually change. When we assume personal responsibility for the character of our own lives, when we find the meaning unique to each of us, we can begin to act in more meaningful ways. We can recognize that our choices, actions, and inactions accumulate to shape our country. It is incumbent upon us all to take those actions and make those choices that protect and enhance the rights of others, not diminish them. We need to remain open to ideas outside of our comfort zone so that we can lead fuller, richer lives by being exposed to new ways of thinking and new experiences, and in order to progress. And we need to choose and become leaders who make pragmatic, informed decisions based in knowledge rather than in ideology, prejudice, or unfounded belief. These things are not inconsistent with maintaining the strength to deal with those who will not respond in kind. They are not inconsistent with those tenets of religion that ask for integrity, understanding, charity, and love of our fellow man. Restoring the promise of our democracy will ultimately benefit all people of faith, regardless of denomination or sect. Finally, we must learn to respect the rights of all people, domestic and foreign, to their own beliefs; to try to learn about and understand the beliefs of others; and to find ways to stand on common ground based on mutual needs so that we can walk forward together. That, more than anything else, will make our world safer by replacing fear with knowledge, and isolation with communication and understanding. We are individually mere pebbles, but together we can shape the course of a mighty stream.

Epilogue

One day we may be forced to put aside our fear and distrust of one another because of a greater fear that will be common to us all: the destruction of our planet's livability. Whether you believe in climate change, the fact remains that we are depleting the earth's resources at an ever-increasing rate. Climate and resource issues and the destruction of species are problems that can be resolved only by the concerted action of all nations and all people. Similarly, the rise of economic globalism has created economic stresses that defy national boundaries and national control. The economic stresses upon some smaller countries can now infect the economies of other countries, and even the entire world, in a significant way. Differing levels of regulation and differing monetary and fiscal policies among countries create competitive friction points between those countries. Left unchecked these stresses and friction points can lead to economic and even real warfare. Warfare in an atomic age should be unthinkable, but it is becoming less so.

The simple fact is that if we do not learn to live together, we will die together. If there is a grand plan for this world, perhaps that is the end game: we have been left to our own devices to learn to coexist in peace for the betterment of all. But if we do not do so, and soon, this ship we call earth will founder upon the rock of our failure, with the loss of all souls aboard.

We have the capacity to shape our growth and change. We have the tools to accomplish great things. So much more good could be created if we were not so focused on negative behaviors rooted in fear and distrust. Force and the imposition of one culture upon another will bring neither understanding nor accomplishment of our objectives. Rather, they will affirm the fears and harden the opposition. We must move away from the politics of fear and diversion towards the politics of understanding and solution. That involves a shift from short-sided reactive behaviors to an ongoing effort to understand and honor our differences and recognize our commonalities. We are so many strangers on this planet, distrustful of one another. We must get to know each other, value each other, and help each other. This is not idealistic prattle. It is our only option if we and this planet are to survive in the long run.

Selected Bibliography

"Adult Literacy, The Readers," The Economist, January 15, 2009. http://www.economist.com/node/12941110

Adults and Children Together Against Violence (ACT). http://actagainstviolence.apa.org/about/what/index.html

Appelbaum, Binyamin, "On Finance Bill, Lobbying Shifts to Regulations,"NewYorkTimes,June 26,2010.http://www.nytimes.com/2010/06/27/business/27regulate.html?pagewanted=all

Brandt, Allen. *The Cigarette Century*. New York: Basic Books 2007

Brill, Steven, "Government for Sale: How Lobbyists Shaped the Financial reform Bill," Time Magazine, July 1, 2010. http://www.time.com/time/magazine/article/0,9171,2001015,00.html

Bureau of Labor Statistics, US Department of Labor. Databases, Tables & Calculators by Subject. http://www.bls.gov/data/

Burns, James MacGregor, *Roosevelt the Lion and the Fox*. New York: Harcourt, 1984

Center for Responsive Politics, http://www.opensecrets.org/index.php

Centers for Disease Control, US Government. *National Center for Injury Prevention and Control. WISQARS Injury Mortality reports, 1999-2007.* http://webappa.cdc.gov/sasweb/ncipc/mortrate10_sy.html

Danforth, John C. "Onward Moderate Christian Soldiers," New York Times, June 17, 2005. http://www.nytimes.com/2005/06/17/opinion/17danforth.html

Dyer, Dr. Wayne. *The Power of Intention.* New York: Hay House, 2004

FactCheck.Org

The Federalist Papers, The Library of Congress, THOMAS online http://thomas.loc.gov/home/histdox/fedpapers.html

"Financial Regulatory Reform Update," New York Times, September 20, 2011. http://topics.nytimes.com/topics/reference/timestopics/subjects/c/credit_crisis/financial_regulatory_reform/index.html

Frank, Thomas. *What's the Matter with Kansas?* New York: Henry Holt and Co., 2004

Guindon, Mary H., PhD, Green, Alan G., PhD, and Hanna, Fred J., PhD. "Intolerance and Psychopathology: Toward a General Diagnosis for Racism, Sexism, and Homophobia." *American Journal of Orthopsychiatry Mental Health and Justice.* Wiley Online Library, 2010. http://onlinelibrary.wiley.com/doi/10.1037/0002-9432.73.2.167/abstract

Hayek, Friedrich. *The Collected Works of F.A. Hayek*. Chicago: University of Chicago Press, 1989

Hoffer, Eric. *The True Believer- Thoughts on the nature of mass movements.* New York: Harper Perennial Modern Classics, 2002

Hofstadter, Richard. *The American Political Tradition.* New York: Vintage Books, 1961

Keynes, John Maynard. *The general Theory of Employment, Interest and Money.* United Kingdom: Palgrave Macmillan, 1936

Morgenson, Gretchen and Rosner, Joshua. *Reckless Endangerment.* New York: Times Books, Henry Holt and Co., LLC, 2011

National Commission on Law Observance and Enforcement Report on the Enforcement of the Prohibition Laws of the United States Dated January 7, 1931 National Prohibition.

Phillips, Kevin. *American Theocracy.* New York: Viking Press, 2006

Phillips, Kevin. *Wealth and Democracy.* New York: Broadway Books, 2002

Pierce, Charles. *Idiot America.* New York: Doubleday, 2009

Ricks, Thomas E. *Fiasco.* New York: Penguin Books, 2007

"Raising children to resist violence: What you can do," American Psychological Association. http://www.apa.org/helpcenter/resist-violence.aspx

Roubini, Nouriel and Mihm, Stephen. *A Crash Course in the Future of Finance.* New York: The Penguin Press, 2010

Smith, Adam. *The Wealth of Nations.* London: W. Strahan and T Cadell, 1776

Steinbeck, John. *The Grapes of Wrath,* United States: Viking Press, 1939

Steinbrook, Robert, M.D., "Lobbying, Campaign Contributions, and Health Care Reform," The New England Journal of Medicine, December 3, 2009. http://www.nejm.org/doi/full/10.1056/NEJMp0910879

Stiglitz, Joseph E. and Members of a UN Commission of Financial Experts. *The Stiglitz Report- Reforming the International Monetary and Fiscal Systems in the Wake of the Global Crisis.* New York: The New Press, 2010

Treaty of Peace and Friendship between the United States of America and the Bey and Subjects of Tripoli of Barbary

United States Senate, "Lobbying Disclosure, Registrant/ Client List." http://www.senate.gov/pagelayout/legislative/one_item_and_teasers/clientlist_parent.htm

Wyatt, Edward and Lichtblau, Eric, "A Finance Overhaul Draws a Swarm of Lobbyists,"The New York Times, April 19, 2010. http://www.nytimes.com/2010/04/20/business/20derivatives.html